The Educational Book Division of Prentice-Hall, Inc., is committed to the publication of outstanding textbooks. One important measure of a book's excellence is how well it communicates with its readers. To assure a highly readable book, the content for this text was selected, organized, and written at a level appropriate for the intended audience. The Dale-Chall readability formula was used to control readability level. An inviting and meaningful design was created to enhance the book's visual appeal as well as to facilitate the reading process. The authors, editors, and designers are confident that the students for whom this book is intended will read it, comprehend it, and learn from it.

The following features were incorporated in the content and design of this text. A page reference is given to provide an example of each feature.

- A scope and sequence table, located at the beginning of the book, acts as an overall guide to the book's basic concepts (pp. 8–9).

- The book is organized into fifteen chapters, each based on an occasion in which food is the focus—after-game snacks, school lunches, a cookout, a holiday meal, for instance. Real-life situations introduce each chapter, rouse interest, and motivate by presenting characters with whom readers can identify (p. 50).

- Learning objectives are listed at the opening of each chapter (p. 51).

- The text's dialogue, or question-answer approach, discusses the concepts in a conversational way that readers can easily understand (p. 51).

- Photographs were chosen and drawings and tables designed to reinforce and expand the concepts introduced in the text. Captions include thought and review questions (p. 62).

- Key terms are defined in text and are in boldface type at first appearance (p. 58). These terms are also listed at the chapter's end (p. 70) and in the glossary (pp. 312–316).

- Vocabulary terms that may be unfamiliar or difficult to pronounce appear with pronunciations in color blocks at the foot of pages where defined (p. 55) and in the glossary. The pronunciation system is both comprehensive and simple. The key to the system is located just before the glossary (p. 312).

- Each chapter concludes with materials that review, reinforce, and enrich key concepts (pp. 70–73):

Words to understand	Things to do
Food and equipment to know	Careers to consider
Questions to discuss	

- Metric measurements are given with customary measurements throughout (p. 64).

turn to page 36

EXPLORING FOODS

EXPLORING

PRENTICE-HALL, INC., ENGLEWOOD CLIFFS, NEW JERSEY

FOODS

DONNA NEWBERRY CREASY JOHN A. CREASY

CONSULTANTS

MICHELE J. CHIAVETTA, Home Economics Specialist
Allegheny County Intermediate Unit, Pittsburgh, Pennsylvania

ARLENE M. KIRMAN, Home Economics Teacher
Tenafly Public Schools, Tenafly, New Jersey

OPAL MASSEY
Oakland Unified School District, Oakland, California

MARILYN L. MEYER
Shawnee Mission School District, Shawnee Mission, Kansas

JOYCE E. NIEDENTHAL, Home Economics Curriculum Supervisor
School Board of Broward County, Fort Lauderdale, Florida

EXPLORING FOODS

Donna Newberry Creasy
John A. Creasy

Donna and Jack Creasy, a wife-husband team, have combined their talents in writing this text. Donna's background is in home economics education and in nutrition; Jack's is in English literature. Both have taught—Donna, in high school home economics, and Jack, in English. Donna has written and edited educational filmstrips and teacher guides and has served as food and nutrition editor of a home economics periodical. She is active in several organizations concerned with nutrition education and consumer interests and has been a college lecturer and public speaker in these areas. Jack is a free-lance writer and editor. Both are involved with young people through scouting and sports activities. Their interest in and knowledge of young people has helped them develop a new approach to teaching about foods.

SUPPLEMENTARY MATERIALS

Teacher's Guide

SDMs for Activities and Evaluation

10   9   8   7   6   5   4   3

Cover photo by Reginald Wickham

PRENTICE-HALL INTERNATIONAL INC., London
PRENTICE-HALL OF AUSTRALIA, PTY. LTD., Sydney
PRENTICE-HALL OF CANADA, LTD., Toronto
PRENTICE-HALL OF INDIA PRIVATE LTD., New Delhi
PRENTICE-HALL OF JAPAN, INC., Tokyo
PRENTICE-HALL OF SOUTHEAST ASIA PTE. LTD., Singapore
WHITEHALL BOOKS LIMITED, Wellington, New Zealand

Contents

Foods index

(RC) indicates a recipe card in the text.

SCOPE AND SEQUENCE	1 NUTRITION	2 CHOOSING FOODS	3 SNACKS WITH FRIENDS	4 BREAKFAST	5 BRUNCH	6 LUNCH	7 KEEPING FOOD SAFE
CAREERS	nutrition and dietetics	farming	teaching	food processing	food preparation	food marketing	food inspection
CONSUMER INFORMATION	enriched, restored, fortified foods		carrots, celery, fresh fruits, cheese buying "in season"	grain products	eggs mixes vs. homemade	salad ingredients salad dressings	choosing lunchbox foods for keeping qualities
EQUIPMENT			for cutting for measuring for mixing and baking cookies		for range-top cooking for measuring for broiling for baking	for salads and dressings for soups	for wrapping food for carrying food
FOOD PREPARATION			fruit and vegetable snacks; dips cheese other simple snacks cookies beverages	cereals breakfast ideas	equivalent measures; changing recipe quantities egg dishes sausage, bacon leavenings quick breads	main dish salads, fruit salads salad dressings soups garnishes	sandwiches, sandwich fillings
KITCHEN MANAGEMENT			storing fresh produce using leftovers; improvising	do-ahead breakfast tips	storing eggs and breakfast meats do-ahead organization and preparation	do-ahead salad tips storing salad ingredients storing soup	principles of safe food storage cleanliness serving and storage temperatures
MEAL PLANNING AND SERVICE	dietary needs using the Basic Four vegetarian diet	sensory qualities of food combining foods for interest and variety food habits	serving snacks	breakfast pattern applying the Basic Four to breakfast planning	planning variations on basic recipes	salads in menu planning using leftovers family-style service	packing and carrying foods planning for variety
NUTRITION	energy; digestion nutrients the Basic Four health; weight control	nutritional variety empty calories (nutrient density)	snacks	importance of breakfast metabolism grain products fiber	protein source: eggs	protein sources: main dish salads and soups	
SAFETY			cutting safely				food poisoning, food spoilage packing and carrying foods safely
SOCIAL ASPECTS OF FOOD		variety in foreign dishes food traditions influences on food habits	foods for informal get-togethers improvising for unplanned events	breakfast traditions and habits		arranging and garnishing foods	

8 EASY SUPPERS	9 ENERGY MANAGEMENT	10 COOKING OUT	11 PARTY TIME	12 A HOLIDAY MEAL	13 FEEDING CHILDREN	14 EATING OUT	15 FOOD IS NEWS
consumer education	consumer affairs	raising food animals	owning a business	food economics	writing about food	food service	food technology
unit pricing, brands, label information, product dating ingredients for pasta supper, beef stew	major appliances small appliances	chicken	cake flour vs. all-purpose flour	turkey and accompanying foods		restaurant practices paying and tipping	evaluating information and advertising world food supplies; cost of food food technology; organic farming FDA and FTC
for cooking pasta for freezing food miscellaneous	major appliances small appliances microwave ovens materials for microwave cooking	for barbecuing for serving outdoors	for making cakes	for roasting for baking for range-top cooking	for warming foods for range-top cooking for feeding babies	special pieces of flatware and tableware	
pasta meat sauce garlic bread beef stew accompaniment salads	fish general microwave cooking	grilling chicken, meats, and other foods	cake, frosting punch	turkey, stuffing, gravy mashed potatoes green beans cranberry sauce, table relishes yeast rolls pie dough	warming foods panbroiling meats fixing babies' formulas and solid foods		
shopping list staples and kitchen supplies meal management storing leftovers do-ahead steps	managing household energy, personal energy work centers defrosting a refrigerator dishwashing	storing chicken organizing indoor and outdoor preparation for a barbecue	organizing for a party	organizing a holiday meal— preparation and time schedule putting away leftovers	checking for safety hazards to children managing food preparation during child care		
planning supper menus serving family meals		planning a cookout foil cooking	party foods buffet-style service	planning a large meal table setting English and family-style service clearing dishes	making children's meals special feeding babies table service and manners for children	restaurant menu terms table settings	
protein sources: casseroles and one-dish meals nutrition labeling menu samples		menu sample for nutritional balance and variety		menu sample for nutritional balance and variety	applying the Basic Four to planning meals for children baby foods and formulas		evaluating weight-loss diets evaluating "health foods"
	kitchen safety	barbecuing and fire safety		food safety: handling leftovers	accident prevention emergency measures for choking, etc. baby-sitting tips	preventing/ handling table accidents	preservatives and other food additives
			party planning; invitations hosting a party		mealtime psychology children's eating habits baby-sitting tips	table manners and customs American and European eating styles	

To the student

All your life you've been eating food. Most of the time it's been food that someone else prepared for you. You probably didn't see the food when it was bought in the store or cooked in the kitchen. The first time you saw it was when someone put it down in front of you for you to eat.

By now, you may have a lot of questions about that food. Where did it come from? Why should you eat it? How can you make it taste better? Here are some questions about food that this book will answer for you.

Why do you need food, anyway? What does your body do with it? The first chapter in this book describes how your body uses food to keep you alive, to help you grow, and to give you energy. It explains why it's important to use the Basic Four food groups to choose good foods. In later chapters, you'll find ideas about how to combine foods into snacks or meals with delicious and nutritious variety.

How do you know what to do with all the tools and equipment in the kitchen? Many chapters include descriptions and explanations of the kitchen equipment you need to prepare the foods discussed. When you've finished the book, you'll understand how to use basic kitchen tools and appliances.

How can you use recipes when they're full of special words only a cook can understand? Throughout this book cooking terms and expressions are explained in simple language. A glossary of these words is included at the back of the book for easy reference.

How do you know when foods are cooked? Guidelines are given for cooking meat, poultry, fish, vegetables, eggs, cakes, cookies, pies, and breads. In these guidelines, you'll find out how to test for doneness.

How do you choose good-quality fruits and vegetables and serve them? You'll find general guidelines as well as specific things to look for in choosing fruits and vegetables. You'll learn how to clean, trim, and cut them up for serving.

How do you decide what to buy when you go shopping? Throughout the book you'll find shopping tips and suggestions: how to make up a shopping list; how much to buy; which package has the lowest cost; how to judge quality; how to understand nutritional labeling; how to use ads and coupons.

How do you keep foods from spoiling? How do you know if they're safe to eat? Food safety is a very important subject. It is covered in detail in the chapter on keeping foods safe and in other chapters. You'll find out about food spoilage and poisoning, and the best ways to handle and store foods.

How do you plan foods for a party? Whether it's a party, a holiday meal, a cookout, or simply snacks with friends, entertaining with food is an age-old custom. Several chapters in the book deal with the subject of preparing and serving foods that you can be proud of.

What should you know when you go out to eat? Customs and procedures in restaurants can often be confusing. So are manners and rules of table etiquette. A separate chapter on eating out gives you simple guidelines to follow that will help you relax and enjoy eating in public.

What's good to fix for small children, and how do you go about feeding them? As a baby sitter, you may be faced with feeding babies and young children. A chapter in the book gives suggestions on what to fix, how to fix it, and how to serve it.

How can you save energy in the kitchen? Two kinds of energy are used in the kitchen. One is household energy and the other is personal energy. You'll learn how to organize your work to save both kinds of energy.

How do you know what to believe in the news stories you see about food? One chapter examines some of today's major food issues and gives guidelines that can help you decide whether or not the stories you read are accurate.

What jobs are there in the food business? At the end of each chapter, you'll find a discussion of career opportunities in the food industry. Among other things, you'll find out what experience and educational requirements are needed for these positions.

It would be easier to answer these questions for you if we, the authors, could actually talk with you instead of writing down everything in a book. You've probably noticed that it's easier to understand a subject if you can ask questions about it. So we've tried to guess what your questions would be, and to answer them through the special way we've written this book.

You'll notice that each chapter begins with a group of students facing a situation involving food. This leads to a discussion in the book of certain important points about buying, preparing, serving, or eating food. The students in the opening situation take part in this discussion, too. They stop the discussion at important points to ask questions and get additional explanations before going on to the next point. They ask the kinds of questions that you, the reader, may have about the material in the chapter. We think you'll find this dialogue approach interesting and enjoyable. But more importantly, it makes the book easier to follow and to understand.

We have organized the book around food occasions, instead of around different kinds of food. You'll find a chapter on breakfast, another on brunches, others on lunch, snacks, parties, cookouts, and so forth. This makes it possible to talk about all the food groups in the same chapter and to emphasize the importance of variety and balanced nutrition in menu planning.

We hope you enjoy reading and using this book. We hope, too, that all your life you'll enjoy using your new knowledge about food and cooking.

Donna and Jack Creasy

1

HAS THIS EVER HAPPENED TO YOU?

Members of the music club are having a beach party. They decide to have a race to see who's the best swimmer.

TIM: *Okay, we'll swim out to the raft and back. Last one in is a lead balloon!*

As they swim back from the raft, Diane is well ahead of the others.

PAUL: *Huh! Why'd we ever let Diane get in the race? She always wins when it comes to swimming!*

TIM (never eats breakfast or lunch, and then stuffs himself at dinner): *I started getting a cramp on the way back!*

MARIA (a thin girl, who doesn't eat enough): *I was doing all right till I started to sink!*

PAUL (eats all the wrong things): *I must have swallowed some water, 'cause I got a stomachache!*

JUNE (an overweight girl sitting on the blanket, eating cookies): *I knew I didn't have a chance, so why bother?*

PAUL: *Why does Diane always win at swimming?*

EVERYBODY: *Yeah! WHY DOES DIANE ALWAYS WIN??*

12

NUTRITION

Exploring . . .

Personal energy—where you get it and where it goes

Calories and nutrient groups

What carbohydrates, fats, protein, vitamins, and minerals do

How to plan for good nutrition

Have you ever wondered why some people always seem to come out ahead in sports? They're often good in other physical activities, too, whether it's dancing, hiking, biking, or what-have-you. What's their secret?

DIANE: *In my case, it's no secret at all. Swimming is my thing, and I work at it. I'm on the school team, and I practice every day.*

Winning at a particular sport takes a certain amount of basic ability, of course, and a lot of practice. Swimmers often do dozens of laps each day, practicing for a race of just one or two laps.

PAUL: *Look, I know that practicing is the secret to winning. But what's the secret to practicing? I always get worn out before I get through enough practice to do me any good!*

Running is one way to get into good physical shape. What rules should you follow to insure safety and good health?

Getting into good physical shape takes more than just practice—it takes training. Coaches know that it's not enough for their athletes to exercise and work out at their sports. They have to treat their bodies right, too, with enough rest and the proper things to eat.

The difference food makes

What you eat makes a big difference in how you feel and what your body can do. Sometimes it makes a difference in the short run, and you'll notice it right away. One example is when you skip a meal and run out of steam later in the day. Or sometimes your stomach starts growling and even cramping up and hurting. Or maybe you eat too much, or eat the wrong things, and you feel sick because of it.

Take a minute and ask yourself what you had to eat today.

MARIA: *I didn't have breakfast, but I had a peanut butter cracker around lunch time. That filled me up.*

TIM: *I don't remember what I had. Maybe nothing. I do all my serious eating at dinner time.*

JUNE: *I wish I could forget! I had ten pancakes with butter and syrup and six strips of bacon, along with three muffins with jelly, a glass of orange juice, two glasses of milk, and a cup of cocoa. That was for breakfast. For lunch, I had a ham and cheese sandwich, a peanut butter and jelly sandwich, three cupcakes, a banana, and a pint of chocolate milk. In between, I had a couple of little boxes of cookies.*

PAUL: *I like to eat enough, but not too much. I had two jelly doughnuts and a cola for breakfast, and a bag of cheese puffs, a bag of potato chips, and a root beer for lunch. In between I had a couple of soft drinks, a box of caramel corn, and some corn chips to snack on. I don't think I overstuffed myself, but I don't feel too good anyway. It must be the water I swallowed in the swimming race.*

It's not surprising for people to notice short-run effects—such as tiredness, lack of energy, or stomach pains or upset—from eating too much or too little, or the wrong things at the wrong time. But even more dangerous are the long-range effects of a poor diet. They may be harder to notice, but they're often more serious and take longer to correct. In fact, some problems may be impossible to correct completely, especially if they happen during the growing years.

That sounds like my mother. She's always telling me, "Eat all your meals so you'll grow up big and strong." Is this really true? Won't I grow up no matter what I eat?

As long as you eat enough to stay alive, you'll grow up—one way or another. But you won't grow up as "big and strong," or as healthy, as you would if you ate the right things in the right amounts.

What do you think your body is made of? Every part of your body is built from things in the food you eat. The better that food is, the better off your body will be, and the better you'll feel and act.

Nutrients   The things in foods that your body needs are **nutrients**. The main groups of nutrients are carbohydrates, fats, proteins, vitamins, minerals, and water.

I know all about nutrients. I take a vitamin pill every day to make sure I stay healthy.

Nutrients are much more than just vitamins. A vitamin pill has some of the things your body needs, but it doesn't do the whole job,

---

nutrients (NOO trē ənts) For pronunciation key, see page 312.

These two pigs are the same age, but the smaller pig was fed a diet lacking a B vitamin. The other was fed all the required nutrients.

by a long shot. For one thing—and this is very important—a vitamin pill doesn't have any protein to build new cells with. And it doesn't contain any form of food energy. **Energy** is the power to do work. The body needs food energy to work and to play, the way a car needs fuel in order to move.

Where does food energy come from?

Three of the nutrient groups can supply food energy. Those groups are carbohydrates, fats, and proteins. Each is made up of different amounts of carbon, hydrogen, and oxygen. Proteins have nitrogen, as well, and sometimes other chemical elements. **Nutrition** is the study of nutrients and how the body uses them.

Digestion When your body **digests** food, it breaks it down into small, simple units. It can even rearrange molecules to form new kinds of units, if needed. (Molecules are two or more atoms joined together. Atoms are tiny particles of chemical elements.) These molecules of digested food are joined with oxygen in the body cells. This produces energy for the muscles to move and for the body organs to do their jobs. It's a little bit like a car, again, which burns gasoline—that is, mixes it with oxygen—to make the energy needed for it to move.

Carbohydrates: Food energy in quick form

Sugars **Carbohydrates** supply energy. Grain products, fruits, and vegetables are carbohydrate sources. Sugars are the simplest kind of carbohydrates. Your body can use sugar as fuel fairly quickly. That's why you hear sweet foods described as a supply of "quick energy."

Glucose is a kind of sugar. The body breaks down many kinds of food and changes them into glucose. It uses glucose to make energy.

I've heard of glucose! My grandmother was given that when she was in the hospital.

A person who is getting well from an operation or serious illness often is given glucose directly into a vein in an arm. The blood then carries it all over the body to the cells that need it. The body doesn't have to do any work to digest it. It's a good way to supply energy to patients, especially if they can't eat or don't have any appetite.

Starches Starches are another kind of carbohydrate. A starch is a lot of glucose units joined together to form a single molecule shaped like a long chain. The molecules are finally broken down into glucose molecules when you digest the starch.

Glucose is often given to hospital patients. Why?

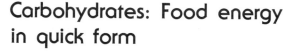

| nutrition (noo TRISH ən) | digests (dī JESTS) |
| carbohydrates (CAHR bə HĪ drāts) | glucose (GLOO kōs) |

Fiber A third kind of carbohydrate is fiber. Grass-eating animals such as cows and horses can use fiber for food, but people can't. It's useful to us because it helps the intestines to move waste materials out of the body. But we can't digest it to provide our bodies with food energy, or calories.

Who wants calories anyway? Don't they make you fat?

Calories **Calories** are simply the units used to measure the amount of energy a food will produce. It's like using "degrees" to measure temperature, or "grams" or "pounds" to measure weight. Calories measure food energy. Scientists use the metric "kilojoule" to measure energy. One calorie equals about 4.2 kilojoules.

Your body combines food with oxygen in the cells to produce energy. Most of the time, you don't realize your body is using energy. Maybe you only think about it when you feel tired and don't seem to have enough energy to do the things you want to. Actually, your body is using energy all the time.

Each part of your body uses energy just to stay alive and do its job. You need energy to breathe, to move muscles, to keep your heart beating, to think, to grow, to digest food, and so on. You also need energy in the form of heat to keep your body at its normal temperature.

The amount of energy you need is really a personal matter. The bigger you are, the more energy (calories) you need—just because your body has more cells using it. Boys tend to need more than girls. When you're growing, that takes extra energy. The more active you are, the more energy you need, and the more calories you "burn up." That's why exercising helps to get rid of extra fat.

Too many calories will add fat to the body. But how many calories are too many? That depends on the person. When you eat more food than your body can use up, your body changes the food to fat and stores it in an energy "piggy bank." Whenever it needs to, your body can deposit more fat or use up some of it.

Body fat has a bad reputation with many people who would like to be thin. *Extra* fat is a problem. It means the body has to carry around extra weight. But everybody needs *some* fat. It helps to cushion parts of your body. It helps your body keep its temperature constant by acting as a kind of insulation material. And don't forget that fat is your reserve energy bank.

Which foods are the most fattening?

No food is fattening all by itself. Almost any food can be fattening if you eat more than your body can use. Generally speaking, proteins and carbohydrates have about the same number of calories per gram. **Fats** have more, and are thus a concentrated form of food energy.

calories (KAL ə rēz)

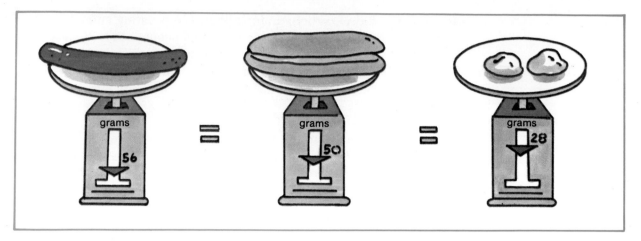

A hotdog (protein) supplies 170 calories. A hotdog roll (carbohydrate) supplies 120 calories. But fats are concentrated energy. Only 2 tablespoons of mayonnaise yield 200 calories.

Fats: Food energy in stored form

Concentrated calories Since stored food energy must be carried around, it needs to be in a concentrated form. That is, it must pack as much energy as it can into as little weight and as little space as possible. A single pound of body fat, for instance, contains 3,500 calories. It takes a long time to store up a pound of fat, and a long time to get rid of it. When you eat fat, therefore, you are getting calories in their most concentrated form.

Yechh! Who eats fat, anyway? Who likes it?

What fat adds to food You may think of fat as just a part of the meat that you cut off and don't eat, but it's much more than that. A lot of your favorite foods contain fat that you can't see. Fat makes a lot of food taste and "chew" better. It carries a lot of the flavors and smells that make some foods, such as peanut butter and chocolate, so appetizing. The "invisible" fat in meats makes them more tender and juicy.

Fat takes longer to digest than other nutrients, so you don't feel hungry again right away. Some important vitamins come dissolved in the fats and oils found in various foods.

Foods that contain fat Oil, such as the kind used in cooking foods or in salad dressings, is simply liquid fat. Butter, margarine, and mayonnaise are mostly fat. So is bacon. Many other foods—such as nuts, potato chips, candy bars, cheese, and eggs—contain quite a bit of fat. Many of the foods that contain fats and oils—such as meat, milk, nuts, cheese, and eggs—are also good sources of protein.

Protein: The body's building blocks

Like carbohydrates and fats, **protein** can provide us with food energy. But protein is much more important to us in other ways. Except for water, your body is made mostly of protein. Good-quality protein is absolutely necessary to build new cells for all parts of your body and to keep them in good repair. If you don't eat enough fats and carbohydrates to supply the energy your body needs to stay alive and working, your body will use protein for energy. This may mean there won't be enough protein to meet the needs for growth and repair.

Fortunately, most people in the United States can get enough food. But we do have nutrition problems in our country. People with little money sometimes don't get enough protein. They tend to buy as much inexpensive food as they can, to keep from feeling hungry. But this food may be low in protein. High-quality protein is found in many foods, but those foods tend to cost more than others.

What does "high-quality" protein mean?

Amino acids   High-quality protein has all, or most, of the amino acids your body needs. **Amino acids** are the small units that go together to make up protein. At least twenty-two amino acids are important in nutrition.

The body is an efficient factory. It can break down molecules, move the parts around, and build new molecules out of them. This happens with amino acids. If your body needs a certain amino acid, it may be able to take parts of other amino acids to make that one.

But the body isn't perfect. It just can't produce some amino acids. You have to get those, called essential amino acids, in the foods you eat. Foods that have all the essential amino acids are called complete

protein (PRŌ tēn)   **amino acids** (ə MĒ nō   AS ids)

High-quality protein foods are more expensive than most other foods.

Here are some sources of protein. Which are complete? Which are incomplete?

protein foods. If the proteins in a food are missing one or more of those essential amino acids, we call them incomplete proteins.

How do you know what's complete protein and what's not?

Sources of complete protein Generally, the protein in meat, milk, eggs, fish, and poultry is complete protein. But here's an interesting thing. You can eat one food with incomplete protein together with another food that also has incomplete protein, and wind up with all the essential amino acids. Rice, for example, contains incomplete protein. Beans are incomplete, too—but they are not missing the same things that rice is. These are complementary proteins. When you eat rice and beans together, as many people from the Caribbean do, you have a meal with a very good protein content.

Split peas are a variety of legume. Split-pea soup is a source of vegetable protein.

Vegetarian diets   People on vegetarian diets (all plant, no meat) need to know quite a bit about nutrition to make sure they get enough good protein. Some eat eggs and milk products, which are very good protein sources. (In fact, eggs contain the best-quality protein of all!) But some vegetarians eat only food from plants. Their best sources of protein are nuts and legumes. Legumes are different kinds of peas and beans, often sold dried. All sorts of interesting soups, salads, and casseroles can be made from legumes.

I didn't know vegetables had protein. I thought they had vitamins.

Many vegetables have large amounts of protein. However, vegetables are even more important as a source of vitamins, because vitamins are often hard to find in other foods. A shortage of vitamins can affect your whole body chemistry.

Vitamins: The body's regulators

Vitamins are complicated molecules. You need them in very small amounts. A pile of all the vitamins your body uses in one day would amount to little more than a pinhead. Vitamins contain materials that take part in many of the chemical reactions that are needed for your body to work properly. They make it possible for your body to do the thousands of little jobs that go on all the time. Most vitamins have many jobs, and they often work together.

We don't know, yet, all of the jobs each vitamin does. In fact, scientists aren't even sure they've discovered all the vitamins. There are a lot of ideas about vitamins going around today—and some of them may not be right.

What about the story that vitamins in carrots are good for your eyes? Is that true?

Vitamin A   The claim that carrots are good for the eyes is true. Carrots are a very rich source of vitamin A. In your eyes, this vitamin is changed into a substance that helps your eyes adjust to light and dark. For example, when you come out of an afternoon movie, it takes a moment or so to get used to the bright sunlight. Vitamin A makes it possible for your eyes to make this adjustment. People who don't have enough vitamin A may find that a sudden change of light hurts their eyes very much. They may have a hard time seeing at all in a darkened room. They are very likely to have trouble driving at night. This problem is sometimes called night blindness.

Vitamin A does a lot of other important things for your body, too. It's very important in building many body parts and keeping them

vitamins (VĪ tə minz)

22

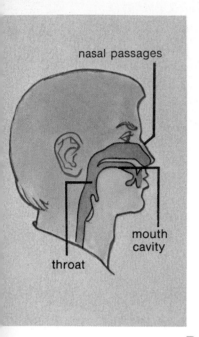

Vitamin A is needed to keep mouth, nose, and throat linings healthy.

healthy and strong. This is especially true of the skin and the mucous membranes such as the lining of the mouth, nose, and throat. This helps the body fight many diseases.

But it is possible to get too much vitamin A. Too much can be toxic, or poisonous. Eskimos, for example, avoid eating polar bear liver because it is extra rich in vitamin A. The body reacts to too much vitamin A as it would to a poison. This is true for many nutrients. A certain amount is good because it's needed. But too much can actually hurt you.

Vitamin A can be made in your body from carotene, a dark yellow substance found in many vegetables. Color is an important clue to foods that have lots of carotene. Yellow vegetables contain good supplies. The darker the color, the more carotene, and the more potential vitamin A. Dark green, leafy vegetables are also good sources. (The yellow color of the carotene is covered over by the dark green.) Eggs and organ meats are good sources. You should be sure to eat one good source of vitamin A at least every other day.

Is there a vitamin B as well as a vitamin A?

B vitamins Vitamin B is actually a whole family of vitamins. Sometimes they are given numbers, such as B_1 or B_2. At other times you'll see their scientific names. Thiamin, riboflavin, and niacin are the best known. But other B vitamins are important, too.

The vitamins in the B group help your body to break down food and use it. This means they help to change food to energy and to build new cells for the body. Some play special parts in the nervous system, which affects the way you feel and act.

Did you ever hear of a disease called beriberi? It used to be very common in the southeastern part of Asia. Beriberi means "I cannot." This was a good description of how the disease made its victims feel. It affected the body's nervous system and energy production. Those who got it became more and more helpless and soon died. The problem turned out to be a **deficiency** (lack) of thiamin, sometimes called vitamin B_1.

We've never had any nutrition diseases in the United States, have we?

The United States has not had the serious hunger and famine that have plagued many parts of the world. We have also had fewer serious nutrition diseases in our history. But there have been some. The most widespread was pellagra. This is caused by a lack of the B vitamin called niacin. In the early 1900s, pellagra was a major cause of death in the South, mostly among poor people. People with pellagra developed a strange red rash and became depressed. Some became mentally ill. Often they had diarrhea and other troubles with

deficiency (di FISH ən se)

Find the souces of vitamin A here. What other nutrients do these foods contain?

their digestive systems. It took doctors several years to figure out that a poor diet was the problem.

It sounds very complicated. How can you tell what foods have B vitamins?

B vitamins are found in many foods. Grain products are the most common source of these vitamins. Grain products are foods such as cereals, breads, and pasta (spaghetti and macaroni, for example).

Some vitamins are lost or destroyed when different foods are processed. The word **restored** on a food label means that certain

restored (ri STORD)

Grain products furnish carbohydrates and proteins. They are also good sources of vitamin B. (Also see page 79.)

nutrients have been put back into the food to make up for those losses. **Fortified** means extra nutrients have been added that may not have been in the unprocessed food. **Enriched** means that certain amounts of iron and three of the B vitamins (thiamin, riboflavin, and niacin) have been added. The word "enriched" appears on the labels of many foods made from grains. Choose enriched foods when you can, even if they cost a few cents more.

Vitamin C must be next. I already know it's good for colds.

Vitamin C Vitamin C is good for colds—but it's not a cure, as many people believe. If you understand a little about what vitamin C does, it will help you figure out if what you hear is correct.

Vitamin C is needed for your body to form collagen, a substance that holds cells together. You might think of it as a kind of cement or glue. If you don't have enough, the tissues in your body are not as strong as they should be. They can't resist or fight infection well. Vitamin C also helps keep hard tissues, like bones and teeth, strong. And don't forget blood vessels—they're tissues, too. Lack of vitamin C will make them weak. Someone who bruises easily or has trouble with bleeding gums may need more vitamin C.

It's easy to get enough vitamin C. There's a lot in all citrus fruits—oranges, grapefruit, lemons, and so on. Vitamin C is found in many other fruits and vegetables, too, such as broccoli, strawberries, and tomatoes. Even potatoes have some. The amount of vitamin C in only 125 milliliters (1/2 cup) of orange juice is enough for your body's normal needs in a day. If you should get extra amounts one day, your

fortified (FOR tə fīd)   **enriched** (in RICHT)

Citrus fruits are excellent sources of vitamin C. What does this vitamin do?

Mackerel is one of the few foods that contain some vitamin D. What are some others?

body won't save it for the next day. This means you should eat a good source of this vitamin every day.

I didn't know bones needed vitamin C!

Bones need vitamin C and various other nutrients to make sure they grow to the proper size and strength. Vitamin D, the "sunshine" vitamin, is especially important. Lack of it causes rickets.

Vitamin D Vitamin D is an interesting vitamin because one of the best sources of it is sunshine. Sunlight actually changes certain substances in your skin into vitamin D. There are several other ways to get vitamin D. Milk that has been fortified with vitamin D is the best food source. Eggs, liver, and fish such as tuna, salmon, sardines, and herring also contain some vitamin D. Salt-water fish can make vitamin D and store large amounts in their livers. Maybe you've heard your grandmother talk about how good cod-liver oil is for you.

Vitamin E What vitamin E does for people is still not clear. There are many ideas about how it works, but very little is known for sure. It is found in a lot of foods, especially green, leafy vegetables, nuts, and various oils. Getting enough is not likely to be a problem.

Vitamin K Vitamin K is found in green, leafy vegetables and in cauliflower. But we get vitamin K another way, too. Certain bacteria in the intestines manufacture it. Vitamin K helps blood to clot. For this reason, people are sometimes given extra vitamin K after surgery or a serious injury.

Is there a vitamin for every letter of the alphabet?

The vitamins that have been discovered so far are A, the B group, C, D, E, and K. But there may be more that we don't know about. Nutrition is really a very young science. Most of the research has been done in this century. In fact, most vitamins were discovered between 1920 and 1940. We may discover many more things in food that are important, in tiny amounts, to life. That's one reason why it's best to get your vitamins from foods. Vitamin pills don't have everything that food has. We don't even know what "everything" means, in terms of the vitamins and minerals the body needs.

What's the difference between vitamins and minerals?

Vitamins are complicated molecules. They are "organic"—that is, they were first made by plants and animals. Minerals, on the other hand, are made of materials that were around long before life even existed.

Minerals: Special materials for special needs

Compared to vitamins, **minerals** are rather simple. In chemistry they are called elements. Elements are the most basic kind of matter. All of the substances on earth are made of some combination of elements. Oxygen, iron, copper, and calcium are examples of elements. Over a hundred elements have been discovered so far. Several of them are important in nutrition. Many of the others may be needed, too, but no one is certain which ones, yet.

I know calcium is important. That's what bones and teeth are made of.

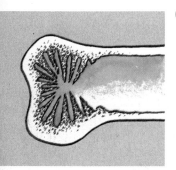

Calcium deposited in bones makes them strong.

Calcium Calcium makes bones hard and strong. The body makes bones by depositing calcium in a special, lacy, protein network. If young children don't get enough calcium, their leg bones don't become strong enough to hold up the tops of their bodies. Their leg bones bend outward, making them bow-legged.

People need calcium most when their bones are growing. But even when they're not growing, bone cells wear out. Replacement cells are made in your body. Those new cells need calcium, too. Many adults make a big mistake in believing they don't need calcium because they've finished growing. Older people may have very weak bones if they don't get enough calcium.

Calcium has other jobs in your body, too. It's necessary in order for your muscles and nerves to work properly. It even helps keep your heart beating. It is involved in the process of blood clotting, too. Often, it works with another element—phosphorus. There is some phosphorus in every cell in your body.

As you probably know, the very best source of calcium is milk. Young children need the amount of calcium in two or three servings of milk. (One serving of milk is 250 milliliters, or 1 cup.) For teenagers, it's at least four servings; for adults, two servings. Other dairy

minerals (MIN ər əlz)

products (such as yogurt, cheese, and ice cream) are fairly good calcium foods. Other good sources are spinach, canned salmon, shrimp, clams, and some green, leafy vegetables. Phosphorus is found in many of the same foods.

Iron Another important mineral found in leafy vegetables is iron. Spinach is famous for its iron (thanks in part to the "Popeye" cartoons). If you don't get enough iron, you're likely to feel tired and look pale. Doctors call this iron-deficiency **anemia.**

What exactly does iron do to give you energy?

Iron becomes part of the red blood cells. The iron attracts oxygen from air that you've breathed into your lungs. Then it helps the blood deliver the oxygen to cells all over your body. Those cells use oxygen to change the food you eat into energy. The iron-oxygen mixture in blood cells is what makes red blood cells red. Arteries carry blood from the heart and lungs to the body cells. The blood from your arteries is bright red because it has just picked up fresh oxygen in the lungs. Veins carry blood back to the heart. Blood from the veins

anemia (ə NĒ mē ə)

Which of these foods are sources of calcium, iron, or iodine? (Hint: some contain more than one of these nutrients.)

looks purplish because carbon dioxide was picked up from the body cells in exchange for the oxygen delivered to them. A doctor can often tell if you have anemia by looking at the color of your blood. If it's a pale red, you may need more iron. A blood test will tell for sure.

You get iron in many of the same foods that contain protein—meat, poultry, eggs, shellfish, nuts, and legumes. Organ meats, especially liver, are excellent sources. So are green, leafy vegetables, as we have already seen. Some fruits—such as prunes, raisins, grapes, apricots, and peaches—have iron. And remember that iron is added to enriched breads and cereals.

Your body recycles quite a bit of iron. As red blood cells wear out, your body saves much of the iron for the new cells. But you still need a constant supply. And whenever a person loses blood—such as through an injury or in menstruation—iron is lost, too. Extra supplies of iron are needed then.

Iodine Another important mineral, iodine, is found only in seafoods and in foods grown in iodine-rich soil, such as along the seacoast. People living in the middle part of the United States once had trouble getting iodine. Food scientists tried for a long time to figure out the best way to make sure everybody could get enough. They even thought about putting it in chewing gum or candy. Finally they decided to put it in salt, because most people use salt every day, but in small amounts. This is important, because too much iodine is poisonous.

I thought iodine was medicine that you put on cuts and scratches.

An iodine solution is generally used as a medicine to prevent infection. As a nutrient, iodine becomes part of a substance made by your thyroid gland.

Maybe you've read about the thyroid gland in one of your science books. It is a small gland in your neck. The substance it produces regulates how your body uses energy. When a person doesn't get enough iodine, the gland works harder and harder. All the extra work doesn't help make the substance, but it does make the gland get bigger and bigger. After awhile, the enlarged gland sticks out as a lump on the throat. This is called a goiter. It used to be a common and serious problem around the Great Lakes area. Now people avoid the condition easily, by using iodized salt.

Wouldn't it be easier just to put iodine in the water people drink?

Putting minerals into the water supply is another way of distributing them. But it is sometimes hard to control the water supply. Many people, particularly in rural areas, get their water from their own wells.

Thyroid gland

Fluorine In many areas fluorine, another mineral, is being added to the water supply. Fluorine seems to be useful in preventing cavities—especially in the teeth of children.

There's so much to remember about nutrition! How can you ever figure out what you need?

There's no doubt about it: nutrition is complicated. Professional nutritionists realized long ago that it was going to be hard for most people to remember and understand it all. So a group of nutritionists made up a simple kind of guide for people to use. This guide is known as the "Basic Four."

The Basic Four: A guide to good nutrition

These big groups of foods make up the **Basic Four**: (1) the Milk Group, (2) the Fruit and Vegetable Group, (3) the Meat Group, and (4) the Bread and Cereal Group. If you regularly eat foods from each of these groups, the chances are that you're getting all the nutrients you need.

Almost all those groups have some things I like and some I don't. Does it matter how I mix them up?

The Basic Four

MILK GROUP

Eat four or more servings a day (teenagers).
1 serving = 250 mL (1 cup) milk
OR
250 mL (1 cup) yogurt
OR
30 g (1 oz) Cheddar cheese
OR
375 mL (1½ cups) cottage cheese
OR
500 mL (2 cups) ice cream

FRUIT AND VEGETABLE GROUP

Eat at least four servings a day.
1 serving = 125 mL (½ cup) fruit or vegetable
(Include a good source of vitamin C every day. Eat a good source of vitamin A at least every two days.)

MEAT GROUP

Eat at least two servings a day.
1 serving = 85 g (3 oz) cooked meat
(This group includes all meats, eggs, poultry, fish, and shellfish. It also includes nuts and peanut butter, and dried beans and peas.)

BREAD AND CEREAL GROUP

Eat at least four servings a day.
1 serving = 1 slice of bread
OR
1 tortilla
OR
30 g (1 oz) cold cereal
OR
about 180 mL (¾ cup) cooked cereal, rice, grits, or pasta
(Be sure to look for "enriched" on the label—or choose "whole grain" or "restored" products.)

Minestrone, an Italian soup served with cheese, is another dish that combines foods from all the Basic Four groups.

You can mix the foods around almost any way you want, just as long as you do mix them up. The most important thing to remember about nutrition is to eat a variety of foods.

Most people get tired of eating the same thing all the time, anyway. Variety is more than a key to good nutrition—it's one of the important keys to enjoyable eating as well.

Speaking of enjoyment, is that so bad—eating food just because it tastes good when you're hungry?

There's nothing wrong with enjoying food. In fact, many of the things you do to make food more enjoyable also make it more nutritious—especially if they add some variety to what you eat.

Take a pizza, for instance. The crust gives you a serving from the Bread and Cereal Group. By itself, that's not too exciting. But if you add melted cheese from the Milk Group, it becomes much more enjoyable—and more nutritious, too. Add some tomato sauce and maybe green pepper from the Fruit and Vegetable Group, and it's even better! Some people like to add sausage or anchovies from the Meat Group.

Hey! That covers all the food groups! Do you mean I could live on just pizza?

You can't live on just one thing, no matter what it is—even if it includes all the food groups. You need to eat other things from each group, too. Still, pizza is a good example of how the different groups go well together to create variety. A cheeseburger with onions, lettuce, and tomato would be another example. Many other foods make good combinations, too. Later on, we'll take a look at a lot of things you can do to fix delicious, nutritious, and exciting foods for yourself, your family, and your friends.

Words to understand

nutrient	amino acid
energy	vitamin
nutrition	deficiency
digest	restored
carbohydrate	fortified
glucose	enriched
calorie	mineral
fat	anemia
protein	Basic Four

Questions to discuss

1. What does your body use for fuel?
2. What does your body use food energy for?
3. Name the groups of nutrients. Which ones supply energy?
4. Why is the fat in foods useful? Can you name four foods that contain quite a bit of fat?
5. What nutrient group do sugars, starches, and fiber belong to? Why is this group important?
6. Why is protein especially important?
7. Explain the difference between complete and incomplete protein.
8. How does vitamin C help to keep you healthy?
9. What is the "sunshine" vitamin? Why does it have that nickname?
10. Why does everyone need some calcium? What is the best source of calcium?

11. How does a person with anemia feel? Why?

12. Why do some towns put fluorine in their water?

13. Name the Basic Four food groups. How many servings does a teenager need from each group every day?

Things to do

1. Make a list of everything you ate yesterday. Use the Basic Four as a guide to evaluate what you ate. Did you meet your needs for good nutrition? Compare your results with the findings of other students.

2. If you were trying to lose weight, what changes would you make in the list of foods you ate yesterday? What if you were trying to gain weight? Write down the changes you would make.

3. Ask your teacher to help you find a list of the calories contained in common foods. Make a poster showing five of your favorite foods. Label each one with the number of calories per serving. Put a star next to the foods you think are good sources of important nutrients.

4. Make a poster about one of the nutrients discussed in this chapter. Include information on why it is important and what foods are good sources of the nutrient.

5. Look for newspaper and magazine articles about nutrition. The articles may be about nutrition problems in the United States or the world, about nutrition research, or about particular foods. Share the information with your class.

6. Conduct a fruit and vegetable poll. Ask ten or more students what fruits and vegetables they ate in the last two days. How many ate four servings every day? Which fruits and vegetables were the most popular?

Careers to consider

Would you like to help people solve diet problems?

If you are interested in helping people choose the foods they need, consider a career in nutrition.

Dietitians are experts in nutrition planning. Dietitians always have a college degree. **Registered dietitians** have "R.D." after their names. This means they have met the professional standards of the American Dietetic Association (ADA). With less education, you might work as a helper to a dietitian. **Dietetic assistants** and **technicians** work under the supervision of a dietitian.

Hospitals hire dietitians to plan meals for their patients. People who are sick or recovering from an operation usually need special diets. A dietitian visits patients to discuss special food problems and help them plan their eating when they go home.

Dietitians also work in local health clinics and other community programs that involve diet planning. They may be found in a variety of places that serve well-planned meals—public schools, colleges, company cafeterias, and military bases, for example.

A **nutritionist**, according to the ADA, is a registered dietitian with an advanced college degree. Nutritionists are often found in health clinics, advising people on how to eat. Many are teachers, especially at the college level.

Dietitians and nutritionists also work in *research*. Some study particular diet difficulties, such as diabetes or weight problems. Some study nutrients, trying to learn more about what they do in your body. Some dietitians and nutritionists look for new ways to help people improve their eating habits.

2

HAS THIS EVER HAPPENED TO YOU?

Jason's five-year-old brother, Mark, is having a birthday. As a surprise for him, Jason is helping his mother fix dinner with all Mark's favorite foods. Jason has been talking to Mark, and has secretly made a list of the things he likes most.

JASON (reading from his list): *Here it is, Mom. He likes macaroni and cheese best. His favorite vegetables are mashed potatoes and cream-style corn. We should have bread and butter, too, and milk to drink. For dessert, he likes angel food cake with vanilla ice cream.*

MOTHER (looking at list): *I know each one of these may be favorites of his, but I don't think they'll go too well together in the same meal.*

JASON: *Aw, come on, Mom. It's his birthday— let him have what he wants. Besides, I like all those things, too!*

Later, at the dinner table, Mark stirs at his plate of food with his spoon.

MARK: *Look, Mommy! This looks just like the library paste we use in kindergarten!*

Still later, Mark picks at his dessert.

FATHER: *I guess Mark was too excited to eat. He didn't even finish his ice cream.*

JASON (confused): *I know he liked everything, 'cause I checked it all out with him first. What went wrong?*

CHOOSING FOODS

Exploring . . .

What makes food appealing

The importance of variety

Food traditions, customs, and habits

Other influences on food choices

The trouble with Jason's meal is that he picked the foods out separately, because he knew that his little brother liked each one. He didn't stop to think how they would all look, taste, or "chew" when he put them all together in the same meal. If he had, he probably would have realized that the appearance of the foods was boring. They were almost all the same color—off-white or pale yellow. They were mostly the same shape and texture, too—roundish and "globby." And the flavors were all mild.

Food and the five senses

When we think of food, we tend to think only of how it tastes. But food also appeals to our other four senses—smell, sight, touch, and even hearing. Each sense offers ways in which variety can be added to a meal.

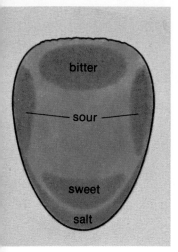

Taste and aroma Actually, there are only four things that the **taste buds** on your tongue can taste—sweet, sour, bitter, and salty. The rest of the flavor you get from the food comes from the **aroma**, or smell, which goes from the back of your mouth into your throat, and up into your nose. That's why you can't "taste" anything when you have a bad cold and your nose is clogged up. That's also why you might hold your nose when you swallow medicine or something else that you don't like. It might even help if you closed your eyes!

I can understand about holding my nose, but what good would it do to close my eyes?

Appearance Appearance is very important to food or anything else you put into your mouth. If it looks good, you will expect it to taste good. But if it looks bad, the chances are that your *mind* will make it taste bad, even if your taste buds don't!

Think about a cheeseburger with lettuce, onions, and tomato, fresh from the grill. On a toasted bun, with a pickle on the side, it might look good enough to make your mouth water! But suppose someone threw it onto a plate, pulled it apart, and messed it around, and then he scooped it up and handed it to you in a broken heap. It would still taste the same, but it would *look* so "yucky" that you probably wouldn't want to eat it.

On the other hand, eye appeal can help make food appetizing. Foods of different colors on a plate make the meal look interesting. Color variety is likely to mean that the meal has a variety of nutrients, too.

Another way to add interest to a meal is to serve foods in different shapes and sizes. For example, corn on the cob and peas are more interesting together on a plate than little piles of peas and corn kernels next to each other. Food can be fixed and cut in many different ways for variety.

All right, so appearance is important. But who cares what food feels like or sounds like?

Texture, temperature, and sound Your senses of touch and hearing tell you the difference between a crisp potato chip and a soggy one. Or a crunchy stalk of celery and a limp one. The feel, or **texture**, of food is sometimes more important to us than anything else. We want steaks to be tender, for instance. Pie dough should be flaky. Cake should be light and moist.

Temperature is a touch, or feeling, sensation too. Soft drinks should be cold. Soup should be hot. Tea should be either hot or cold, but not in between.

Many foods make sounds, too. You need to watch television only for an hour or two to realize that some foods are sold on their sound

turn to page 57

aroma (ə RŌ mə) **texture** (TEKS chər)

Flavor depends on appearance, taste, texture, temperature, and sound.

appeal. Potato chips and corn chips, crackers, breakfast cereal, apples, fried chicken, and fried fish are all sold on the promise of more crunch to the munch.

Your eyes, ears, nose, tongue, and teeth all work together when you eat food. And that's all to the good. It makes eating a fuller, more exciting experience. At the same time, it makes for variety in your food. And variety, more than anything else, makes for good nutrition. If you have variety, it means that you are eating different foods with the different nutrients that you need.

Importance of food variety

We sometimes put so much emphasis on how foods taste that we overlook some of these other important things that make us want to eat them. Jason's brother liked the taste of each of his favorite foods, but each one was pretty much like the other—more or less **bland** (mild, not spicy) and more or less sweet. The texture was monotonous (dull, everything the same), too. All the foods were soft. Most were creamy. Each one by itself might seem smooth and satisfying, but when they were served all together they produced a mushy feeling in the mouth.

MARK: *Well, I liked everything okay. I just got tired of eating.*

Even Jason's little brother got bored. All together, the meal was dull.

When you plan meals, try to include a variety of flavors. Creamed chicken on toast, for example, would be nicely **complemented** (filled out, completed) with a crisp green salad and Italian dressing. This combination is also a good balance of textures, or the "feel" of foods in the mouth. A soft food is much more interesting if you serve something crisp or crunchy along with it.

complemented (KAHM plə MEN tid)

Left: *Tacos* are delicious with fruit punch, refried beans, *tortilla* chips, and a green salad—a combination of flavors and textures. Right: *Linguine* with red or white clam sauce is an Italian specialty.

Monotony, or sameness, in colors, textures, and tastes can often result in monotony and lack of balance in nutrition, too. Jason's meal of soft, bland, whitish foods had a definite imbalance. Except for the milk and ice cream (which was heavy on sugar), they were all very heavy on starch.

Italian food If you look at the favorite foods of many countries, you'll notice how important variety is to nearly everyone. Pizza, as we have seen, is a good example of food variety. So are many of the Italian pasta dishes—such as lasagna, manicotti, ziti, and stuffed shells. Prepared with a meat and tomato sauce, they have a variety of colors and textures. They are often served with a salad of crisp greens, black olives, and bright red peppers for even more variety in the same meal.

Chinese food The Chinese plan especially carefully for variety. They like to combine opposite textures and flavors to create an appetizing taste sensation. Sweet-sour sauce is a good example. Chinese cooking traditionally tries to combine five flavors: sweet, sour, bitter, and salty, plus hot (look out for that spicy mustard!).

Meats and vegetables are combined to give variety in color and texture—from soft rice to chewy pork or beef to crunchy water chestnuts.

Mexican food Or take Mexican food. The *taco* (TAH kō), for instance, combines a crunchy golden shell with chewy brown meat, tangy

Rice, winter melon soup, and fish in sweet-sour sauce are a Chinese feast.

white onions, creamy yellow cheese, crisp green lettuce, and juicy red tomatoes. It's all topped off with a hot, spicy sauce.

Spanish food   Spanish *paella* (pah YEL ə) is another good example of variety. All kinds of delicious things are buried in a pan of saffron-colored (yellow) rice. One forkful will come up with a piece of hot, chewy *chorizo* (kor Ē zō), or Spanish sausage. Another will have a piece of tangy, red tomato. Another will lift a piece of white or dark meat chicken. Another will get a pink shrimp, a clam, or a mussel. Even the shells are left in the dish. They aren't eaten, of course, but they still add variety to the eating experience with their interesting shapes and even with their sound, as the fork clinks against them.

Wow! These dishes really turn a meal into something special!

Paella, a Spanish dish, combines a variety of foods. What foods do you see here?

When you think about it, eating is always a special occasion. Just look at all the things that happen when you eat. In the first place, eating satisfies your hunger and makes you feel better. It can stimulate all five of your senses, which adds to your enjoyment of life. It gives you energy, builds up your body, and keeps you healthy, all at the same time. Now, that's something special!

We show that eating is a special occasion in our lives by making it a part of many of our traditional events.

Food traditions and customs

Holidays Food is closely tied to our celebrations of many holidays. Some of these holidays have particular foods associated with them. A traditional Thanksgiving dinner includes many of the new foods the Pilgrims found in the New World, such as turkey, cranberries, pumpkins, and corn. What would Halloween be without candy corn and other "treats" to go trick-or-treating for? We associate brightly colored eggs with Easter, and ribbon candy with Christmas.

Many Jewish holidays have food symbols. During Passover, for example, it's traditional to eat flat, unleavened bread. This represents the bread baked by the Hebrews as they left Egypt over 3,000 years ago. They had to flee so quickly that they had no time to let their bread rise before baking it. In the Catholic religion, many saints have special days that are celebrated with feasts in which traditional foods are served.

Food get-togethers The Spanish *fiesta* (fẽ ES tə), or feast, has become traditional in many parts of the United States. So have other food get-togethers, such as clambakes, ox roasts, corn roasts, wiener

Salmon is being barbecued for a sea festival in Vancouver, Canada. Grilling is a traditional native North American method of preparing fish and meat.

Food gifts, such as this fruit basket, are suitable for a variety of occasions.

roasts, barbecues, pot-luck suppers, fish fries, wine-and-cheese parties, ice cream socials, and Fourth-of-July picnics.

All sorts of meetings are built around food. What would a club or business association luncheon meeting be without the lunch? A testimonial luncheon or dinner is often held to honor someone who is retiring.

Foods and food occasions are often the central feature of fund-raising drives, from Girl Scout cookies and bake sales to pancake breakfasts and spaghetti dinners. And don't forget the $100-a-plate dinners that raise money for political campaigns!

Special celebrations Since prehistoric times, people have held feasts to celebrate weddings, birthdays, harvests, victories, and other important events. Today's wedding reception isn't always a real tribal feast, but it still includes food and beverages. Most of the time there is a fancy wedding cake.

Food gifts Food is often used as a gift at holidays or as a "thank you" for some favor. Sometimes a gift of food is an expression of sympathy. In the Jewish religion, it is traditional to give something sweet to a family in mourning to "sweeten the sorrow." At other times, food is used to express joy, happiness, or simply friendship. A basket of fruit may say "Get well soon," or *Bon voyage!* A cake may say "Happy Birthday," "Happy Anniversary," or "Welcome to the neighborhood." A box of candy may say "Be my valentine" or "It's a girl!"

Food is usually associated with pleasant, happy occasions. **This fact sometimes plays an important part in the eating habits that people form.**

Food habits

A **habit** is something you do over and over again until you do it without thinking about it. Usually, you don't even realize that you are forming a habit. For instance, some people tend to eat more when they feel sad. They associate food with parties, social get-togethers, and other happy times, so they feel better when they eat. Without knowing it, they may get into the habit of eating to relieve feelings of loneliness or sadness. This isn't always bad, but if it happens too often, they can gain a lot of weight.

Food and emotions Food satisfies physical hunger very well. But some people eat to satisfy emotional needs, too. What they are really "hungry" for is love or friendship or success or admiration. The saddest part of all is that overeating and overweight often handicap them in getting these things.

Habits are hard to change. That's why it's especially important to form good food habits from the start. Once you do, it's relatively easy to keep to a proper diet.

Do you have to go on a diet to get into the right eating habits?

Diet A **diet** is simply a list of the foods you eat, whether by habit, by plan, or because that's all you can get. There are two kinds of diets— good ones and poor ones. A good diet contains the right foods in the right amounts. A poor diet contains too much of the wrong foods, or too little of the right foods, or both. Whether a particular amount is too much or too little depends on the individual person.

Don't think of a diet as simply eating less in order to lose weight. A diet should be part of an overall plan. It may be designed for a particular purpose, such as to lose or gain weight. But regardless of

These cyclists are burning about 2.2 calories per hour for every pound of their body weight. How many calories would you burn in one hour? For safety, bicycle on bikeways or roads closed to traffic (as shown here) whenever possible.

What kinds of problems can empty-calorie snacks cause?

its particular purpose, it must stick to the general aim of all diets. This aim must always be to provide the basic nutrients essential to good health and body activity.

I guess you can't just eat anything you like, can you?

You can eat almost anything you like—if you like enough different things and you like to combine them in a variety of ways. You also need to make a habit of eating in the proper amounts for your age, size, and level of activity.

What about snack foods with "empty calories"? Aren't they bad for you?

Empty-calorie snacks   Snack foods can be bad for you—if that's all you eat and you eat the wrong kinds. Snacks and other foods with **empty calories** have food energy (calories) but very little else in the way of nutrition. They are often high in starch, fat, or sugar, and low in vitamins, minerals, and protein.

Such foods can be bad for you if either of two things happens. If you are overweight, the extra calories will add to your problem. Or if you eat so much of them that you have no appetite left over for foods with protein, vitamins, and minerals, snack foods are bad for you.

However, if you eat enough of the things you need and are active enough to use up the extra calories from snack foods, they won't hurt you nutritionally. Of course, a particular food may contribute to problems of a particular individual—such as stomach problems, tooth decay, allergies, and skin problems. Obviously, you shouldn't make a habit of eating anything that adds to these problems.

Most of your food habits are probably pretty good. Any habit that gets you eating a variety of foods in reasonable amounts is a good habit. If you eat breakfast, that's a good habit. So is the habit of eating lunch and dinner. The habit of snacking can be good, too, if

it's not overdone and doesn't interfere with your regular meals. In fact, you can use snacks to fill in nutritional gaps. The habit of eating foods from the Basic Four Food Groups is a good one—and there are probably at least *some* foods that you like in each group.

Other influences on eating habits

Geography A lot of things influence your eating habits. Your background is one. We've already mentioned religion and national origin as possible influences on what you eat. Your geographical area is another. For instance, if you are from New England, you are most likely used to eating lobster, codfish, and scrod. In Maryland, you would be used to eating crab cakes. In Louisiana, it might be crawfish and red beans with hot pepper sauce. Throughout most of

Food is often a part of celebrations, as at this Italian festival in Edison, New Jersey.

the South, hominy grits are served regularly with breakfast and other meals. In the Southwest and California, you would probably be used to Mexican food: tortillas, enchiladas, and tacos.

Advertising Advertising plays an important part in influencing food choices, too. A great deal of television time is devoted to convincing you that a certain brand of cereal, soup, soft drink, snack, or sandwich spread will help make your life healthy and happy. Critics of advertising claim that too much of the satisfaction consumers get from their purchases has been created by the ad rather than by the product.

Other people Even more important than advertising is the influence of other people—friends, neighbors, and social "trend setters." Most people like to keep up with current styles and tastes, in food as well as clothes, furniture, and automobiles. As we have seen, eating is something that people like to do together. They like to talk about food, too. Exchanging favorite recipes with friends and acquaintances is a tradition as old as cooking itself.

Climate and seasons Climate, weather, and the season of the year also influence what you eat. To the pioneers, these factors were probably the most important of all. They had to settle for whatever would grow locally—and wait until harvest time to pick it. If they wanted fruits or vegetables at other times, they were pretty much out of luck. Some fruits and vegetables would keep fresh for a while in "root cellars." These were small rooms dug down below the frost line—the level where the ground normally freezes. But most fruits and vegetables had to be canned, dried, or pickled to keep them from spoiling. Many recipes resulted from the search for new ways to liven up the limited choice of foods available in a particular region at a particular time of year.

Apples, nuts, and other foods that ripen in the fall were once associated with harvest time. Nowadays, foods from various climates can be shipped anywhere and anytime, so no one in any region has to depend on a single harvest season.

Because of transportation and refrigeration, lettuce grown in California is at markets in other parts of the country year round.

Transportation Because of improved transportation and refrigeration, foods like Florida oranges, Texas grapefruit, Idaho potatoes, and Georgia peaches now can be found in stores all over the country. California lettuce is available in northern supermarkets year-round. So climate, weather, and season of the year are not as important as they once were. However, these factors still affect the price. Local fruits and vegetables in season are much less expensive, and usually tastier, than those that are picked green and shipped long distances.

Food processing and equipment Transportation and refrigeration aren't the only technological changes that have affected our eating habits. New developments in food processing, packaging, and freezing have also influenced what we eat. Methods of preparing food have been influenced by new home equipment, too—the pressure cooker, the slow cooker, the Japanese hibachi, the Chinese wok, and the microwave oven, for example.

Eating out The rise of fast-food restaurants serving hamburgers, hot dogs, chicken, fish and chips, pizza, and the like has increased the number of meals eaten out.

Life style Most of these developments have fit in with a general trend toward informality in our **life style** (the way we live). Dining, in particular, has become more casual than in the past. The formal dining room and living room have given way to the more relaxed "family room."

You are what you eat. As you learn more about food and nutrition, you can take care of your health and learn to enjoy a wide variety of foods.

Income Personal or family income is another factor that influences many diets. Some foods are too expensive to fit into low-income budgets. We have already mentioned the fact that some of the high-quality protein foods—especially high-priced meats—cost too much for low-income families to buy often.

No wonder people can't control their eating habits. With all that hitting them, they don't stand a chance!

Education Many of the things that influence your eating habits are very hard to control. But there's one other thing that plays an important part: education. The more you know about yourself and the food you eat, the better equipped you'll be to make wise food decisions. By using this knowledge, you will get not only the most nutrition from your food, but the most pleasure and enjoyment, too. It will help you make every food occasion a special occasion.

Words to understand

taste buds
aroma
texture
bland
complement

habit
diet
empty calorie
life style

Questions to discuss

1. How can you make food look interesting?
2. What are the five senses? Give an example of how food appeals to each.
3. What four tastes can taste buds sense?
4. Why does food lose its flavor when you have a cold or if you hold your nose?
5. Why does variety in color, taste, and texture make for good nutrition?
6. List four holidays and some foods that you associate with each.
7. Name three occasions when you might give a gift of food. What would you give?
8. How would you describe a good diet? A poor one?
9. Are "empty-calorie" foods good for you? Make a list of foods that provide calories and few, if any, other nutrients.
10. List five or more things that influence your food choices.

Things to do

1. Plan a meal based on your favorite foods. Describe the colors, tastes, and textures. Do the foods go well together? Is there nutritional variety?
2. Make a list of ten foods that have strong associations or memories for you (for example: popcorn, watermelon, hotdogs, cheeseburger with everything on it, jelly beans). Read your list to five other people. Ask them to write down the things that first come to mind when they hear each food named. Compare their responses. Which food associations were the most common? Which were very different? What might explain the differences?
3. Analyze your eating patterns. For one day, every time you eat, write down when you ate, what you ate, and why you ate it. How many times did you eat something during the day? Were you really hungry each time? Did you ever eat to be sociable, or because you were nervous, unhappy, or bored? Which eating patterns are about the same every day? Would you call them habits? Which of your food habits are good? Which habits should you try to improve?
4. Analyze a lunch served at your school. List the foods served. Identify the food groups involved. Did the lunch contain at least one food from each group? Did it have other kinds of variety?

5. Try to think of at least five things you eat now that you did not eat five years ago. When did you first eat each food? What caused you to try it? (Did you see the food advertised? Did a friend introduce you to it? Did a parent make you eat it?) Trying to answer these questions will help you become aware of some of the things that affect your food choices and habits.

6. Describe to your class a favorite family meal—if possible, one that represents your ethnic heritage. Discuss the variety of colors, tastes, textures, and nutrients. You may want to compile a class cookbook of favorite recipes.

Careers to consider

Would you like to grow food?

If you are interested in working with plants, consider a career in agriculture.

Many agricultural jobs are on some kind of farm. Maybe it's a wheat farm in Kansas, a citrus grove in Florida, a grape vineyard in California, or an apple orchard in New York. Almost every state has some farm specialties.

Not everybody can run a farm, of course. Successful farming today takes a technical knowledge of agriculture plus know-how in running a business. After-school clubs such as 4-H and the Future Farmers of America (FFA) can help you learn more about farming.

Farmers need a lot of help. **Farm hands** help the farmer from planting to harvesting, and in protecting the crops from diseases and insects in between those times. **Business managers** are hired by some farmers to help them handle the financial end of farming. Farmers also depend on the help and advice of experts in plant science.

Botany and *horticulture* are two common names for the science of plants and how they grow. There are a number of different careers in plant science. For example, there are **plant pathologists**, who study plant diseases. They may work on developing a substance that prevents or cures a particular disease. Or they may try to create a new variety of plant that has built-in disease resistance. **Plant ecologists** study the environment plants grow in. They are interested in how such things as weather, soil conditions, and fertilizers affect plant growth. **Plant geneticists** work on improving plants by developing new varieties. Improvements might include better flavor, more nutrition, or easier harvesting.

In counties across the country, there are **agricultural extension agents** ready to help farmers and home gardeners with advice on growing foods in each area. They are part of our federal government's Department of Agriculture.

3

HAS THIS EVER HAPPENED TO YOU?

Jim and some friends walk past Jim's house on their way home from a basketball game.

JIM: *Come on in, gang. I'll put some records on the stereo. You've got to hear my new Paul Richmond album!*

They all go into the family room. Jim puts a record on the stereo.

TOMMY: *Hey, Jim! Do you have anything in the kitchen to chew on? I like to eat while I follow the beat!*

Jim goes into the kitchen and searches through the cupboard.

JIM: *Huh! Nothing here. No corn chips, no Cheesies, no Fluffies, no Twirpies, no Snookies. Just some plain old crackers.*

MICHELLE: *Nothing in the fridge, either. No ice cream, no Slurpies, no Chirpies, no Fudgies, no Sludgies. Just some raw vegetables and a package of cream cheese.*

JIM: *Hey, gang–I guess I goofed. There's nothing here we can eat. I'll have to wait till my Mom gets home to fix something.*

Everyone moans.

ANNE: *Sorry, Jim. I can't listen to music on an empty stomach. All those in favor of going over to Hamburger Heaven, say "Me!"*

EVERYONE: *ME!!*

50

SNACKS WITH FRIENDS

Exploring . . .

Easy snacks for all occasions

How to trim and cut vegetables

How to choose fresh fruits

How to measure ingredients

Recipe language: baking and mixing terms

Have you ever had friends over at your house and found suddenly that there was "nothing around to eat"? If you're like most young people, you and your friends are hungry a lot of the time. You spend a lot of time eating and snacking together. That's partly because your bodies are growing and need nutrients to build new tissues, and partly because you're physically active and need lots of energy. But it's also because eating is a social occasion. Eating is something that all people, young and old, enjoy doing together.

It's too bad Jim's party broke up before it even got started. It didn't really have to. There were actually lots of good things around to snack on, but he didn't see them.

JIM: *What do you mean, I didn't see them? I looked all through the cupboard and the refrigerator!*

The problem is, some people don't know what to look for, because they don't know what can be done with the things they find. For instance, let's see what you can do with those "plain old crackers," and the raw vegetables and cream cheese that Michelle found in the refrigerator.

> JIM: *Well, I'm certainly not going to serve my friends plain cream cheese on crackers. And I can't throw a clump of celery and a bunch of carrots at them, either. They're kids, not rabbits!*

The only thing those vegetables need is a little cleaning and cutting to give them some "style." You can also add some excitement to the taste of vegetables if you know your way around the kitchen.

Fruit and Vegetable Snacks

The first things you'll need are some tools—a cutting board, a large kitchen knife (sometimes called "chef's knife"), and a vegetable peeler.

Cleaning and cutting celery Let's start with the celery. Pull a stalk off the bunch and rinse it under cold water, rubbing it with your fingers. You may notice some gritty dirt down at the base of the stalk. If this does not come off easily, rub it with a vegetable brush.

Now lay the stalk down on the cutting board. Trim off the bottom edge, along with the hard "knuckle" where the trunk of the stalk divides into branches, and the leaves. Throw these parts away. Save the branches. Some may be used as celery sticks. The smaller ones can be saved and chopped up later for salads, casseroles, or soups.

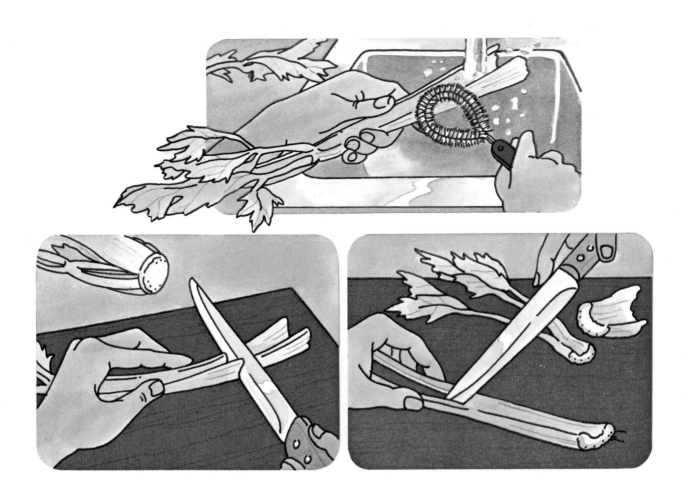

Now cut the stalk and the very thick branches into sticks about a centimeter (1/2 inch) wide. Cut the very long sticks in half so they'll be easier to handle.

Suppose the celery is all droopy?

Keeping celery crisp Fresh, good-quality celery should not be droopy. Certainly never buy any that is all wilted. Look for celery with green, fresh-looking leaves and stiff stalks. It shouldn't have any brown or dark-colored areas. To keep it fresh and crisp once you get home, trim off the ends, rinse well, and store in a covered container or plastic bag. If your celery does get a little limp, you can freshen or "crisp" it by putting the thick end in water. Since you're in a hurry, try putting the celery sticks in some ice water while you get the carrots ready.

Okay, now what do I do with the carrots—slice them up into little round chips?

Choosing carrots Carrots are easy to serve and eat in stick form, like the celery. If you have a lot of carrots to choose from, pick out the slightly smaller, thinner ones. They're younger and more tender. They're also sweeter and milder in flavor. Use the larger carrots for cooking.

Fresh carrots are smooth, firm, and bright orange. Don't buy ones that look tired, have spots of decay, or have a lot of green on the carrots themselves. You can keep carrots at their best by storing them in their original package in the vegetable section of your refrigerator. If they aren't packaged when you buy them, put them in a plastic bag.

Making carrot sticks To make the carrot sticks, first peel off the skin with the vegetable peeler. Next, cut off the tip and the thick end. Rinse with cold water. Cut the carrot crosswise in half, or into 8- to 10-centimeter (3- to 4-inch) lengths. Now cut each piece lengthwise into sticks. This often means cutting the thin end of the carrot lengthwise into halves (making two carrot sticks) and the thick end into quarters (making four sticks).

Now put your carrot and celery sticks in mugs or short glasses, and you're ready to pass them around to your friends. If you want to give them some extra flair, try making a dip out of leftover cream cheese.

How do you make a dip?

Making dips First, soften the cream cheese by mashing it with a spoon. Then thin it with milk, adding a few drops at a time and mixing until the cream cheese has about the **consistency**, or texture

consistency (kən SIS tən sē)

and thickness, of mayonnaise. Now look around for some seasonings to add. Chives would be good, or onion salt, or garlic salt. A little seasoned salt will add quite a bit of flavor.

How much seasoning should you use?

The amount of seasoning depends on your taste and on how much cream cheese you have. The best approach is to add a few shakes at a time, mix it in, and taste it. Be sure to taste it *on* the celery and carrot sticks, because they will add their own flavor to the dip. If you're not sure what a certain seasoning will taste like, put a spoonful of the dip on a separate plate and test out the seasoning. That way, if you don't like what it does, you haven't ruined the whole dip.

If you want to add an extra taste, see if you have any dry onion soup mix in the house. Add it to the dip a couple of milliliters (half a teaspoon) at a time until it's as strong as you like it.

Or perhaps you can turn it into a tuna fish dip. A 185-gram (6½-ounce) can of tuna fish will be about right for a 230-gram (8-ounce) package of cream cheese. If you have less cream cheese than that, use proportionately less tuna fish. Add 45 milliliters (3 tablespoons) of mayonnaise, too. This dip could also use 15 milliliters (1 tablespoon) of lemon juice and 1 milliliter (1/4 teaspoon) of hot pepper sauce, but they're not essential.

Serve the dip in a small bowl. You might put the bowl on a platter or tray and surround it with some of those crackers you found in the cupboard. Those crackers won't be plain and ordinary anymore!

Suppose I have time to go shopping ahead of time. What else would be good to nibble on?

Cream cheese dip makes these crackers and vegetables extra special.

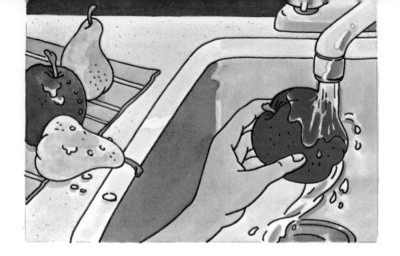

Serving fresh fruits Any kind of fresh fruit makes a good snack. Most of your friends probably like fruit. Apples, pears, grapes, peaches, plums, and nectarines are all good. These fruits are especially delicious in the late summer and fall, when they are most plentiful. You can serve them without any special preparation. Just wash them off under cold water.

Won't they taste like soap if you wash them?

Do *not* use soap. Directions in a cookbook or other recipe to "wash" foods mean simply to rinse them in clean water, rubbing them with your fingers or scrubbing with a vegetable brush, if needed.

Your fruits will look best when heaped up in a bowl, with all sorts of sizes, shapes, and colors. If you're willing to go to a little extra effort, cut the fruit up into chunks (with or without the peel) and serve them with toothpicks. (The cut edges of apples, pears, and bananas can be dipped in lemon or orange juice to keep them from turning brown.) You can even prepare some melon balls for variety in shape and color.

How do you make melon balls?

Making melon balls There is a kitchen tool made just for this job, called a melon baller. But if you don't have one, you can use a round measuring spoon. Simply cut off a slice of melon about 8 centimeters (3 inches) wide. Then take the measuring spoon and press the hollow side very firmly down against the flesh of the melon. This forms the top of the melon ball. Now twist the spoon down into the melon, scooping out the bottom of the melon ball, and lift it out.

Melons are most plentiful in the summer. You'll find cantaloupes from May through September. Honeydews are available from July through October. Watermelons are at their best in June, July, and August.

When these fruits are out of season, turn to other kinds. Many varieties of oranges and tangerines come into season in the winter, when other fruits are going out. Bananas can be found throughout the year. So can pineapples, though they are most plentiful in April and May.

How do you peel a pineapple? I know you can't eat that prickly skin.

Making pineapple chunks   The simplest way to trim a fresh pineapple is to cut it first into round slices, from 1 to 2 centimeters (1/2 to 1 inch) thick. Use the large kitchen knife. Then lay each slice on its side and trim off the rind with a smaller sharp knife. Don't forget to go back and dig out any "eyes" that you miss the first time around.

Now cut each slice in half and cut out the tough core from the center. Cut the slices into chunks and serve them with toothpicks. You might like to use colored cocktail toothpicks, but plain round

ones will work just as well. You can serve canned pineapple chunks the same way.

I like pineapple—and other fresh fruits, too. But I hate to pick them out. Sometimes they turn out to be soft and mushy, and sometimes they're hard and sour.

Each fruit has its own special things to look for, but there are a few things that can be said about almost all fruits.

Buying fresh fruits

In general, look for fruits that are heavy for their size. The heavier they are, the juicier they are. They should be **mature**—that is, fully grown. Most fresh fruits are picked when they are mature but before they are ripe. They still must develop in sweetness and flavor. They will do this if they are mature, but if they are picked too early, they may never ripen properly. Mature fruits are round and full, and usually bright in color.

Peaches, nectarines, pears, and plums will feel just a little soft when mature and ripe. But when checking, be sure *not* to bruise the fruit. Damaged fruit must be thrown out, which raises the cost of food to everyone.

Remember also to look for fruits at the time they are harvested, when they are **in season**. They are usually cheapest and best tasting then. Do not buy more than you can use. Fresh fruit may spoil rather quickly. If you end up throwing out half of what you bought, it's as if you had paid twice as much for what you did use. Most fresh fruits will keep for two to five days, especially in the refrigerator. Apples, citrus fruits, and melons will keep in the refrigerator for one to two weeks.

Avoid fruits that have large bruises, cuts, watery spots, or mold. Even if they are on sale, they may not be a bargain by the time you trim off the bad parts. Remember: good-quality fresh fruits *look* fresh. If your fruit does have any bruises, cut them out and eat the good fruit immediately. If you don't, the spot will spread.

The **U.S. Department of Agriculture (USDA)** publishes information on buying and storing fresh fruits and vegetables. You can get copies from home economists working in Cooperative Extension offices all over the country. Many cookbooks also contain information about particular fruits. Here are some tips about a few of the fruits you may want to buy for snacking with your friends.

APPLES Look for firm, full, well-rounded, and well-colored apples. Most eating apples start out green and turn red or yellow as they mature and ripen. Some kinds, such as McIntosh, may have large

mature (mə CHUR)

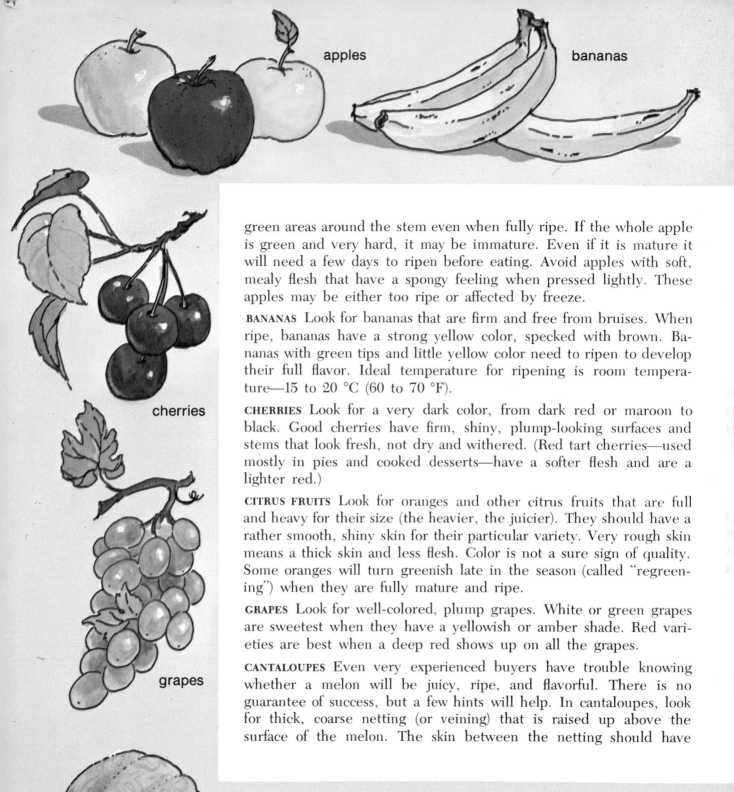

apples

bananas

cherries

grapes

cantaloupes

citrus fruits

green areas around the stem even when fully ripe. If the whole apple is green and very hard, it may be immature. Even if it is mature it will need a few days to ripen before eating. Avoid apples with soft, mealy flesh that have a spongy feeling when pressed lightly. These apples may be either too ripe or affected by freeze.

BANANAS Look for bananas that are firm and free from bruises. When ripe, bananas have a strong yellow color, specked with brown. Bananas with green tips and little yellow color need to ripen to develop their full flavor. Ideal temperature for ripening is room temperature—15 to 20 °C (60 to 70 °F).

CHERRIES Look for a very dark color, from dark red or maroon to black. Good cherries have firm, shiny, plump-looking surfaces and stems that look fresh, not dry and withered. (Red tart cherries—used mostly in pies and cooked desserts—have a softer flesh and are a lighter red.)

CITRUS FRUITS Look for oranges and other citrus fruits that are full and heavy for their size (the heavier, the juicier). They should have a rather smooth, shiny skin for their particular variety. Very rough skin means a thick skin and less flesh. Color is not a sure sign of quality. Some oranges will turn greenish late in the season (called "regreening") when they are fully mature and ripe.

GRAPES Look for well-colored, plump grapes. White or green grapes are sweetest when they have a yellowish or amber shade. Red varieties are best when a deep red shows up on all the grapes.

CANTALOUPES Even very experienced buyers have trouble knowing whether a melon will be juicy, ripe, and flavorful. There is no guarantee of success, but a few hints will help. In cantaloupes, look for thick, coarse netting (or veining) that is raised up above the surface of the melon. The skin between the netting should have

honeydews

plums and prune plums

dried fruits

watermelons

nectarines

changed from green to a yellowish color. (However, a very yellow, soft rind—the skin—may mean overripeness.) When ripe, the melon will have a pleasant cantaloupe smell when held close to the nose. It will feel a little soft to the thumb at the blossom end (opposite the dimpled end where the stem fell off). Small bruises won't hurt, but avoid large damaged areas or mold.

HONEYDEWS Look for melons with a soft, velvety feel, a yellowish-white or cream-colored rind, and a slight softening at the blossom end. Ripe melons will have a faint, pleasant, fruit odor. Avoid melons with a pale white or greenish-white color and hard, smooth feel. They were picked too early.

WATERMELONS The easiest and surest way to pick a watermelon is to have it cut so you can see what it looks like on the inside. Look for firm, juicy flesh with good red color and a thin rind (white part). The red flesh shouldn't have any white streaks. Seeds should be dark brown or black. White seeds are a sign of immaturity.

If you can't have the watermelon cut first, here are a few tips. Look for a rather smooth surface. It should be slightly dull (neither very shiny nor very dull). The ends of the melon should be filled out and rounded. The underside should have a creamy color. While these are qualities that the "experts" look for, they don't always guarantee a melon at its peak of ripeness and flavor. It is therefore a good idea to do as the experts do when they choose an uncut melon—cross your fingers!

NECTARINES This delicious fruit has the flesh of a peach and the skin of a plum. Look for rich color, plumpness, and a slight softening along the "seam." Most varieties are orange-yellow between the red areas. Avoid rock-hard, greenish, or dried up fruits. These are immature and may never ripen properly.

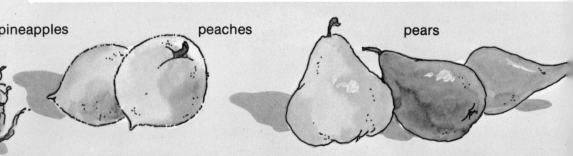

pineapples   peaches   pears

PEACHES Look for peaches which are fairly firm or just a little soft. As with nectarines, the skin between the red areas should be yellow or creamy. Avoid rock-hard peaches with a greenish color. These are usually immature and won't ripen properly.

PEARS Look for firm or medium firm pears. Color depends on the variety—from greenish yellow to brown. Pears that are rock-hard may ripen at room temperature, but sometimes they won't. It is better to select ones that have already begun to soften, to be sure that they will ripen properly. Avoid limp or shriveled pears. Also avoid pears with spots on the sides or blossom end (away from the stem). This means that brown, dried up tissue may lie beneath.

PINEAPPLES Look for sweet-smelling pineapples that have leaves or "spikes" that can be pulled fairly easily from the top. Mature pineapples are dark green in the hard stage. As they ripen (at room temperature) most varieties turn to a golden yellow or reddish brown color. Avoid pineapples with a dull yellowish-green color, dried appearance, or unpleasant smell.

PLUMS AND PRUNE PLUMS Most plums are rather round in shape and vary from yellow to red to purple. Prunes are flatter, with a purplish-black or bluish-black skin. Look for plums and prunes that have a good, full color for the particular variety. They should be fairly firm to slightly soft when ripe. Avoid fruits that are very hard, or poorly colored. These may be immature, which means they will not ripen properly.

DRIED FRUITS Less trouble to fix and to eat are dried fruits, especially raisins. These are also very good mixed with peanuts or other nuts. Serve them in little bowls—one for every three or four people.

Another good snack item—one that goes very well with fruit—is cheese.

Cheese and other snacks

Cheese is very versatile—that is, you can serve it in a lot of different ways. You can cut it into little chunks and serve it with toothpicks. You can slice it with a knife or a cheese wire and put it on crackers. Cheese spreads can be scooped out with a knife and spread on crackers, pumpernickel or rye bread, or what-have-you.

The problem with cheese is, there're some that I like a lot, but most kinds are too strong for me.

Kinds of cheese There are a lot of mild but flavorful cheeses you can choose from. The best-liked cheeses in this country are Swiss, Cheddar, and American. Swiss is a mild, firm cheese with a nutty flavor. Cheddar comes in mild, medium, sharp, and very sharp varieties. If you don't like cheese with a "bite" to it, get the mild.

One of the best ways to be sure you will like the cheese you pick out is to shop at a cheese store or delicatessen where the cheese is

Here are some different kinds of cheese. Which ones can you identify?

kept in large pieces, rather than already cut and prepackaged. Salespeople in these stores are often willing to cut off a little slice for you to taste before you buy.

American cheese and process cheese are very mild cheeses. They're used a lot in casseroles and grilled cheese sandwiches, but they're also good on crackers or with fruit.

Pizza snacks   Another cheese that you've probably had and liked is mozzarella (MAHT sə REL ə). It's used in a lot of Italian dishes, including pizza. That's another good snack item, by the way. You can heat up a frozen pizza and cut it into little squares to snack on. Or you can make "pizza toast" on your own. Simply spoon some pizza sauce (available in jars at your grocery store) onto a piece of toast, English muffin, or hamburger bun. Sprinkle it with grated mozzarella cheese. Then put it under the broiler for just a few minutes, until the cheese bubbles (but don't let it burn!). Serve open-faced, like a slice of pizza, with milk or fruit juice to drink.

You can buy the grated mozzarella cheese in the store, but it may cost more that way. You're better off grating your own. There are many kinds of graters. The most common kind is called a "stand-up" grater. The stand-up grater is inexpensive and easy to use. For grating mozzarella cheese, use the side with the large round holes. Simply rub the cheese firmly down over the cutting edges—but watch your fingers! The very fine side is good for grating things like Parmesan cheese into very fine pieces. The side with medium-size holes cuts things into small shavings (such as grated orange or lemon rind). The side with the large slits is good for shredding things—such as cabbage for cole slaw or lettuce for tacos.

Hotdog snacks If you don't have pizza makings, try pigs in a blanket. They're quick to cook and delicious to eat. Simply cut a few frankfurters in half—or use small "cocktail" frankfurters. Wrap the hotdog pieces in pieces of refrigerated biscuit dough. Stretch the dough around the frankfurter so that it overlaps, and press it together with a fork.

Put the "pigs" on a cookie sheet and bake in the oven at 200 °C (400 °F) for about 10 minutes. Serve them with mustard and catsup and a dish of pickles.

Here's an even easier hotdog snack: first boil the frankfurters. Cut each one into four pieces. Stick toothpicks into the pieces and serve on a plate with a dipping sauce. Your dip might be a barbecue sauce or a spicy mustard mixture. Or maybe you would prefer a sweet-sour sauce.

What if all you've got in the refrigerator is leftovers? What can you do with those?

Snacks from leftovers Almost any kind of leftover meat is good for snacks—sliced and served with crackers and mayonnaise or mustard. Add a side dish of pickles and olives. Ham, turkey, roast beef, and meat loaf are fine with crackers. So are bologna and other luncheon meats. Or put these on bread and make party sandwiches by cutting them diagonally into quarters. And don't forget good old peanut butter and jelly—on crackers or in those little party sandwiches. You've probably got eggs in the refrigerator, too, for a sandwich spread like egg salad. We'll talk later about a lot of tasty but quick

Some tasty treats to fix for your friends include relishes, crackers and dip, party sandwiches, pigs in a blanket, hotdogs on toothpicks, popcorn, or cookies.

things you can do with eggs, when we get into the subject of brunches.

Another snack item that's easy to keep around until you need it is popcorn. It's also easy and fun to make.

Doesn't popcorn have a lot of "empty calories"?

Popcorn Popcorn is actually rather low in calories—if you don't "drown" it in butter. It can be expensive, though, if you buy it already popped. Instead, buy the kernels and pop your own. Directions for popping are usually on the package. The oil you pop it in should be enough to make the salt stick, without adding butter—and calories.

What if you've got a sweet tooth? Are things like cake and cookies always bad?

Like everything else, cake and cookies are fine if you don't overdo it, and if you eat enough other things, too. You'll probably find that cookies taste better and fresher if you make them yourself. Home-made cookies are also a good topic of conversation!

Making and baking cookies

Most cookies are fairly easy to make. There are several kinds. Bar cookies—such as brownies and butterscotch squares—are made in a square or rectangular cake pan, and are more like a heavy, chewy cake. Rolled cookies, as their name suggests, are made from dough flattened out with a rolling pin and cut into various shapes with a cookie cutter.

The simplest of all are drop cookies. A small amount of cookie dough is spooned out or pinched off with the fingers and simply

Oatmeal cookies

about 5 dozen cookies

180 mL	¾ cup shortening	**Cream** the shortening and sugars in a large bowl. Beat in egg, water, and vanilla.
250 mL	1 cup brown sugar	
125 mL	½ cup sugar	**Blend** flour, salt, and baking soda into the creamed mixture.
	1 egg	
60 mL	¼ cup water	
5 mL	1 tsp vanilla	**Stir in** the oatmeal.
250 mL	1 cup all-purpose flour	**Drop** the batter by teaspoonfuls onto greased cookie sheets.
5 mL	1 tsp salt	
2 mL	½ tsp baking soda	**Bake** at 175 °C (350 °F) for 12 to 15 minutes.
.75 L	3 cups uncooked oatmeal	**Cool** on wire racks.

dropped (without being rolled or formed or cut) onto the cookie sheet. Then they are **baked**, or cooked by dry heat in an oven.

An example of a popular and easy drop cookie is oatmeal cookies. To make them, first look at the recipe carefully, to be sure you have all the incredients. (See page 316 for key to recipe abbreviations.) Next, check to see that you have all the equipment.

Measuring, mixing and baking tools Here's what you will need for making oatmeal cookies.

mixing bowl	cookie sheets
measuring cups and spoons	pot holders
electric mixer or large spoon	pancake turner
rubber scraper	wire cooling racks
2 teaspoons	

Hey! We've got two kinds of measuring cups in our cupboard. There's a glass one and a bunch of little ones.

You'll need both kinds of measuring cups. The glass kind is called a *liquid* measuring cup. That's used for measuring water, milk, and

other liquids. The metal cups are called *dry* measuring cups. They are used for measuring dry ingredients like flour and sugar. You'll also need them for measuring that 3/4 cup of shortening.

But I don't have a 3/4-cup cup here. What will I do?

Many dry measuring-cup sets don't have a 3/4-cup measure. In that case, use the 1/2-cup measure (which equals 2/4 cup) plus the 1/4-cup measure—or use the 1/4-cup measure three times.

Measuring dry ingredients   Careful measurements are very important when you're baking. The big problem is that different ingredients pack down differently in the measuring cup. In order to get exactly the same amount time after time, rules have been established for measuring dry ingredients.

1. Brown sugar should be packed down firmly to remove any empty space between lumps. Shortening, or fat, should also be packed down, to get rid of air bubbles.

2. Flour, on the other hand, is measured when it is light and fluffy. If you pack it down, you'll be putting in more flour than the recipe really calls for. This is why many recipes call for "sifted flour." However, you can usually avoid sifting if you spoon the flour *lightly* into the measuring cup.

3. Ingredients that pour easily, such as granulated sugar, need no special handling. The uncooked oatmeal for your cookies is another example. Just let it fall into the cup naturally.

4. To guarantee a standard measure, dry ingredients should always be heaped up *above* the top of the measuring cup and then leveled off with a straight edge such as the back of a knife or the side of a metal spatula.

Measuring liquids   There are no special rules about measuring liquids, such as water and milk, except to be sure that you read the measurement at *eye level*. (If the cup is below eye level, the level of the liquid may appear to be different from what it really is.)

One other thing. Before you start, it's always a good idea to look over the recipe to be sure you understand all the terms and procedures mentioned in the directions.

> *Okay, in the oatmeal cookie recipe, what's the difference between "cream," "blend," and "stir in"?*

Mixing terms   The word **cream** is used when fat is being combined with sugar. It means to make soft and smooth and creamy by beating with a spoon or electric mixer. **Beating** uses a quick, regular motion that lifts the mixture up and over itself. For creaming, work the spoon against the side of the bowl or use the low speed on the electric mixer.

To **blend** simply means to mix two or more ingredients thoroughly. It can be done by beating or stirring. The point is to get the ingredients mixed evenly.

To **stir** means to move around in a circular motion. It is usually less vigorous than beating. The purpose may be to blend, to keep smooth, to keep solids from settling, or to distribute heat evenly so the mixture won't burn.

> *Okay, now it's all mixed. The next step says "drop by teaspoonfuls." How do you do that?*

To "drop" batter, simply scoop up a spoonful with one of your teaspoons and scrape it off with the other, onto the cookie sheet. Place the cookies about 5 centimeters (2 inches) apart.

Greasing pans   Be sure to grease the cookie sheet first. Place a small dab of shortening (a soft, white, solid fat) on waxed paper and spread it lightly over the cookie sheet to produce a thin film of grease. Or you can use cooking oil or one of the new oil sprays.

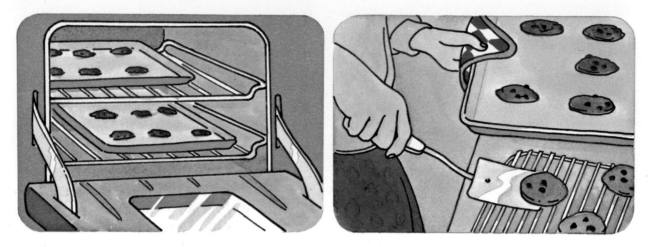

Another thing to remember: *don't crowd the oven*. Too many sheets in the oven at one time will cut down the circulation of hot air. Some parts of the oven will become too hot, while others remain too cool. So pans and cookie sheets should always be placed with space between them.

Baking time You will often see baking time expressed as a range of time. For instance, the oatmeal cookies should bake for "12 to 15" minutes. This means you should set the timer for 12 minutes and check then to see how they are doing. But don't peek too often. Each time you do, the oven loses a lot of heat.

Cooling The cookies will be soft and "droopy" when you first remove them from the cookie sheet. They will become firmer and crisper as they cool. For quick, even cooling, place them on wire cooling racks. Let them cool thoroughly before stacking and storing them.

When they've cooled, heap the cookies up on a plate or tray and serve them with glasses of cold milk.

Hot and cold beverage ideas

There are lots of drinks besides milk that you can serve with your snacks that are nutritious as well as delicious. First of all, there are fruit juices—orange juice, apple juice, tomato juice, and a variety of blends and nectars. You can serve milk with chocolate mix in it, either cold or as hot chocolate. If you want something a little more inventive, try one of the following.

HOT BROTH COCKTAIL Combine equal amounts of beef broth and tomato juice or vegetable juice cocktail. Heat and serve in mugs.

FRUITY ICED TEA Combine equal amounts of iced tea and orange juice or other fruit juice. Serve over ice.

LEMONADE Mix the juice from 2 lemons, 60 milliliters (1/4 cup) of sugar, and .75 to 1 liter (3 to 4 cups) of water. Add ice cubes, and serve in tall glasses.

ORANGEADE Fill a tall glass halfway with orange juice, the rest of the way with water. Add sugar to taste (if necessary). Add ice cubes.

ORANGE JUICE FLOAT Add one or two scoops of vanilla ice cream to a glass of orange juice. Serve the drink with a straw and a spoon.

CHOCOLATE MILK SHAKE In the blender, mix a cup of milk, a heaping teaspoon of chocolate drink powder, and one or two scoops of vanilla ice cream. You can add an egg, if you like—with or without the ice cream. The egg will make your shake thicker and creamier. Mix the drink well. Serve it in a tall glass with a straw.

PEACH OR BANANA MILK SHAKE Follow the chocolate milk shake directions. Instead of the chocolate drink powder, use 125 milliliters (1/2 cup) of canned peaches, or one banana.

HOT CHOCOLATE Mix 80 milliliters (1/3 cup) of dry cocoa, 80 milliliters (1/3 cup) of sugar, and a dash of salt in a saucepan. Stir in 125 milliliters (1/2 cup) of water, and boil the mixture for 1 minute. Add .85 liters (3½ cups) of milk and 2 milliliters (1/2 teaspoon) of vanilla. Heat the drink to the boiling point, but do not boil.

Or dissolve 20 milliliters (1 heaping tablespoon) of chocolate drink mix per 250 milliliters (1 cup) of cold milk. Heat the drink in a saucepan, but do not boil. Serve in mugs or cups with a marshmallow floating on top.

HOT MULLED CIDER Combine 2 liters (2 quarts) of cider or apple juice in a large saucepan with 125 milliliters (1/2 cup) of brown sugar, 5 milliliters (1 teaspoon) of whole allspice, 5 milliliters (1 teaspoon) of whole cloves, 1 milliliter (1/4 teaspoon) of salt, and a dash of ground nutmeg. Bring the mixture slowly to a boil and simmer 15 to 20 minutes. Remove the spices and serve in mugs with a cinnamon stick and an orange slice floating on top.

Drinks for any weather. On cold days, have a mug of steaming hot cocoa or mulled cider. And when it's hot outside, enjoy fruity iced tea or a frosty orange juice float.

We don't usually have all of those things in the house. What do you do if you're missing something—like the oranges or the cinnamon sticks?

Many things can simply be left out. The hot cider will still be good without the orange slices and the cinnamon sticks. Or you can often substitute things that you *do* have. For instance, you could add a dash of ground cinnamon instead of the cinnamon sticks.

In fact, you can try experimenting with new taste combinations and invent new drinks of your own. Just be sure to taste them as you go along to check how they're turning out.

That sounds like fun! Can you do that with other recipes, too? Or do you have to do everything exactly as the recipe says?

With most things, it's better to follow the recipe as exactly as you can, the first time around. Then you know how it's supposed to turn out. The next time you make it, you can experiment. For instance, in a meat stew recipe you might safely add a little garlic—even though it isn't called for—if you know you like this seasoning. Or if you like lots of onions in your meat loaf you might put in more than the recipe calls for.

However, be very careful about recipes for baked goods. Just a little extra baking powder or vanilla or salt may make a big difference in the finished product. That's why careful measurements are so important.

There are a lot of things you can do with food that are simple and fun. With just a little experience you can become very creative. The best part is, if you like what you've done, you can do more than just look at it—you can eat it!

Words to understand

consistency	cream
mature	beat
in season	blend
USDA	stir
bake	

Food and equipment to know

Swiss cheese	bar cookies
Cheddar cheese	rolled cookies
American cheese	drop cookies
mozzarella cheese	shortening

cutting board	measuring cups: dry and liquid
chef's knife	measuring spoons
vegetable peeler	electric mixer
vegetable brush	rubber scraper
melon baller	cookie sheet
cheese wire	pot holder
"stand-up" grater	pancake turner
mixing bowl	wire cooling rack

Questions to discuss

1. How can you make limp celery fresh and crisp again?
2. List three signs that fruit has begun to spoil.
3. Why are "in season" fruits usually a good buy?
4. How should most fruits be stored at home?
5. Name three popular cheeses in the United States.
6. What kind of cheese is usually served on pizza?
7. What is the difference between liquid and dry measuring cups?
8. Describe how to measure 250 milliliters (1 cup) of each of these ingredients: brown sugar, white sugar, shortening, flour, milk.
9. How do you grease a cookie sheet?
10. Why is it important that the oven not be too crowded with pans?
11. Why should you avoid peeking into the oven frequently while something is baking?

Things to do

1. Experiment with some raw vegetables to see what you would enjoy as snacks. You might try these for starters: celery, carrots, asparagus, broccoli, turnips, zucchini, cherry tomatoes. Wash, trim, and cut the vegetables into pieces that are easy to nibble. Arrange the pieces on a plate or serving platter. Compare the taste of each food eaten raw with how it tastes when it's cooked.
2. Make a dip for vegetable snacks. Look through a few cookbooks for dip recipes and choose one that looks interesting to you. Share your dip with other students in your class. Sample the dips they prepare.
3. Choose three fruits and make a platter of snack-size pieces. Most fruits should be cut into bite-size chunks or wedges. Stick toothpicks into the pieces. Some fruits (such as pineapple) will need

peeling. Some (such as oranges) should be carefully pulled apart into sections. Grapes need to be divided up into small clusters. If you choose a melon, cut it into small chunks or make melon balls. Arrange the pieces attractively on a serving platter.

4. Make a bulletin board on how to choose fresh fruits. Show what to look for as signs of freshness and quality. Garden or seed catalogs have very good pictures.

5. Pick one fruit and give a short talk to your class on how to buy and store that fruit.

6. Set up a tasting display of as many different dried fruits as you can find in your area. (Small specialty stores may have a greater variety than the supermarket.) Are there some you haven't tried before?

7. Make up a cheese-tasting game. Set up a serving table with ten different cheeses. Number each cheese. Give everybody a sheet that describes the taste and appearance of each cheese (your teacher can help you find this information). Have students match the descriptions to the samples. Which cheeses are new to you? Which ones would be good served with crackers or fruit? Which do you think would make good sandwiches?

8. Make a list of the leftovers in your refrigerator at home. Bring the list to class. Discuss ideas for snacks you might fix from those leftovers.

9. Hold a "county fair" cookie-baking contest. Choose a drop cookie recipe from your family's recipe collection or a cookbook. Bake the cookies. Bring the cookies and a copy of the recipe to class for judging. Choose winners in each of these categories: (1) best tasting; (2) most nutritious; (3) most unusual.

10. Hold a beverage-tasting event. Choose one of the ideas in this chapter or find a new one in a cookbook. Exchange samples with other members of your class. When might you serve your beverage (for example: winter, summer, at a cookout, at a fancy party)? What foods might be served with it?

Careers to consider

Would you like to teach about food?

If you are interested in working with young people and enjoy talking about food, consider a career in teaching.

Most teaching jobs require a college degree and a state license to teach. If you are especially interested in teaching foods in a school, you should study home economics, with an emphasis in food and nutrition.

Home economics teachers most often teach in junior and senior high schools. Their students learn how to choose foods for good nutrition. They also learn how to plan meals, shop for food, and develop basic skills in preparing food. Many schools offer special food courses that prepare students for jobs in restaurants and other kinds of food service. HERO clubs (Home Economics Related Occupations) can help you learn more about careers in food service.

Teaching means a lot of responsibility and hard work—teachers have homework, too! But there is also a lot of satisfaction. You can help your students improve their lives by learning basic consumer and homemaking skills.

Other kinds of teaching jobs may not require college, but depend heavily on a person's experience. You may teach in a school that trains cooks and chefs, for example, if you are very skilled in preparing and serving food. On a part-time basis, you might give cooking courses for people in your town. In time, you might even open up your own cooking school.

HAS THIS EVER HAPPENED TO YOU?

Jack is taking an important science test. He stayed up till 2:30 in the morning studying for it. He had everything learned, but now he's having trouble on the test. Mrs. Wilcox, his science teacher, informs the class of the time remaining in the period.

MRS. WILCOX: *You have 25 minutes left, class. You should be about halfway through the test by now.*

JACK: *Halfway through! I'm only up to question 3! Why can't I remember anything?*

Fifteen minutes later, Sandra raises her hand.

SANDRA: *I've finished the test, Mrs. Wilcox. Can I turn it in now and go to lunch?*

MRS. WILCOX: *Yes, you may, Sandra. Any others who are finished may bring up their papers, too, and go to lunch early, if they like.*

JACK: *I'll never be finished! I can hardly keep my eyes open. And now I'm getting a headache. That food smell from the cafeteria is driving me crazy!*

Later, in the cafeteria, Phil sits down next to Jack and tries to talk to him.

PHIL: *How'd you do on the science test today, Jack?*

JACK: *What do you care?! I did lousy, if you have to know. The questions weren't fair at all. Why don't you go get lost?*

74

BREAKFAST

Exploring . . .

Why breakfast is important

How to plan a good breakfast

Grains and grain foods

How to make hot cereals

How to put variety into breakfast habits

Do you ever get the feeling late in the morning that someone has "pulled out the plug" on your power supply—that you've got no energy left? Or that you're so nervous and jumpy that you're ready to "blow a fuse"?

JACK: *Yeah, like during that test. But I can't help it. If they give tests, I have to take them.*

Difficult situations often make people tired and nervous. And you can't spend your life trying to avoid these situations. But you *can* make sure that you are prepared for them in every way possible. Your body needs to be prepared, as well as your mind. For instance, you need to have enough rest. How much sleep do you usually get?

JACK: *I usually get eight hours. But I stayed up till 2:30 studying, so I only got four and a half hours last night.*

You can't expect to be clear-headed and alert if you're fighting off sleepiness. To make matters worse, the effort of trying to wake up

and to concentrate makes you all the more tired and nervous. Studying is important, but you can't do it all in one night. It's better to get your studying done ahead of time. Then you can get some sleep the night before and go into your test well rested.

It's also important to go into your test (or any important event) well nourished. What did you have for breakfast this morning?

JACK: *I was too up-tight to eat. I just had a glass of cola to wake up. What difference does that make, anyway? Pushing a pencil doesn't take much muscle!*

Mental effort *does* take energy. Your brain never stops working, even while you're asleep. Other body functions keep working, too. Your heart keeps beating, your lungs keep breathing. Your stomach, kidneys, and other organs keep doing their work. These various activities are needed to support life, even when you are resting. They use up more than half of the fuel you consume each day, if you are an average person. That's one reason why a good breakfast really counts.

Why breakfast is so important

Think about it. When you get up in the morning, it's probably been twelve to fourteen hours since you had your last full meal. Your body has kept on working and using up fuel, but you've been **fasting**— going without food—more than half a day. That's how "breakfast" got its name, by the way. It's the meal in which you *break* the *fast*.

Doesn't your body get any energy if you don't eat breakfast?

Glucose production When there is no food in your stomach, your body uses stored energy—from glycogen or from fat cells. **Glycogen** is a form of starch made by the body from glucose. About a day's supply of energy is stored in the muscle cells and liver as glycogen. It can be quickly broken down to glucose again when needed. But that's a complicated process. Your brain has to send out all kinds of chemical and electrical signals to the rest of the body for food, and then wait for deliveries! In the meantime, your body chemistry is thrown off balance. It's that first food of the day that signals your body that it's time to get "geared up"—to increase the glucose level and get ready for the day's activities.

Metabolism It's all part of a complicated but fascinating process called **metabolism**. That's the name for all the physical and chemical processes that help your body use food to keep you alive. It starts with **digestion**, in which your stomach and intestines break down the food

---

glycogen (GLĪ kə jən) **metabolism** (mə TAB ə LIZ əm)
digestion (dī JES chən)

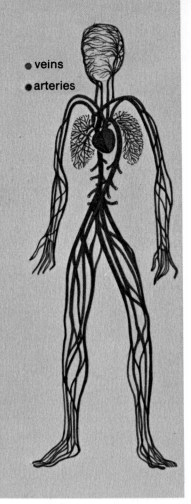

veins
arteries

Circulatory system

you've eaten into nutrients your body can use. These are your old friends—proteins, carbohydrates, fats, vitamins, and minerals. They are **assimilated**, or absorbed, into the bloodstream during the process of metabolism.

In the bloodstream, these nutrients travel around the body to do their different jobs. Then the glucose made from the food you eat will be combined with oxygen in the body cells to produce the energy you need quickly. If you eat the amounts and kinds of foods your body needs, your energy needs will be met by carbohydrates and fats. Amino acids (broken-down proteins) will be used for growth and for the repair of worn-out cells. If you aren't eating enough carbohydrates and fats, your body will use protein for energy needs. This means that the protein can't be used for building or repairing body cells.

Energy storage Any extra calories you eat but do not need will be stored, some as glycogen, but most as fat. If, sometime later, the supply of nutrients in the bloodstream is not enough for the body's energy needs, the body will use some of the stored supplies. In other words, the process of taking glucose out of the bloodstream and storing it as glycogen or fat is reversed.

The bloodstream also carries vitamins and minerals from the food you eat to the cells. These replace the ones used up in the body's thousands of chemical processes. A few vitamins and minerals can be stored for future use. Some are recycled and used again. In general, though, you need a fresh supply often.

Okay, but what does all this have to do with eating breakfast?

Skipping breakfast For this whole process to work smoothly and efficiently, you need a regular supply of nutrients. For instance, if you go too long without eating, the level of glucose in your blood drops. You have less strength, and you get tired more easily. Tests have shown that when people skip breakfast, they become fatigued, less alert, less energetic, and more irritable later in the morning. Their reaction time slows down. Students become less interested in school work, and their grades go down.

Maybe so, but I need to get rid of some of my "stored energy" —which means fat, right? And breakfast is the only meal I don't mind skipping.

Unfortunately, skipping breakfast is a very bad way to get rid of fat. In the first place, it puts a strain on your whole system, including your digestive system. Your stomach goes on producing acids to use in digesting food. If there's no food for them to work on, these acids become irritating to the stomach itself. When your stomach becomes irritated, *you* become irritated!

assimilated (ə SIM ə lāt id)

In the second place, you are depriving your body of some important nutrients it can't store—including vitamin C.

In the third place, people who skip breakfast often end up *gaining* weight rather than losing it!

How can you gain weight by skipping meals?

People who skip breakfast usually do so because they "aren't hungry when they get up," or they "don't have time," or they "don't like breakfast foods." But they usually *are* hungry later on—hungrier than they would have been if they'd had breakfast. So they are likely to eat more for lunch. Worse yet, they may satisfy their hunger *before* lunch with a snack that is high in calories and low in other badly needed nutrients.

Basic breakfast pattern For balanced nutrition, you should get at least one-fourth of your whole day's food at breakfast.

How do you know when you've had a fourth of what you're going to eat all day?

For teen-agers, breakfast should consist of *at least* the following.

One serving from the Fruit and Vegetable Group—for instance, a dish of fruit or a glass of juice.

One or two servings from the Bread and Cereal Group. This might be a bowl of cereal, a slice or two of toast, or two or three pancakes.

One serving from the Milk Group. This might be a glass of milk with your toast, or it could be the milk you put on cereal.

If you like a hearty breakfast, you could have a serving or two from the meat group. Bacon or ham with eggs is a popular breakfast.

Why is it so important to have fruit in the morning?

Fruit as a source of vitamin C Fruit is good for you any time of day. One of the most important nutrients we get from fruit is vitamin C. This vitamin is important for healthy skin tissue and mucous membranes—such as the lining of your mouth, nose, and throat. It helps you fight off colds and other infections, too.

Your body can't store vitamin C. It can't manufacture it, either. That's why it's important to have a good source of vitamin C every day.

Does every fruit have vitamin C?

Not every fruit has vitamin C, but many do. Citrus fruits, such as oranges, grapefruits, lemons, and tangerines, are very rich in vitamin C. About 75 to 125 milliliters (a 3- to 4-ounce glass) of citrus juice will supply your vitamin C need for a full day. So will 250 milliliters (1 cup) of tomato juice, 500 milliliters (2 cups) of pineapple juice, a fourth of a large cantaloupe, or 125 milliliters (1/2 cup) of fresh strawberries.

Would this breakfast supply at least one-fourth of your daily food needs? How?

You don't have to get all your vitamin C at one time, either. There are lots of other things you can eat during the day to put together the amount you need. Broccoli and cabbage are excellent sources. Potatoes are good, too. But most people like to have fruit or juice in the morning because of its refreshing "wake-up" flavor.

Bread and cereal products

Bread and cereal products contain many nutrients that are just as important as vitamin C. Wholegrain and enriched breads are good sources of B vitamins (thiamin, riboflavin, and niacin) and minerals (iron and phosphorus). They also contain carbohydrates and protein.

As the name suggests, **whole-grain** products are made from the whole kernel of grain. Some products are made from refined white flour, which uses only part of the kernel.

Parts of grain kernel The diagram shows a wheat kernel, but the kernels of corn, rice, oats, and other grains look much the same. They all have three parts: the bran, the endosperm, and the germ. The bran and the germ are rich sources of vitamins and minerals. However, these parts are often removed in the milling, or grinding, process.

The **bran** contains fiber, which gives whole-grain flour a rough texture and a dark color that some people don't like. Fiber, also called cellulose, can't be digested, but it provides bulk, which helps move waste materials through the intestines.

The **germ** has a distinctive, nutty flavor. You may have had wheat germ at one time or another—maybe as a topping for pudding or

Wheat kernel

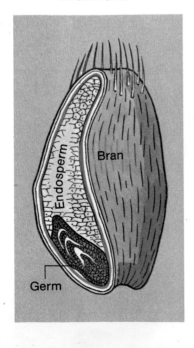

other desserts. The germ has a higher fat content than the other parts of the grain. If whole-grain flour is stored for a long time under poor conditions, the fat turns rancid (stale). The flour sometimes gets a spoiled "off" flavor.

The **endosperm** is the part that is *kept* when making refined white flour. It is made up mostly of starch. It has the delicate flavor and smooth texture that most people like for things they bake. Unfortunately, it is low in vitamins and minerals. Refined flour is often enriched (by adding iron and three B vitamins) to make it more nutritious. Sometimes it is even fortified—extra nutrients are added that may not have been in the grain originally. For example, although vitamin C is not normally found in grain, it is sometimes added to a grain product, such as cereal, to fortify it.

However, remember that even enriched, fortified, and restored grains have had the bran itself removed. And it's the bran that contains the fiber that's so helpful to the intestines in getting rid of body wastes.

What's so important about getting rid of body wastes?

Fiber Think what it would be like to live in a house where you couldn't take out the garbage. It would just keep piling up in one room after another. Or imagine a city that had no wind to blow away the air pollution. It would just keep getting thicker and thicker. Well, your body has "pollution" too—from its many chemical activities, from the by-products of infections, and so forth. Some of these wastes would be very poisonous if they were allowed to build up in the body. They

---

endosperm (EN dō SPERM)

Can you imagine how this sky would look if there were no winds to carry the smoke away?

are cleaned out of the blood by the kidneys and liver. Some of them are dumped into the intestines, where they are moved out of the body along with that indigestible fiber you ate. If you don't have enough of this fiber, the elimination process takes longer, and poisonous wastes remain in your body longer.

Fiber not only makes the elimination process quicker, but makes it easier. Fiber holds water, which keeps the waste products from getting hard and difficult for the body to pass. So the overall result is: fiber helps your body keep itself healthy, and it helps you keep feeling good, too.

Don't most foods have fiber in them?

Most plant foods have at least some fiber. But many of the foods we eat today are highly refined. The fiber is taken out. As a result, many people don't get enough natural fiber in their diets. That's why it's especially important to eat enough fruits and vegetables and whole grain products.

Protein Grains have more than just vitamins, minerals, carbohydrates, fats, and fiber. They also contain good amounts of protein. Even many refined grains do. Grain products should be eaten in combination with other protein foods, especially milk. The reason is that the protein in grains is incomplete. It does not contain all of the necessary amino acids. But when it is eaten along with other protein foods, all of these amino acids can be provided.

Grain foods There are many traditional breakfast foods made from grain products. One of the easiest is simply buttered bread or toast, perhaps with jam or jelly. Cinnamon toast—buttered toast with sugar and cinnamon—is more trouble, but a delicious change.

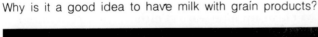

Why is it a good idea to have milk with grain products?

There are many types and styles of muffins, too—corn, bran, whole wheat, English, blueberry. Or you can have pancakes, griddlecakes, flapjacks, hotcakes, or whatever you like to call them. If you're in a hurry, there are dozens of cold, ready-to-eat cereals. If you have a little more time, you may prefer a hot cereal—such as oatmeal, Cream of Wheat, or farina—especially on a chilly morning.

I like hot cereal in the winter, but I don't like the lumps! How do you get them out of cereal?

Hot cereal   The best way to get the lumps out of hot cereal is not to let them get in. And the best way to do this is to read the package directions carefully. Then follow them as closely as you can.

Most hot cereals are made by pouring dry cereal flakes or granules into boiling water and stirring. The trick is to *pour slowly* with one hand and *stir constantly* with the other. Cereal contains a large amount of starch, and starch is sticky when wet. If you've ever mixed flour and water together, you know it makes a very good paste for everything from *papier mâché* objects to wallpaper. Because of this stickiness, it's important to mix the cereal flakes into the water *thoroughly.* Each flake must be completely surrounded by the water. Otherwise, the flakes will stick to each other and form rubbery lumps.

Remember, too, that it's important to measure carefully the amount of cereal and water you use. The more cereal, or the less water, the thicker the finished product will be.

You should also have a timer available, or a clock with a second hand. The length of cooking time will affect the texture of the cereal—how soft or how "chewy" it will be. Most hot cereals cook in 5 to 10 minutes. Some precooked types take only 2 or 3 minutes; others are made right in the bowl, just by adding hot water or milk. Actually, hot cereals are easier to prepare than most people think. And it's not so hard to clean up afterwards, either. Just remember to fill the pot with cold water when you're finished, and let it soak for a while.

Is hot cereal better for you than cold cereal?

Nutrients in cereal   Nutritionally, hot cereal and cold cereal are pretty much the same. But hot cereal is usually less expensive. So it's "better" for you in terms of the amount of nutrition you can buy for your money. Also, some people don't like a cold breakfast on an empty stomach. A hot breakfast gives them a more satisfying comfortable feeling, especially on a cold morning. If you agree, a hot breakfast may be better because it makes you feel better.

But nutrition varies from product to product. You should read the label to see what nutrients your breakfast cereal contains. Don't be alarmed, by the way, if some important nutrients are missing. You can't expect to get your whole day's supply of every nutrient from your breakfast cereal alone. Many "natural" breakfast cereals are

nutrition
information

lacking important vitamins, such as vitamin C and vitamin D. They also lack important minerals, such as calcium. They have a high amount of indigestible fiber, which isn't a "nutrient" at all. And yet these cereals are quite good for you. Cereals have important amounts of carbohydrates, protein, B vitamins, and a little fat. As we've already seen, indigestible fiber is very healthy for you, too.

So don't look for one "super-food" that will give you everything. Once more, the key is to eat nutritious foods in reasonable quantities, and eat a wide variety of them.

All we ever have for breakfast at our house is juice, cereal, eggs, and bacon. How much variety is there in that?

Don't think that breakfast has to be limited to certain foods. Breakfast is monotonous only because people make it that way. They get into the habit of eating the same thing every day. But if you want, you can make breakfast as varied and exciting as any other meal.

Breaking the breakfast monotony

There's no law that says you can't have lots of different things for breakfast. Many people around the world have breakfast habits that are quite different from yours. They eat things in the morning that you probably never have before noon, or even before nighttime. The English enjoy kippers—a kind of smoked, salted fish—for breakfast. Meat, fish, and cheese are popular in Norway.

Eating breakfast outdoors is another way to break the breakfast monotony. This German family is having a hot beverage, rolls, and soft-cooked eggs. Have you ever eaten breakfast outside?

Even inside the United States, regional specialties add variety and zest to breakfast. Apple pie is a favorite in Boston. Bagels (BĀ gəls—chewy, doughnut-shaped rolls) with lox (smoked salmon) or cream cheese are popular in New York. In many southern states, cornbread and hominy (HAHM ə nē) grits are "musts" for breakfast to be complete. Steak and eggs are especially popular in the Midwest and the Southwest.

Won't your stomach get all mixed up if you eat lunch and dinner things for breakfast?

Actually, if you change your breakfast habits, your *head* is more likely to get mixed up than your stomach. For instance, let's say you're used to having juice and cereal for breakfast. Then one morning you have a peanut butter and jelly sandwich instead. You may go to school feeling as if it's one o'clock in the afternoon, because you've just had "lunch." But as far as your stomach is concerned, food is food. And as far as your body is concerned, nutrients are nutrients. As long as you get all the ones you need, in the right amounts, it doesn't matter whether they come from "breakfast foods" or "lunch foods" or "dinner foods."

After all, you already eat "breakfast foods" at other times of the day. You've probably had eggs for lunch, and even dinner. Eggs are often served as omelets or in sandwiches and salads. They are also used as ingredients in meat loaves, cakes, casseroles, and many other dishes.

Bacon shows up in the afternoon and evening, too. You'll see it served lots of ways: wrapped around hotdogs; in bacon, lettuce, and tomato sandwiches; with liver and other meats; or crumbled over salads.

Other traditional breakfast foods are good throughout the day, too. Fruit and fruit juice make refreshing and nutritious snacks any time of day. You can munch on dry cereal in the afternoon—with or without milk—or as a bedtime snack, or even for dessert!

But if you mix everything around at different meals, how can you tell if you're getting the right foods in the right amounts?

Using the Basic Four To figure out whether you're getting a balanced diet, just go back to the Basic Four food groups we discussed earlier. For instance, let's take that peanut butter and jelly sandwich we were talking about before. The two slices of bread give you two servings from the Bread and Cereal Group. Two tablespoons of peanut butter provide about half a serving from the Meat Group. It has a little more protein than a large egg, but it has about twice the fat and overall calories. If you have a glass of milk with your sandwich, and an orange or a tangerine, you've got an excellent breakfast.

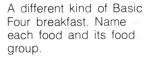

A different kind of Basic Four breakfast. Name each food and its food group.

Hey, that sounds good! Can I have the same thing for lunch and dinner, too?

There's no single food that will supply *all* the variety of nutrients you need, even if it contains a serving from each of the Basic Four food groups. The Basic Four approach is a very simplified way to plan balanced meals. It works only if you choose a *variety* of foods from each group. If you pick the same thing meal after meal, you could cover all the groups and still miss out on a lot of vital nutrients. Besides, having the same thing two and three meals in a row doesn't help to break up breakfast monotony. It just increases it!

But if you like sandwiches a lot, have one kind for breakfast and another kind for lunch. If you had an orange for breakfast, take a raw carrot, celery, or an apple for lunch. Add variety to your milk dish now and then with cocoa, chocolate milk, a strawberry milk shake, ice cream, or a grilled cheese sandwich. All you need is a little imagination to come up with something different for every day of the week—even every day of the month!

Yeah, but my mom would kill me if I asked her for something different every day!

You can't ask your mother to do all the work for you. But if you are able to fix some things yourself, and do the extra planning it takes, and any extra cleaning up, she might enjoy the change herself. And you won't find it so hard if you put a little thought into it and know what you're doing.

Ideas for "different" breakfasts Here are some suggestions that should wake up your appetite and get you thinking of varied and delicious breakfasts that you can look forward to. After you've tried these, you can keep right on going with your own creations! You'll notice that the following suggestions are for single dishes, and do not cover the whole breakfast. Some of the Basic Four food groups may be missing. See if you can figure out which ones they are, and how you might supply them.

Have a fried egg and a slice of bologna or other luncheon meat or cheese on a hamburger bun.

Make an open-face sandwich of scrambled eggs on rye or whole-wheat toast. Sprinkle with cheese, chopped chives, or bacon bits.

Have "cereal à la mode"—your favorite cereal topped with vanilla ice cream and frozen or fresh fruit such as strawberries, blueberries, or peaches.

Make French toast using a different kind of bread—for example, French, Italian, raisin, or whole wheat. Serve with fruit and powdered sugar.

Make a breakfast milk shake with milk, vanilla ice cream, and fruit. Add a little strawberry jam or other preserves, if you like.

How about trying one of these breakfast dishes tomorrow morning? Clockwise from upper left: Hotdog omelet sandwich, breakfast milk shake, cereal *à la mode*, fruit dish.

Mix some chopped fruit and/or nuts into pancake batter. Top the pancakes with preserves or sour cream, or both.

Chill some fruit salad or orange/grapefruit sections and top with sherbet or ice milk.

Make a fruit dish of orange juice, sliced bananas, strawberries, and melon chunks, or other fruits.

Spice up a glass of tomato juice with a dash of Tabasco sauce, some Worcestershire sauce, a sprinkle of salt and freshly ground pepper, a squirt of lemon or lime juice, and anything else you can think of.

Top a bowl of hot oatmeal, Cream of Wheat, or other hot cereal with ice cream, raisins, chopped dates, or nuts.

Make a "hotdog omelet sandwich." The omelet is the same as any other, except that it includes frankfurter slices. Brown the frankfurter slices slightly before adding them to the egg mixture. Serve in buttered hotdog buns. Two eggs and one frankfurter are enough for two sandwiches.

I'd like to try some of those things, but I don't have much time to fix them in the morning. I have even less time to clean up afterwards.

Planning ahead   Most of these things don't take much time to fix or clean up. They'll take even less time if you plan ahead. First, of course, you have to buy any ingredients you don't have on hand. Check the previous day to see whether you have the ice cream, fruit, nuts, cheese sauce, or hotdog buns you want to use the next morning.

Next, do any preparation ahead of time that you can. Peel, cut up, and chill fresh fruits. Put frozen fruits in the refrigerator section to thaw. Shell and chop nuts. Break and mix eggs for scrambled eggs and omelets. Put them in a covered container in the refrigerator.

Also, get out the utensils you will need, so that you won't be sleepily groping through drawers and shelves for them in the morning. Even set the table. Napkins and an attractive centerpiece will make breakfast more pleasant and less like a chore.

You may not have time to wash all the dishes after breakfast. You probably will have time, though, to rinse them and put them into a pan of soapy water or the dishwasher. That will be a big help later to you or whoever else does the dishes. When you're on your own and have a job, do the same thing. It will make doing the dishes much easier when you come home at night.

To make things even easier, go to bed fifteen minutes earlier than you do now. Get up fifteen minutes earlier, too. For most people, that extra fifteen minutes is like a magic wand. It turns a hurried, frantic ordeal in the morning into a time of delicious enjoyment!

Words to understand

fasting　　　　　　　whole-grain foods
glycogen　　　　　　bran
metabolism　　　　　germ
digestion　　　　　　endosperm
assimilated

Questions to discuss

1. Why is it important to eat breakfast?
2. What food groups are represented in a good breakfast?
3. List five foods that are good sources of vitamin C. How often should you eat a good source of this vitamin?
4. Describe the three basic parts of every grain.
5. Why do only whole-grain or enriched grain products count as servings from the Bread and Cereal Group?
6. Why is fiber important?
7. What is the difference between enriched and fortified cereal?
8. How can you find out what's in a cereal?
9. What causes lumps in hot cereal? How can you prevent them?
10. If you plan a meal that covers all the Basic Four food groups, why can't you eat that same meal three times a day, every day?
11. What are some things you can do ahead of time in planning for breakfast?

Things to do

1. Conduct a breakfast survey. Ask ten friends to write down what they ate for breakfast. (If they didn't eat breakfast, they should write down why.) What are the results? How many ate breakfast? How many ate a *good* breakfast? What reasons did people give for skipping breakfast?
2. Plan three different menus for a good breakfast that you would enjoy. Be sure each menu includes a serving from each of the following food groups:

   Fruit and Vegetable Group　　Bread and Cereal Group
   Milk Group

   You may also include foods from the Meat Group, if you wish. Try to use different foods in each menu.

3. Make a report on the breakfast foods and habits of a foreign country. Which ones seem most unusual to you? Which of your breakfast habits do you think these people would consider strange?

4. Prepare a hot cereal. How long did it take you to fix it? List five things you could add to the cooked cereal for variety (for example: sliced peaches, brown sugar). What else would you need to eat to make it a balanced breakfast?

5. Study the nutrition information panel on a box of your favorite cereal. Write down the nutrient values. Would you judge the cereal to be a nutritious food or an "empty calorie" food? Is it enriched, fortified, or restored? Make a list of the other information you can get from reading the package.

6. Make a bulletin board about breakfast. Choose one of these themes: (1) the importance of breakfast; (2) how to plan a balanced breakfast; (3) a variety of foods that would be good for breakfast.

7. Examine the structure of a grain kernel. With a pair of tweezers, pull apart a kernel of canned corn. See if you can identify the bran, endosperm, and germ. What nutrients would you expect each part to contain? Popcorn is corn that has been exploded inside out. What part of the kernel do you think the soft, white part is?

Careers to consider

Would you like to work in a food-processing plant?

If you are good with your hands and enjoy a steady routine, consider a career in food processing.

Food processors take various ingredients and produce a finished food. It may be packaged, canned, bottled, frozen, or dried. The kinds of jobs vary, depending on the kind of food being produced. Jobs in an orange juice plant, for example, are different from jobs in a plant that makes spaghetti.

Production jobs focus on some aspect of processing the food. The work may start with jobs in unloading, trimming, and preparing the ingredients. Down the line, there are jobs in mixing, and often in baking or cooking. Once the food is made, it has to be packaged and stored until it's shipped out of the plant. Many of the jobs are automated (done by machine), but it takes people to run the machinery and keep it in good repair.

If you think about it, you'll realize that running a food plant is a complicated business. Mistakes and delays can be expensive. What would happen in a cornflake plant that suddenly ran out of boxes? What if a vegetable soup plant was late getting its supply of carrots? What would happen in an ice cream plant if all the space in the freezer warehouse was full? Every food plant has a **management staff** to make sure everything goes smoothly.

For most jobs in a food-processing plant, you should have a high school education. Usually new workers are trained on the job. Some employees, such as the mechanics who keep the machinery in good working order, need special skills that can be learned in a trade school. Management jobs often require some college, although many companies prefer to train their own managers.

5

HAS THIS EVER HAPPENED TO YOU?

Karen has had a group of friends over to her house for a slumber party. The next morning, she wants to fix a leisurely brunch. She has written down everyone's food order.

KAREN: *Let's see—some of you want scrambled eggs, some want sunny-side ups, some over easy, some soft-boiled. That's too complicated. Tell you what—I'll fix the pancakes and the bacon, and whatever else you want, you can make it for yourselves.*

DIANE (at the stove): *You don't have enough skillets for everybody, Karen. But that's okay—there isn't enough room on the stove, anyway.*

MARIA: *These must be very cheap eggs, Karen. They broke as soon as I put them in the boiling water. But at least they didn't burn, the way Cindy's scrambled eggs did!*

JUDY: *Darn! The yolks broke when I tried to turn my eggs over, and they got cooked hard as a rock!*

BARBARA: *I'll trade one egg with you, Judy, 'cause mine are both too runny!*

KAREN: *Okay, who wants the raw pancakes, and who wants the burned ones? It's good they didn't all turn out, 'cause that recipe makes twice as many as we could ever eat!*

At the table, everyone agrees that the brunch was a disaster.

KAREN: *You know, I've watched my Mom cook all these things a hundred times. She never has any trouble. What's the trick?*

92

BRUNCH

Exploring . . .

Basic egg cookery

How to buy and store eggs

How to change recipe amounts

Metric measurements

Ways to cook bacon and sausage

How to mix and bake quick breads

Whether to use mixes

The "trick" to cooking anything is simply knowing a little bit about how each food behaves when you work with it. For instance, some things should be handled quickly, for a short time. Others must be handled slowly and gently, over a longer time. Some things are cooked for a long time over low heat. Others take high heat for a short time. Eggs, by the way, should be cooked over low to medium heat. If the heat is too high, they will be tough and rubbery.

KAREN: *Don't I know it! We could have bounced those eggs from the floor up to the ceiling! All except the sunny-side ups, which never did get cooked on the top!*

Cooking eggs isn't difficult, once you know how.

Fried and scrambled eggs

Frying eggs **Frying** means cooking in a pan with a little fat of some kind. To fry eggs, first melt a little butter, margarine, or bacon grease (about 15 to 30 milliliters, or 1 to 2 tablespoons) in a skillet (frying pan) over medium heat. The fat should be hot enough to make a drop of water sizzle but not pop. Crack the egg in the middle with a knife or on the edge of the skillet or bowl. Hold the egg over the skillet and pry the crack apart, letting each egg drop gently into the skillet. Repeat with other eggs to be cooked at the same time. Reduce the heat, and let the eggs cook until the whites are firm around the edges—about 2 or 3 minutes.

If you want your eggs sunny-side up, the best way to get them to cook on top is to put a lid on the skillet after the whites have started to firm up. Add 2 milliliters (1/2 teaspoon) of water for each egg to the skillet before covering. The steam trapped under the lid will cook the eggs on top.

If you want your eggs over easy, wait until the eggs are almost finished cooking. The whites will be firm and opaque, with just a little runny part on top. Now gently slide an egg turner under one egg and turn it over. Repeat with the other eggs in the skillet,

turning one at a time. Remove the skillet from the heat and lift the eggs out onto a plate with the turner. Don't wait too long, unless you want the yolks hard-cooked.

How do you keep the eggs from sticking when you turn them over?

Food sticking to the pan is a problem that many cooks run into. The secret usually lies in the pan. Use a pan with a special "no-stick" finish, or a pan that is well seasoned. A **seasoned** pan is one that has built up a smooth surface. You don't buy pans this way. You have to do it yourself.

Seasoning a pan To season a pan, pour in 2 centimeters (about an inch) of cooking oil. Place the pan over medium heat for 20 minutes. Pour off the oil. (You can save the oil and use it for cooking later.) Wipe the pan with paper towels. The pan is now seasoned. Some chefs keep pans that they use only for eggs and omelets. To keep them properly seasoned, they don't wash them in water, but wipe them clean with paper towels after each use. Never scour an egg pan with cleanser or steel wool. It will scratch the surface and make the eggs stick.

To avoid scratching the pan while cooking, use a rubber turner. Also, be sure you have enough grease in the pan. In some pans, spray-type cooking oils work very well. Finally, be sure the pan does not get too hot. If it does, your eggs may stick even if the pan is seasoned perfectly.

Do you cook scrambled eggs the same way?

Scrambling eggs For scrambled eggs, first break the eggs into a bowl. Mix them well with a fork. If you like your eggs fluffy, add some water, milk, or light cream, and beat the eggs a little longer. *Do not overcook*—it's easy to do. Scrambled eggs can turn very quickly from just right to dry and tough. This is especially true if the skillet is too hot. What's more, the eggs will keep cooking a little from their own heat after you take them out of the skillet.

For specific amounts, look at the fluffy scrambled egg recipe on the next page.

Fluffy scrambled eggs

3 servings

	6 large eggs
80 mL	**⅓ cup milk**
30 mL	**2 tbsp butter, margarine, or bacon fat (about 1 pat of butter per egg)**
1 mL	**¼ tsp salt**
	dash of pepper

Beat the eggs, milk, salt, and pepper together with a fork in a medium-size mixing bowl.

Heat the butter, margarine, or bacon fat until it is just hot enough to make a drop of water sizzle.

Pour the egg mixture into a medium-size skillet. Turn the heat down *low*.

Stir lightly when the eggs start to set (get firm). Fold the cooked edges over and toward the center, allowing the uncooked part to go to the bottom. Do not stir too much, or the eggs will break up and become stringy and hard.

Cook about 5 to 8 minutes, or until the eggs are cooked throughout but still moist.

The only trouble with this recipe is that it's for six eggs when I just want two. What can you do when a recipe makes too much, besides just stuff yourself?

Recipe arithmetic   Most recipes can be cut down with no problem. If you know and understand equivalent measures (equal measurements), the arithmetic is usually fairly simple. A table of equivalent measures will be helpful to you in learning to make more or less of a recipe.

Of course, if you're working with metric measurements, the arithmetic is very simple. There are only two kinds of volume measurements you're likely to encounter in recipes—liters and milliliters. A

Equal volume measurements (U.S. customary system)

1 quart = 2 pints = 4 cups = 32 ounces
1 pint = 2 cups = 16 ounces
1 cup = 8 ounces = 16 tablespoons
½ cup = 4 ounces = 8 tablespoons
¼ cup = 2 ounces = 4 tablespoons
⅛ cup = 1 ounce = 2 tablespoons
⅓ cup = 2⅔ ounces = 5⅓ tablespoons =
　　　　¼ cup + 1 tablespoon + 1 teaspoon
1 ounce = 2 tablespoons = 6 teaspoons
1 tablespoon = 3 teaspoons

Equal volume measurements (metric)

1 liter = 1000 milliliters

liter is a little more than a quart. Metric measuring equipment uses various-size cups (such as 250 milliliters or 125 milliliters) for large measurements. Small amounts are measured in spoons of different sizes, such as 5 milliliters or 15 milliliters. Metric measurements are based on the decimal system.

Using tables of equal measurements, you should find it fairly easy to change the quantities in most recipes. Some recipes, however, do not work well if you increase or decrease the quantities by too much. This is especially true for baked goods. But for most things, the amounts can be changed if you keep the same **proportions**—that is, if the relationship between the amounts of various ingredients remains the same.

For instance, take the scrambled eggs. The recipe is for six eggs, but you only want two. That is, you want only a fraction of what the recipe makes.

To figure out what this fraction is, divide the quantity you want by the quantity the recipe makes, like this.

$$\frac{\text{quantity you want}}{\text{quantity recipe makes}} = \frac{2}{6} = \frac{1}{3}$$

Now, take the fraction (in this case, 1/3) and multiply it by the quantity for each ingredient in the recipe, like this.

6 eggs × 1/3 =	2 eggs
1/3 cup milk × 1/3 =	1/9 cup milk (Your measuring cup probably doesn't have a 1/9 measure on it. Just remember, 1/9 cup is a little bit less than 1/8 cup. Since 1/8 cup = 2 tablespoons, then 1/9 cup will be just a little bit less than 2 table-spoons.)
2 tablespoons butter × 1/3 =	2/3 tablespoon = 2 teaspoons butter
1/4 teaspoon salt × 1/3 =	1/12 teaspoon salt (Since 1/12 teaspoon is very hard to measure, it's better simply to salt "to taste.")
dash of pepper × 1/3 =	very small dash of pepper (to your own taste)

What this comes down to for two scrambled eggs, then, is this.

> 2 eggs
> almost 2 tablespoons milk
> 2 teaspoons butter, margarine, or bacon fat
> salt and pepper to taste

Okay, now what if I want two scrambled eggs and Cindy wants one? That makes three eggs!

proportions (prə POR shənz)

For three eggs, just do the same thing you did before.

$$\frac{\text{quantity you want}}{\text{quantity recipe makes}} = \frac{3}{6} = \frac{1}{2}$$

This is even easier than before. Just multiply everything by 1/2. Try it this time with the metric measurements. See if you come up with the answers at the bottom of the page.

Okay, that's fine if I want less than the recipe calls for. But suppose I want more? What if everybody wants some, and I've got to cook, say, fifteen eggs instead of six?

To make more of a recipe, just do the same as before.

$$\frac{\text{quantity you want}}{\text{quantity recipe makes}} = \frac{15}{6} = 2^3/_6 = 2\frac{1}{2}$$

If you multiply all of the ingredients by 2½, you should come up with the following quantities.

6 eggs × 2½ =	15 eggs
1/3 cup milk × 2½ =	5/6 cup milk
2 tablespoons butter × 2½ =	5 tablespoons butter
1/4 teaspoon salt × 2½ =	5/8 teaspoon salt (a little over 1/2 teaspoon)
dash of pepper × 2½ =	2½ dashes of pepper (about 1/8 teaspoon—a dash is not an exact measurement)

Can you really do all fifteen eggs at once?

You can measure and mix the ingredients all at once. But with this large a quantity, it would be better to cook half or a third at a time.

When you change the amounts, do you change the cooking time, too?

Adjusting cooking time If you change the quantity of eggs that you put into the pan at one time, the cooking time will change a bit. Of course, if you cooked twelve eggs in two batches of six each, the cooking time for each batch would be the same as in the original recipe for six eggs. If you cooked seven or eight eggs at a time, they would take a little longer—about 6 to 9 minutes instead of 5 to 8 minutes. For only two eggs, it would be about 1½ to 3 minutes.

There's really no set rule about how cooking time changes when you change the amount you're cooking at one time. If you have some

6 eggs × ½ = 3 eggs   1 mL salt × ½ = .5 mL salt (or to taste)
80 mL milk × ½ = 40 mL milk   dash of pepper × ½ = pepper to taste
30 mL butter × ½ = 15 mL butter

Easy omelet

2 servings

	3 large eggs
30 mL	**2 tbsp milk**
15 mL	**1 tbsp butter, margarine, or bacon fat, salt and pepper to taste**

Beat the eggs and milk together with a fork in a small mixing bowl.

Heat the butter in a skillet or omelet pan until it sizzles. Tilt the pan to grease the sides.

Pour the egg mixture into the pan. Turn the heat down to medium.

Tilt the pan when the edges start to set. Lift (but do not break up) the cooked edges with an egg turner, to let the uncooked, runny part run to the bottom.

Add a filling, if you wish, when the egg is set, but still moist and shiny. The filling might be jelly or bits of cheese, or sautéed mushrooms, green peppers, or onions.

Fold the omelet gently in half with the spatula. Slide the folded omelet onto a warm plate. Add salt and pepper to taste.

way besides time by which to judge when the food is done, use that. You should remove scrambled eggs, for instance, from the heat when they're solid throughout, but still moist—no matter how long they've been cooking!

Omelets and other egg dishes

Omelets The main difference between scrambled eggs and an omelet (AHM lit) is that the omelet is left in one piece. It isn't mixed up at all, once it's in the pan. But it has about the same ingredients as scrambled eggs. You can cook an omelet in a skillet, but an omelet pan is easier. An omelet pan is like a skillet, but it has sloping sides. This makes it easy to slide the omelet out of the pan.

What about soft-cooked eggs? How long should they be cooked? And how do you keep them from cracking when you put them in the water?

Soft-cooked eggs   The best way to make soft-cooked eggs is to place them in a saucepan and cover them with *cold* water. If the water is hot when you put them in, the shells will expand too rapidly, causing them to crack. (The same thing can happen if you pour boiling water into a cold glass. The rapid expansion can cause the glass to crack.) Moreover, eggs have an air sac inside. Air expands very quickly when it is heated, causing pressure that will crack the eggshell.

Bring the cold water quickly to a boil over high heat. Since you started with cold water, the shell has time to expand. The air trapped in the air sac has time to escape through the porous egg shell without cracking it. When the water reaches the **boiling** point (100 °C, or 212 °F—the point at which the water bubbles), cover the pan with a close-fitting lid and take it off the heat. Leave the eggs in the hot water for 2 to 4 minutes, depending on how well done you like them. Most people like soft-cooked eggs so that the whites are just firm but the yolks are still runny.

If you are cooking more than four eggs at a time, don't turn off the heat. Cover the pan as before, and turn down the heat to just below **simmering**. (When water is simmering, small bubbles form on the bottom. Some will rise slowly, but will collapse before they reach the surface.) Let the eggs cook in this way for 3 to 6 minutes. Serve the eggs immediately, or cool them a little bit in cold water. If eggs remain hot, they continue to cook and harden in their shells, even when removed from the hot water.

To eat soft-cooked eggs, first break the shell through the middle with a knife. Scoop out the egg with the knife or a teaspoon. If you like, crumble pieces of buttered toast and mix them with the egg. If you're using an egg cup, slice off the large end of the egg with a knife. Stand the egg in the egg cup and eat from the shell with a teaspoon.

Hard-cooked eggs   To prepare hard-cooked eggs, begin the same way you did for soft-cooked eggs. When the water starts to boil, cover the pan and turn the heat down to just below simmering for 15 to 20 minutes. Then cool the eggs immediately in cold water. This helps to make the egg peel more easily.

Sometimes I have a lot of trouble with the shell sticking to the egg when I try to peel it. Does this mean the egg isn't fresh?

Actually, the egg white sticks to the shell more in very fresh eggs than in eggs that have been stored awhile. To make even "farm-fresh" eggs peel more easily, try these tricks.

1. Puncture the shell at the large end (where the air sac is) before cooking. You can do this by using a gadget called an egg punch, or by striking the egg gently on the point of a thumb-tack stuck through a piece of cardboard.
2. Be careful not to overcook the egg.
3. Cool the egg immediately and thoroughly after cooking.
4. Crackle the shell all over before peeling.
5. Start peeling at the wide end of the egg. Holding the egg under cold water sometimes helps to remove stubborn shells.

Why do people say "hard-cooked" and "soft-cooked" eggs? I always thought it was "hard-boiled" and "soft-boiled."

Eggs really should not be boiled. The minute the water reaches the boiling point, it should be turned down to simmering or turned off completely. Water boils at 100 °C (212 °F). This temperature can make eggs tough and rubbery. Egg white will actually begin to cook at a temperature of 60 °C (140 °F), and egg yolks at 65 ° C (149 °F). The hot water that comes out of your kitchen faucet is probably this hot. It's too hot to hold your hand in, but well below the boiling point.

Isn't a poached egg cooked in water, too? Why does it look so different from a soft-cooked egg?

Poached eggs   Poached eggs and soft-cooked eggs are both cooked in water, but that's where the similarity ends. Soft-cooked eggs are cooked in their shells. A poached egg is removed from the shell first. Poached eggs are really not hard to make, especially if you start with very fresh eggs. Fresh eggs hold their shape better than older eggs.

1. Put 8 to 10 centimeters (3 to 4 inches) of water into a saucepan. Heat the water just to the boiling point.
2. Crack an egg into a small bowl or dish.
3. Slip the egg into the water. Reduce the heat to simmering.
4. Let the egg cook for 3 to 5 minutes, depending on how done you like it.
5. Remove the egg with a slotted spoon. Blot some of the excess water with a paper towel, still holding the egg on the spoon.

Top: Why should you use a slotted spoon to remove a poached egg from the cooking water? Bottom: Name the nutrients in quick eggs Benedict (next page).

6. Serve the egg on a slice of buttered toast or a toasted, buttered English muffin.

For a special treat, make quick eggs Benedict. Place a thin slice of cooked ham or Canadian bacon on a toasted English muffin. On top of the meat place a poached egg. Top with prepared Hollandaise sauce or a dab of mayonnaise.

That looks kind of tricky to make for a bunch of eight people.

For a party, scrambled eggs or omelets may be better. They're not hard to fix, and they have lots of variations.

Omelet variations   In addition to the omelet fillings already mentioned, you could try the following.

Add corn, string beans, or other vegetables to the omelet mixture before cooking.

Add orange juice to the omelet mixture instead of milk. Use sections or slices of peeled, fresh orange for filling. **Garnish** (decorate) with more orange sections or slices, and dust with powdered sugar.

Spoon marinara or pizza sauce over the omelet. Sprinkle with grated cheese. Fold the omelet in half and slip it onto a serving plate. Garnish with more sauce and cheese.

Spread a couple of tablespoons of sour cream over the omelet. Then spread sliced fresh or canned peaches (drained) or fresh, sliced strawberries over the sour cream for filling. Save a few fruit slices for garnish. Fold the omelet in half and slide it onto a serving plate. Garnish the omelet with sour cream and the remaining fruit slices.

That sounds good! Can you do the same thing with scrambled eggs?

garnish (GAHR nish)

These omelets have a filling of freshly cooked mushrooms and are topped with hotdog pieces. What are some other ways to serve omelets?

Scrambled egg variations   Scrambled eggs don't take a filling the way omelets do, because they aren't folded over in one piece. But you can put lots of things in the egg mixture that will add a variety of tastes and textures. Here are just a few suggestions.

When the eggs begin to thicken, add 125 milliliters (1/2 cup) of shredded Swiss, Cheddar, American, or other cheese.

Instead of cheese, stir in some chopped, cooked meat. You might use bacon, ham, bologna, hotdogs, or cooked, crumbled hamburger.

Lightly brown some sliced or chopped mushrooms or onions in the butter, margarine, or bacon fat before adding the egg mixture to the pan.

Add something to the egg mixture that is characteristic of a particular country or area of the world. For Indonesia, add a dash of curry powder. For Mexico, try a dash of chili powder or some chopped hot peppers. For Hawaii, add some drained, crushed or chunk pineapple. For China, use some bean sprouts and a dash of soy sauce.

I'm not very efficient first thing in the morning. Is there any way to keep it simple?

You can save time in the morning and reduce confusion by doing some of the preparation the night before. You can break and mix the eggs, for instance. Refrigerate them in a covered bowl until you're ready to use them. You can peel and slice fruit, chop nuts, dice ham, cook bacon, grate cheese, and so forth, for omelet fillings and extra ingredients for scrambled eggs.

If you're having something that uses hard-cooked eggs, you can cook the eggs the night before and refrigerate them in their shells.

I did that one time, but I got the cooked eggs mixed up with the raw ones. I had to crack them all to tell them apart!

It's easy to tell a cooked egg from a raw one without cracking it. Just set it on a flat surface and spin it gently. If it spins easily, it's cooked. If it doesn't, it's raw. A raw egg is runny inside. When you spin it, the insides slip and slide against the side of the shell at first. A cooked egg is hard. It spins right away as one solid piece.

If you don't want to take any chances, you can peel the hard-cooked eggs before you put them in the refrigerator. Store them in the refrigerator in a closed container, covered with water.

Deviled eggs   A good way to use hard-cooked eggs is to make deviled eggs out of them. (See the recipe on page 104.) You can do all the preparation ahead of time and store the finished eggs in a covered container in the refrigerator. That way, all you have to do the next morning is wake up and eat!

French toast   If you're willing to do just a little cooking in the morning, try French toast. (See the recipe on page 104.) Once you've

Deviled eggs

	4 hard-cooked eggs
7 mL	1½ tsp vinegar or lemon juice
5 mL	1 tsp prepared mustard
1 mL	¼ tsp salt
2 mL	½ tsp Worcestershire sauce
	dash of pepper
30 mL	2 tbsp mayonnaise or salad dressing
15 mL	1 tbsp pickle relish

Cut the eggs in half lengthwise.

Remove the yolks, and crumble them into a small mixing bowl.

Add the rest of the ingredients. Beat until smooth.

Fill the egg whites with the yolk mixture. For extra color, sprinkle with paprika.

Store the eggs in the refrigerator, in a tightly covered container or on a plate well covered with plastic wrap.

French toast

2 slices

	1 egg
60 mL	¼ cup milk
	dash of salt
	dash of nutmeg
15 mL	1 tbsp butter or margarine
	2 slices of bread

Beat the egg, milk, salt, and nutmeg together with a fork in a small bowl.

Melt the butter or margarine in a skillet until it sizzles.

Pour the egg mixture into a shallow dish large enough for you to lay the bread flat, one slice at a time. Put a slice of bread into the egg mixture, and gently turn it to cover both sides.

Place the bread gently into the hot skillet. Turn the heat down to medium. Cook until the bread turns light brown. You can check by lifting up the edge of the bread with a turner. Then turn the bread over, and cook the other side.

Coat the second slice of bread with the egg mixture, and cook it as you did the first piece.

Serve the French toast right away. Some people like to eat French toast with syrup, powdered sugar, or some jam or jelly.

mastered scrambled eggs, you should have no trouble making this old favorite. Serve French toast with some fruit or juice and a glass of milk. You've got a fine breakfast—with foods from each of the Basic Four food groups. Eggs, by the way, are an excellent source of high-quality protein and other important nutrients.

The inside facts about eggs

Nutrients in eggs   Eggs are rich in protein, vitamins A and D, and iron, among other things. Because they have such high-quality protein (well balanced in the essential amino acids), they are used as the standard in judging other protein sources. In fact, the white is practically pure protein—plus water. The yolk has protein, fat, and almost all of the vitamins and minerals found in the egg.

Do eggs lose vitamins and minerals as they get older?

Eggs lose very little of their nutritional value in storage. What they do lose is water and carbon dioxide. This affects the texture and appearance of the egg somewhat, but not the vitamin or mineral content.

Parts of an egg   The yolk of an egg is actually one giant cell. It's millions of times larger than most of the cells in your body, but a single cell, nevertheless. If the egg had been fertilized and incubated (kept warm), the yolk would have divided thousands of times until it developed into a baby chick. Look at the diagram of an egg.

The **yolk** is the part that develops into a chicken. The white is food on which it lives. An egg contains all the nutrients necessary to nourish the chick until it is fully developed and ready to hatch.

The egg shell is porous. It can "breathe." As the egg gets older and loses water and carbon dioxide, the air cell grows larger. In a fertilized egg, this is the air that the developing chick breathes.

In addition, the thick white gradually gets smaller as the egg gets older. The egg becomes thinner and runnier. The yolk becomes flat and breaks easily. Eggs in this condition may be used for omelets or scrambled eggs, or as ingredients in baking. But only fresh Grade AA or Grade A eggs should be used for fried and poached eggs. Fried and poached eggs need firm, round yolks and high, thick whites.

The diagram shows "chalaza." What's that?

The **chalaza** is simply a ropelike strand of thick protein that holds the yolk in place, in the center of the egg. Some people believe that if an egg has a chalaza, a baby chick has started to develop. But the chalaza has nothing to do with it. All fresh eggs have a chalaza.

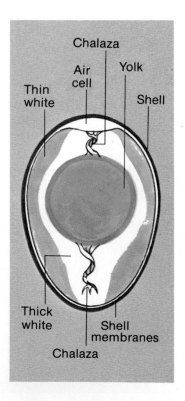

Chalaza

Air cell

Yolk

Thin white

Shell

Thick white

Shell membranes

Chalaza

chalaza (kə LĀ zə)

Have you ever tried to stand a raw egg on end? With a little skill and luck, you can. First shake the egg vigorously to break the chalaza, loosening the yolk from the white. Stand the egg up on the large end. The yolk will sink to the bottom and act as a ballast. This makes it possible, with a little skill and a great deal of patience, to stand the egg on end.

As an egg gets older, the internal structure gets weaker. The thick white, including the chalaza, is less firm. It may not be able to hold the yolk in the center of the egg. You may have noticed fried or hard-cooked eggs that had the yolks off-center. Eggs in this condition are no longer Grade A.

Are Grade A eggs better for you than Grade B?

Egg grades   Grade A eggs are not more nutritious than Grade B eggs, though they should be fresher. Eggs are graded on the condition of the yolk and white. The yolk should stand up high in a top-quality egg. The egg should have mostly thick white, and very little thin white. The condition of the shell is also important. It should be clean, with no cracks or weak spots. Eggs are graded AA (or "Fresh Fancy"), A, and B. The higher the grade, the higher the price. Grade B eggs are fine for scrambling and as an ingredient in cooking, where the appearance of the egg is not important. They are just as nutritious as other eggs.

Are Grade AA eggs larger than other eggs?

Egg sizes   The grades AA, A, and B have nothing to do with size. Eggs are given separate classifications for size. The most common sizes are extra large, large, medium, and small. Extra large eggs must weigh 756 grams (27 ounces) per dozen. Large eggs weigh 672 grams (24 ounces) per dozen (or an average of 56 grams—2 ounces—per egg). Medium eggs must weight 588 grams (21 ounces) per dozen. Small eggs weigh 504 grams (18 ounces) per dozen. The size you buy is up to you—although cost is likely to influence your decision. Standard recipes usually call for large eggs.

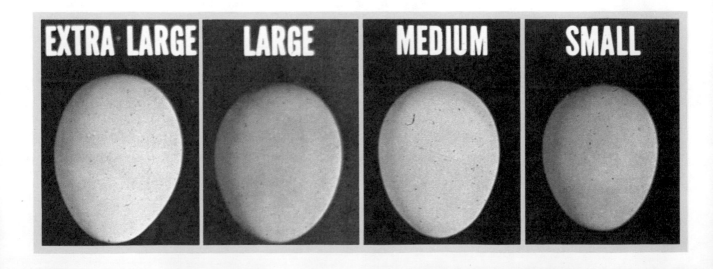

When buying eggs, it's a good idea to open the carton and check them for cracks. Even Grade AA eggs can get broken after they're packed in the carton. Move each egg slightly to be sure it isn't stuck to the carton. If it is, you may not be able to remove it without breaking it.

How long can you store eggs before they spoil?

Storing eggs   Eggs can be kept in the refrigerator for several weeks if they're fresh to begin with. However, they will lose some of their "eye appeal" with time. The yolks will flatten, and the whites will spread. It's best to use raw eggs within two or three weeks.

The best way to store eggs is in a covered container on a shelf of the refrigerator. Actually, the egg carton you buy them in is an excellent storage container.

Like most protein sources, eggs are a good place for bacteria to grow under warm, moist conditions. One bacteria family is salmonella, which causes a food poisoning that produces nausea, vomiting, and diarrhea. Salmonella in eggs is rare, but it can grow there—especially if eggs are not handled and stored properly.

Meat products must be handled even more carefully than eggs. They are rich in protein, as eggs are, but they don't have a protective shell to keep them clean.

Bacon and sausage

Even smoked and cured meats, like bacon and sausage, need to be kept cold. They should be eaten within two or three weeks from the time you buy them. They should be wrapped in film or sealed in plastic bags to keep from drying out in the refrigerator.

When you take bacon out of the refrigerator, the slices are often stuck together in a solid clump. If you can, pry the slices apart gently with your fingers or a table knife. If that doesn't work, pry off a whole clump and put it all in the skillet at one time. As the strips become warm, they become easy to separate with a knife and fork, or tongs.

How do you cook bacon so it's not all greasy? When I tried it, no one would touch it, let alone eat it!

Cooking bacon   There are several ways to cook bacon and various ways to get rid of the fat. To fry bacon, place the strips in a cold skillet. You don't need to add any fat, because bacon already contains quite a bit. Cook over moderate heat for about 5 to 7 minutes. Turn often. If you like bacon crisp instead of chewy, spoon off some of the grease and cook a minute or two longer. Drain the bacon on paper towels, blotting the grease if necessary.

Broiling is a popular way to cook bacon. When you broil a food, you expose it directly to the source of heat. It's not cooked with any added fat (as in frying) or water (as in boiling or simmering), or by

hot air (as in baking). In your oven broiler, the broiling unit produces heat above the food.

To broil bacon, place the slices on a rack in a cold broiler pan. Place the pan in the oven with the surface of the bacon 8 to 12 centimeters (3 to 5 inches) from the heat. Broil the bacon for about 5 minutes and turn it over. Broil the other side about 3 minutes. If you like bacon crisp, broil it another minute or two. Watch closely to be sure it doesn't get too done, no matter how long it's been cooking.

You can also cook bacon successfully in a microwave oven. We'll talk more about how to do that in Chapter 9.

How do you know when bacon is done?

For chewy bacon, the strips should be shriveled to about three-fourths of their original length. They should have lost the "glassy" look they had when the fat first started to melt. But they should be limp and curly when you lift them with a fork or tongs.

For crisp bacon, continue cooking until the fat begins to have a grainy look and a slightly golden color. The strips will be stiffer (but will still bend) when you lift them.

If the bacon smokes, that means it's too done. It also means the heat is too high. The bacon is in danger of becoming hard and shriveled, or even burned. You can run into the same kind of problems with sausage.

Do you cook sausage the same as bacon?

Cooking link sausage   Sausage requires its own special cooking methods. Link sausage (shaped like little hotdogs), should be cooked as follows.

1. Place the sausages in a cold skillet. Add 60 milliliters (1/4 cup) of cold water.

2. Cover the skillet and cook the sausages 5 minutes over medium heat.

3. Drain off all the water and grease.

When you fry link or ground sausage, avoid hot grease spatters by cooking at a low temperature. Blot excess grease by placing cooked sausage on paper towels.

4. Continue cooking the sausages with the skillet uncovered, over low heat, for 12 to 15 minutes. Turn the sausages occasionally until all sides are browned.

If you buy a package of sausage labeled "precooked," follow the package directions for heating.

Cooking ground sausage Ground sausage (which looks like hamburger) should be cooked as follows.

1. Shape into small, thin patties.
2. Place the patties in a cold skillet and cook them over low heat for 10 minutes.
3. Turn the patties once and continue cooking them for an additional 5 to 10 minutes.
4. Drain the patties well on paper towels.

Yum! I love sausage with pancakes and syrup! If I just knew how to make pancakes!

The combination of sausages and pancakes is not only a favorite but easy to prepare. Pancakes are really quite simple to cook. In fact, the hardest thing about them is deciding what to call them. Sometimes they're called pancakes, and sometimes griddlecakes, flapjacks, hotcakes, or wheatcakes. Whatever they're called, they're popular across the country. The expression "selling like hotcakes" refers to something that sells very quickly because everyone likes it.

Pancakes

Dependable basic pancakes Pancakes are easy to make, but like most other things they need two things for success: a good recipe, like the one on page 110, and a little practice. The key to cooking pancakes is the heat of the griddle (a pan without sides). Test the

Basic pancakes

18 medium pancakes: 6 servings

625 mL	**2½ cups all-purpose flour**
30 mL	**2 tbsp baking powder**
30 mL	**2 tbsp sugar**
5 mL	**1 tsp salt**
	2 eggs, beaten
500 mL	**2 cups milk (a little more milk for thinner pancakes)**
60 mL	**¼ cup salad oil**

Mix the dry ingredients thoroughly with a fork, in a large mixing bowl.

Beat the eggs in a separate bowl. Add the milk and salad oil.

Add the liquid mixture to the dry ingredients. Stir the batter only until the dry ingredients are mixed in. (It will still be lumpy, but that's all right. Avoid overstirring.)

Cook the pancakes on a greased, hot griddle or skillet.

heat by sprinkling the griddle with drops of water. The drops should "dance" on the griddle.

For 8-centimeter (3-inch) pancakes, use a ladle or a measuring cup. Pour about 60 milliliters (1/4 cup) of batter onto the griddle. For "silver-dollar" pancakes, use a tablespoon.

How can you tell when pancakes are done, but not too done?

After you pour the batter onto the griddle, start looking for bubbles. When bubbles form over the whole pancake, turn it over. Don't wait for all the bubbles to pop. By then the pancake will be too done.

Let the other side cook for a little less time than the first side, and remove the pancake from the griddle. Pancakes can be stored in the oven for a short time, on a rack or in an ovenproof dish, at 125 °C (250 °F).

KAREN: *The trouble with this recipe is the same as with the one I used. It makes twice as many pancakes as we wanted!*

Pancakes with meat, grapefruit, and milk make a delicious wake-me-up breakfast.

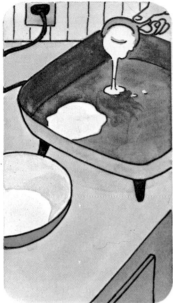

If you want nine pancakes (three each, for three people) instead of the eighteen that the recipe makes, use your old formula to cut the recipe in half.

$$\frac{\text{number you want}}{\text{number recipe makes}} = \frac{9}{18} = \frac{1}{2}$$

Multiply all of the ingredients in the recipe by 1/2, and you should come up with just the right number of pancakes.

Wouldn't it all be a lot easier if you used a pancake mix?

Pancake mixes   With pancake mixes you usually have to add your own milk, eggs, and oil anyway, so you still have to do some recipe arithmetic on those ingredients. Since a pancake recipe is fairly simple to begin with, there's little advantage to using a mix.

In deciding whether to use a mix for pancakes or any other item, you should consider three things: (1) convenience (savings in time and trouble), (2) cost, and (3) quality. If it's a lot quicker and easier to use a mix than to start from scratch, and the differences in cost and quality are not great, using a mix makes sense. Otherwise, you're better off using a recipe.

Pancake variations   For variety, make blueberry pancakes. Cook the pancakes as usual, but just before you turn them over, sprinkle each one with a few fresh or frozen (and thawed) blueberries. Turn the pancakes and brown the second side as usual. Or invent your own ingredient to use instead of blueberries. You can use lots of special and creative ingredients for other quick breads, too.

Other quick breads

Pancakes are one kind of quick bread. Waffles are another. So are muffins, biscuits, banana bread, many coffee cakes, and popovers. A quick bread is any leavened bread that uses a quick method of rising instead of yeast, which takes a long time to grow.

What's a "leavened" bread? And how does bread rise?

Almost all breads are leavened. This simply means that they are "fluffed up," or filled with air bubbles, to make them light and easy to chew. When bread dough fills with air bubbles, it expands—we say it "rises."

If breads weren't leavened, they would be flat and hard. An example of unleavened bread is *matzo* (MAHT sə). Matzo is eaten by Jewish people during Passover. In the flight from Egypt during Biblical times, the Jews didn't have time to let their bread rise before baking it. They had to eat unleavened bread. The thin wafers eaten by Christians during Communion are unleavened, too.

What does yeast have to do with it?

Leavening agents **Yeast** is a harmless kind of microscopic plant. It is one kind of **leavening agent**—an ingredient that makes a food rise. When yeast is mixed into bread dough, it grows and gives off carbon dioxide, a gas. The gas forms bubbles in the dough. When the dough is baked, the bubbles are baked into the bread, too. This makes it light and easy to chew.

But yeast dough takes time to rise—often from 1 to 3 hours, sometimes longer. There are quicker ways to get air bubbles into doughs and batters. One is to fold fluffy, beaten egg whites into it. Another is to fold and beat a batter to trap air in it.

The most common quick leavening agents are baking soda or baking powder. **Baking soda** reacts with the acid in buttermilk, vinegar, fruit juice, or other ingredients. It forms carbon dioxide the way yeast does.

Baking powder contains baking soda, plus its own acid in a dry form. When it is mixed with liquid, the acid reacts with the baking soda, forming gas bubbles. Baking powder acts again when the dough or batter is heated. For this reason, it is called "double-acting."

Are quick breads easy, as well as quick?

There are hundreds of different quick-bread recipes. Some are fairly easy, and some are a little tricky. A couple of basic recipes will give you some practice and experience. Then you can try others from your favorite cookbook. Let's start with muffins.

leavening agent (LEV ən ing   Ā jənt)

Muffins

12 muffins

430 mL	1¾ **cups all-purpose flour**
60 mL	¼ **cup sugar**
12 mL	2½ **tsp baking powder**
4 mL	¾ **tsp salt**
	1 egg
180 mL	¾ **cup milk**
80 mL	⅓ **cup salad oil**

Combine the dry ingredients thoroughly in a medium-size mixing bowl. Then make a well, or hole, in the center.

Beat the egg well in a small bowl. Mix in the milk and oil.

Pour the liquid mixture into the center of the dry ingredients. Stir quickly for only a few strokes, until the dry ingredients are moistened. The batter will look very lumpy. Do not overstir. This would make the muffins tough.

Line the muffin pans with paper baking cups. Or grease the pans. With waxed paper, coat the inside of each cup in the pan with a thin film of oil or shortening.

Fill the cups 2/3 full with batter.

Bake at 200 °C (400 °F) for about 25 minutes.

Muffins Look at the muffin recipe for a minute. Notice how the ingredients are mixed. All of the dry ingredients are mixed in one bowl, and all the liquids in another. Then the liquid mixture is quickly added to the dry mixture and stirred briefly. The batter should be lumpy. This way of mixing ingredients is called the **muffin method**. It is used in making pancakes and in many cake recipes.

Muffin variations To turn plain muffins into blueberry muffins, gently stir in 250 milliliters (1 cup) of fresh or frozen (thawed and drained) blueberries. Once again, do not stir the batter any more than necessary.

If you get tired of blueberries, try raisins, chopped nuts, or chopped dates. Or try this. Fill the muffin pans 1/3 full. Put a teaspoon of tart jelly or jellied cranberry sauce in the middle. Add the remaining batter and bake as usual. Or think up your own "surprise" filling.

What about biscuits? I tried to make some once, and they turned out as hard as hockey pucks! What happened?

Biscuits Several things can make biscuits too hard. If the dough is mixed too much or baked too long, the biscuits will be hard and tough. Or there may be too much flour in proportion to the other ingredients. If there isn't enough baking powder, or if the baking powder is old, biscuits won't rise enough to make them tender.

Easy drop biscuits

18 biscuits

500 mL	**2 cups all-purpose flour**
15 mL	**1 tbsp baking powder**
1.5 mL	**⅓ tsp salt**
60 mL	**¼ cup shortening**
250 mL	**1 cup milk**

Mix the dry ingredients thoroughly in a medium-size mixing bowl.

Cut in the shortening. Make a well, or hole, in the center of the mixture.

Add all the milk. Stir quickly with a fork until the mixture is moistened evenly.

Scoop out a heaping measure of dough with a teaspoon. With another teaspoon, scrape off the dough and "drop" it onto a greased baking sheet. Continue with more biscuits, placing them 2 to 3 centimeters (1 inch) apart.

Bake at 225 °C (450 °F) for 10 to 12 minutes, or until evenly browned on top. Serve hot.

Muffins and biscuits are called quick breads. Why?

Some recipes call for biscuit dough to be **kneaded**. This means folding and pressing the dough. This kind of biscuit dough is then rolled out and cut into biscuits. If you handle the dough too much, though, the biscuits may turn out hard. A simpler and easier method is to make drop biscuits. These are simply spooned out and dropped onto a baking sheet. They don't have to be kneaded.

The biscuit recipe on this page tells you to **cut in** the shortening. To do this, first distribute the shortening around the bowl. Then use a pastry blender or fork to cut the shortening into small pieces, and to coat the pieces with flour. Do this until the whole mixture looks like large, coarse crumbs.

Biscuits are delicious for dinner, too. They are a good way to add a serving from the bread and cereal group to the evening meal. For that matter, they make a good bread to serve at lunchtime. To eat

kneaded (NĒD əd)

Left: Cutting in.
Right: Dropping.

them, split them through the middle and spread them with butter or margarine.

Don't you already get enough bread at lunchtime, in sandwiches?

You don't have to have sandwiches every day for lunch. There are lots of other delicious and nutritious foods you can have. We'll take a look at some of them soon.

Words to understand

fry	chalaza
seasoned pan	broil
U.S. customary system	yeast
metric system	leavening agent
proportion	baking soda
boil	baking powder
simmer	muffin method
garnish	knead
yolk	cut in

Food and equipment to know

eggs sunny-side up	quick bread
eggs over easy	
scrambled eggs	skillet
omelet	omelet pan
soft-cooked eggs	egg turner
hard-cooked eggs	saucepan
poached eggs	egg cup
deviled eggs	broiler pan
French toast	griddle
link sausage	muffin pan
ground sausage	pastry blender

Questions to discuss

1. What happens if eggs are cooked at high heat or for a long time?
2. How can you prevent eggs from sticking to the pan?
3. How do you "season" a pan?
4. Why should you start with cold water when you're cooking eggs in their shells?

5. What can you do to make it easy to peel hard-cooked eggs?

6. What's one way to tell if an egg is raw or hard-cooked without cracking the shell?

7. What does the grade on an egg carton mean? Describe a Grade AA egg. What could you use Grade B eggs for?

8. Describe the parts of an egg. What makes an egg so nutritious?

9. How many milliliters are in a liter? How many teaspoons are in a quart? Which is easier to figure out?

10. How can you separate cold bacon into strips?

11. What is the difference between link sausage and ground sausage patties?

12. What does a leavening agent do? Name three leavening agents.

13. What is the "muffin method" of mixing ingredients?

14. What happens if you mix biscuits or muffins too much?

Things to do

1. Break an egg onto a saucer. Identify the yolk, thick white, thin white, and chalaza. What grade would you give this egg? Why?

2. Plan the menu for a family brunch. Include an egg dish and a quick bread. What else do you need to make it a balanced meal? Make a list of all the ingredients you would need to prepare this meal. Check the supplies in your kitchen at home. Make a shopping list of the things you would need to buy.

3. Mix 30 milliliters (two tablespoons) of vinegar with 15 milliliters (1 tablespoon) of baking soda. What happens? Now explain what happens in a quick bread when you add baking soda or baking powder.

4. Prepare a hard-cooked egg by the method described in this chapter. Cook another egg in boiling water for 20 minutes. Cool both eggs. Cut them in half. Describe the differences between the two eggs. Which egg is more tender? Does one have a green ring around the yolk?

5. Prepare the pancake recipe in this chapter, but don't add the baking powder. Take out 125 milliliters (1/2 cup) of the batter. Add the baking powder to the batter that is left. Now cook pancakes from both batters. Describe the differences between the two sets of pancakes. Can you explain what happened?

6. One trouble new cooks have is timing—getting everything ready to serve at the same time. Plan a time schedule for this meal:
Orange juice   Muffins
Scrambled eggs   Milk
Start by making a list of every step and how long it will take.

Example: getting out muffin ingredients   5 minutes
greasing muffin pan   3 minutes
cracking and beating eggs   3 minutes

Set a serving time. Figure out when you would need to do each step to have everything ready at that time.

7. Figure out how much it would cost to make the pancake recipe in this chapter. Buy a pancake mix. Figure out how much it would cost to make the same number of pancakes that are the same size as your homemade ones. Compare the costs. Time how long it takes you to prepare homemade pancakes, and how long it takes to make them from the mix. Compare the cooked pancakes (looks, taste, texture, etc.). If you were making pancakes for friends, would you make them "from scratch" or from a mix? Why?

Careers to consider

Would you like to work in a kitchen preparing food?

If you enjoy cooking and creating food ideas, consider a career in food preparation.

People are eating out more often. This means there are a lot of jobs in the kitchens of restaurants, fast-food chains, cafeterias, and other places that serve food. These kitchens depend on the skill and speed of **cooks** or **chefs** and various helpers. A large restaurant may have several chefs who each specialize in something—such as a salad chef or a pastry chef. **Kitchen helpers** are assistants. They may handle jobs from cleaning vegetables to mixing ingredients to washing dishes. Many vocational schools offer basic training programs for jobs in food service. You can get an excellent background in schools that specialize in training chefs. Some colleges offer programs in restaurant management. Skilled chefs are more than good cooks; they know about kitchen management and the art of serving food attractively. Generally, the more skilled you are, the more money you can make.

There are, however, other kinds of careers in food preparation. If you like experimenting with food ideas, perhaps you would enjoy developing recipes as a career. **Test-kitchen home economists** do just that. They may work in a food company, on the staff of a magazine, or in an advertising or public relations agency.

If you have artistic talents, think about how to apply them to foods. Specialists in **food photography** prepare and arrange food so that it looks appealing in a photograph.

With basic skills in decorating food, you might work in a bakery—decorating pies, cakes, and other desserts. The same skills are needed by **caterers**—people who provide food for special occasions. Caterers pay careful attention to how their food looks, as well as how it tastes.

HAS THIS EVER HAPPENED TO YOU?

Kim's photography club is having a luncheon meeting with a guest speaker. The club has twelve members and operates on a very small budget. Kim and David are trying to decide what to serve for lunch.

DAVID: *I vote for hotdogs or hamburgers!*

KIM: *That's fine for the kids, but what about the guest speaker? It should be something a little more elegant.*

DAVID: *But we can't have a seven-course meal, either. We'd have more people waiting on table than sitting and eating! We need a one-dish meal—something like shrimp curry.*

KIM: *That's fine—except that no one likes it but you! We've got to have something everyone likes. How about T-bone steak?*

DAVID: *Everyone would like that, all right! And it would certainly be elegant enough. But who can afford it? We need something cheap, like chicken croquettes.*

KIM: *That takes too long. We have only two periods to fix everything, eat, hold the meeting, and listen to the speaker. Besides, we don't have an oven.*

DAVID: *Okay, I give up! What can you serve that's elegant and popular, but doesn't take too much time, trouble, money, attention, or equipment?*

118

LUNCH

What you need for this occasion is something inexpensive that looks bright and colorful, that can be prepared in advance, and that can be served all at once. That's just what makes main dish salads such favorites for luncheons.

Main dish salads

A main dish salad—or **entrée** salad—is one that includes greens and other vegetables and a source of protein. It should have 60 to 120 grams (2 to 4 ounces) per person of meat, poultry, eggs, fish, seafood, or cheese. All you need to complete the meal is a serving from the Bread and Cereal Group, and one from the Milk Group.

entrée (AHN trā)

119

Tuna fish salad

8 servings

370 g	**13 oz canned tuna fish**
375 mL	**1½ cups chopped celery**
	3 hard-cooked eggs, cut into quarters
125 mL	**½ cup mayonnaise or salad dressing**
30 mL	**2 tbsp pickle juice, lemon juice, or vinegar**

Drain the oil or water from the tuna fish. In a medium-size mixing bowl, break up the fish with a fork, stirring and mashing lightly.

Mix in the chopped celery.

Mash the eggs lightly with a fork, breaking them up into small pieces. Add them to the tuna.

Moisten the salad with mayonnaise or salad dressing until the desired consistency (thickness or firmness) is reached.

Cover and refrigerate until ready to use. The salad is now ready for sandwiches or to be made into a main dish salad.

One example that you're probably familiar with—and which makes a good luncheon item—is tuna fish salad.

Sure, I've had it. I even like it. But tuna fish doesn't sound very special to me.

Tuna fish salad   Tuna fish can be plain or fancy, depending on how you serve it. A tuna fish sandwich is—well, just a sandwich. But tuna in a salad! Surrounded by sparkling red tomato wedges and bright yellow and white egg slices, garnished with radish flowers, and sprinkled with paprika, it is a feast to the eyes as well as the taste buds. Once you have the idea, you can change some of the ingredients if you like, and make up your own salads.

The celery for tuna fish salad should be chopped into fairly small pieces. But the pieces should not be so tiny that you lose the texture or "crunch" of celery as you eat the salad. That "crunch" adds a **contrast** (difference) in texture to the salad, which makes it more enjoyable to eat.

How do you **chop** foods? Perhaps you've seen professional chefs at work in a restaurant or on television. Here's how they might chop or dice celery.

1. Place the trimmed stalks on a cutting board. Using a chef's knife, cut the celery crosswise into half-centimeter (quarter-inch) slices.

2. Turn the knife at a right angle and cut across the celery slices. With one hand hold the handle of the knife, and place the other over the top (dull side) of the blade. Cut across the celery slices with a light chopping motion. Chop coarsely.

contrast (KAHN trast)

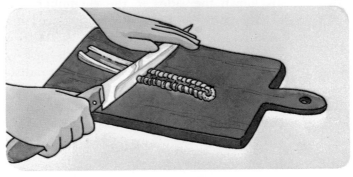

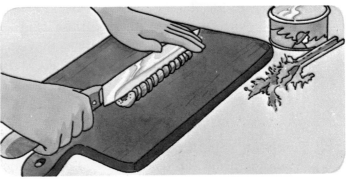

With the tuna salad all mixed, you're ready to make up the salad plates. The salad plate in the recipe on this page has a tempting variety of colors, shapes, tastes, and textures. It combines tuna salad with lettuce, tomatoes, eggs, cucumbers, and radishes.

To wash the raw vegetables, use cold water. Do *not* use soap! To **score** the cucumbers, take a fork and scrape the tines (the pointed

Main dish tuna salad plates

8 servings

	1 **medium head iceberg lettuce**
	8 **medium-size tomatoes**
	8 **hard-cooked eggs**
	1 **large cucumber**
.50 kg	1 **lb medium to large radishes**
	tuna fish salad for 8 people (see recipe)

Tear the lettuce into bite-size pieces.

Cut out the stem base from the center of each tomato. Cut each tomato into 4 wedges.

Peel the hard-cooked eggs and cut them into quarters.

Wash the cucumbers. Score them lengthwise with a fork and cut them into thin slices.

Wash the radishes and cut off the ends. Cut the radishes into "flowers."

Make a bed of lettuce pieces on each plate. Place a rounded portion of tuna fish salad in the center of the bed. (A large ice cream scoop is helpful.) Surround the tuna fish with 4 tomato wedges. Next to each tomato wedge, place a quarter of an egg. Next to the egg, place a cucumber slice. On each cucumber slice, place a radish flower.

Can you find the safety hazard in the pictures above? Why is this dangerous?

tips) down the sides of the cucumber, cutting through the skin in parallel grooves. Before slicing, place the cucumbers on a cutting board and cut off the ends. The ends are often bitter. The best part of the cucumber is the long middle part with the large seeds.

To make a radish flower, stand the radish on one of its cut ends on a cutting board. With a paring knife, slice halfway down the skin on all four sides of the radish. The cut marks will make a square out of the flat, white top of the radish, instead of a circle. The partly cut red skin will look like the petals of a flower.

Chicken salad   The basic salad plate is very flexible. Just change the tuna to .75 liter (3 cups) of cubed cooked chicken, and your main dish tuna salad becomes main dish chicken salad. To cube chicken, cut chicken pieces into strips and then cut the strips into cubes. If you like, add 60 milliliters (1/4 cup) of pickle relish or two sweet pickles, chopped into small pieces.

We don't have much time to work on the food at school. Can much of this be done ahead of time?

Do-ahead salad tips   Just about everything except the final assembly on the plates can be done ahead of time, even the night before. Store everything in the refrigerator.

Store the tuna (or chicken) salad in a dish with a close-fitting cover.

Store the torn lettuce pieces, cucumber slices, and radish flowers in plastic bags that you can close tightly. To keep them crisp, put a wet paper towel into each bag before closing.

Cut the stem base out of the tomatoes and store the whole tomatoes in a plastic bag.

Cook the eggs and refrigerate them. Carry them to school in the original egg cartons.

After you get to school, everything should be refrigerated or put into an ice chest until you're ready to arrange the salad plates. Most of your work has been done ahead of time, except for peeling the eggs, cutting the eggs and tomatoes into quarters, and arranging the individual salads on plates. Even this last-minute work can be reduced by serving the salad "family style" on a single, large platter.

Serving family style   In family-style serving, each person helps herself or himself from one serving platter. To serve salad this way, lay a bed of lettuce on the platter and spoon tuna or chicken salad into the lettuce in a rounded heap. Surround it with cucumber slices topped with egg and tomato wedges. Distribute radish flowers around the salad. You might even press some into the tuna or chicken salad itself. Each platter should serve four to eight people. Serving more than eight people with only one platter is awkward and difficult.

Chef's salad   A really hearty main dish salad that's still elegant and easy to serve is a chef's salad. This is a large tossed salad of greens,

This "tuna for four" salad plate is garnished with carrot curls—shavings made by scraping a vegetable peeler down a carrot. What other garnishes could you add to a tuna fish salad?

tomatoes, and other crisp vegetables. It usually has strips of ham, cheese, and turkey laid across the top. Over it all goes a dressing of your choice.

You can use other meats besides the traditional ham and turkey. Leftover roast beef, pork, or chicken is just as good. Cut it into strips or cubes. Lay the meat on top of the salad or toss it along with the other ingredients.

Salad plates can be as simple or exotic as you want them to be. If you want something new and different, look through cookbooks and magazines for interesting ideas. You'll find all sorts of foods used in salads and dressings. For example, you could add chopped nuts, diced apples, and even a small can of mandarin oranges to your basic tuna salad. Then you would have an unusual tuna salad full of new flavors and textures.

Apples and oranges! This is beginning to sound like a fruit salad!

You can put a little fruit into many kinds of salads, just to add variety in taste and texture. Sections of oranges, tangerines, or grapefruit, for example, will give a pleasant tang to an ordinary mixed green salad. The fruit may also add some important vitamins and minerals.

Fruit salads Fruits are useful in salads as more than an accent. Fruits are the main ingredients of some delicious salads. Waldorf (WAL dorf) salad (apples, nuts, raisins, mayonnaise) is a common favorite. A large scoop of cottage cheese placed on a bed of lettuce and surrounded by sections or pieces of different fruits makes a good main dish salad. The cottage cheese provides the protein missing in the fruit.

Both this Waldorf salad and the cottage cheese platter provide variety in texture, color, and taste. Which fruit salad do you prefer? Why?

Fruit salads are often used as a light dessert after a hearty meal. They also make good appetizer salads, because the tangy taste stimulates the appetite. Of course, many people enjoy fruit salads for breakfast. Fruit salads can be prepared in advance, covered, and refrigerated until breakfast time.

You can't fix all fruits in advance, can you? I cut up some apples for a salad one time, and they all turned brown!

Some fresh fruits—such as apples, bananas, pears, and peaches—will turn brown if you cut them and leave them exposed to the air. But this is easy to prevent. Just protect the cut edges from the air. This is best done by covering them with some kind of acid. Any citrus juice will do. So will the liquid that comes with most canned fruits. You could also drop the pieces into a bowl of water mixed with 30 milliliters (2 tablespoons) of lemon juice. If you plan to use salad dressing, you can toss the fruit pieces with the dressing right away to keep them from browning.

Salad dressings won't hurt fruits and most other foods that are fairly firm—such as meats, celery, green peppers, and cucumbers. But lettuce or other leafy greens will get limp and lifeless if you put dressing on too far in advance. You should wait till the last moment to add dressing to lettuce or other salad greens.

Salad ingredients

You have a great variety of salad greens to choose from. Get to know them all, and buy them as a change from iceberg lettuce—especially when iceberg lettuce is out of season.

Kinds of salad greens We really must start with iceberg lettuce because it is by far the most popular.

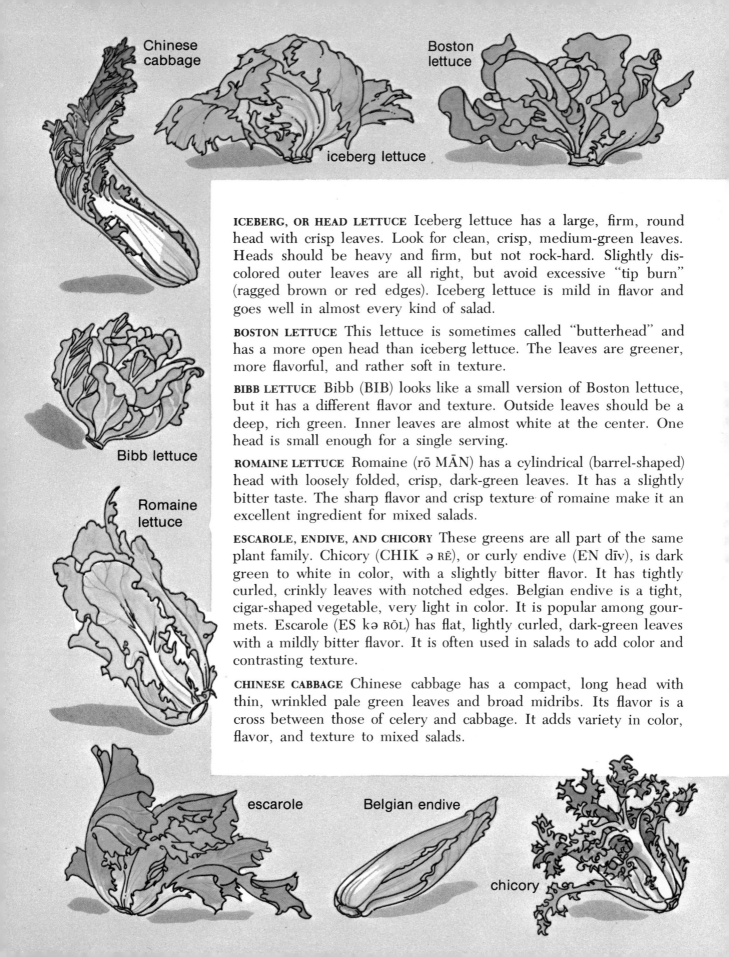

Chinese cabbage

iceberg lettuce

Boston lettuce

Bibb lettuce

Romaine lettuce

ICEBERG, OR HEAD LETTUCE Iceberg lettuce has a large, firm, round head with crisp leaves. Look for clean, crisp, medium-green leaves. Heads should be heavy and firm, but not rock-hard. Slightly discolored outer leaves are all right, but avoid excessive "tip burn" (ragged brown or red edges). Iceberg lettuce is mild in flavor and goes well in almost every kind of salad.

BOSTON LETTUCE This lettuce is sometimes called "butterhead" and has a more open head than iceberg lettuce. The leaves are greener, more flavorful, and rather soft in texture.

BIBB LETTUCE Bibb (BIB) looks like a small version of Boston lettuce, but it has a different flavor and texture. Outside leaves should be a deep, rich green. Inner leaves are almost white at the center. One head is small enough for a single serving.

ROMAINE LETTUCE Romaine (rō MĀN) has a cylindrical (barrel-shaped) head with loosely folded, crisp, dark-green leaves. It has a slightly bitter taste. The sharp flavor and crisp texture of romaine make it an excellent ingredient for mixed salads.

ESCAROLE, ENDIVE, AND CHICORY These greens are all part of the same plant family. Chicory (CHIK ə RĒ), or curly endive (EN dĭv), is dark green to white in color, with a slightly bitter flavor. It has tightly curled, crinkly leaves with notched edges. Belgian endive is a tight, cigar-shaped vegetable, very light in color. It is popular among gourmets. Escarole (ES kə RŌL) has flat, lightly curled, dark-green leaves with a mildly bitter flavor. It is often used in salads to add color and contrasting texture.

CHINESE CABBAGE Chinese cabbage has a compact, long head with thin, wrinkled pale green leaves and broad midribs. Its flavor is a cross between those of celery and cabbage. It adds variety in color, flavor, and texture to mixed salads.

escarole

Belgian endive

chicory

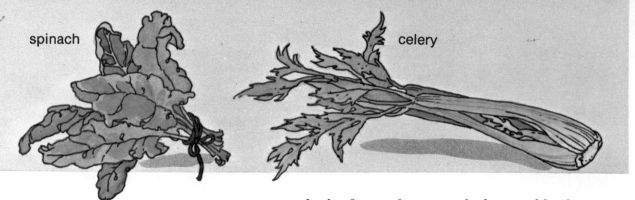

spinach

celery

SPINACH You may think of spinach as a cooked vegetable that comes from a can (Popeye-style) or the freezer. But one of the most delicious ways to eat spinach is fresh and raw, as salad greens. Look for rich, dark green color and shiny, fresh leaves with no decay.

CELERY You know all about celery as a snack, but don't forget about using it in salads. Celery may vary in color from green to white. All-green celery is usually called Pascal. Choose celery for overall crispness and freshness. Stalks should feel solid and rigid, and should have no pithy, hollow, or discolored areas. For salads, chop stalks and branches into pieces about a half centimeter (a quarter inch) long.

CABBAGE Cabbage makes an inexpensive and nutritious vegetable salad, high in vitamin C. It can be served by itself as coleslaw or mixed in with other salad greens to add body and flavor. Look for solid, heavy heads with no large splits and no worm damage on the outer leaves. New cabbage is green and not as dense as cabbage from storage. Cabbage that has been stored is firm and tightly packed. It ranges from pale green to white. It is usually somewhat crisper and juicier than new cabbage.

WATERCRESS This green has small, round, bright-green leaves, branching from slender stems. Both the stems and the leaves have a distinctive herbal flavor, slightly bitter. Watercress is often used as a garnish.

PARSLEY Like watercress, parsley is often used as a garnish, as well as in mixed salads. It has curly, lacy leaves that are bright green in color. Parsley has a fresh, zesty flavor. In fact, some people nibble it to freshen their breath.

Parsley and watercress should be stored in airtight containers in the refrigerator. Put a small amount of water in the container before closing it. If sprigs become slightly wilted (limp), they can be freshened by trimming the stems and placing them in cold water.

cabbage

watercress

parsley

What about lettuce? How can you keep that from wilting?

Storing salad greens   Lettuce and other leafy greens should be thoroughly rinsed (but not soaked) in cold water before storing. Remove discolored or wilted leaves. Drain or shake off excess water. Store greens in the crisper section of the refrigerator in covered containers or plastic bags. This prevents evaporation, drying out, and wilting.

If you plan to use lettuce for tossed salad, you will want to take out the core. Bang the core sharply on the kitchen counter. This breaks the core loose so that it twists out easily. Run cold water down into the hole to rinse and freshen the leaves. Drain the lettuce. If you plan to serve lettuce wedges, leave the core in to hold the leaves together.

I like lettuce, but I like other things in salads, too. What can you put in that you can really sink your teeth into?

Other salad ingredients   There are many salad ingredients that add variety in taste and texture. We've already mentioned celery, eggs, radishes, tomatoes, cucumbers, meat, cheese, and fruit. There are also onions, chives, scallions (green onions), green peppers, and olives. Or try raw cauliflower, carrots, broccoli, zucchini squash, or asparagus. Just break or cut the vegetables into bite-size pieces.

How do you know what things to put into what kind of salad?

Choosing salad ingredients   Salads come in all shapes and sizes. The things you put in a salad will depend somewhat on the purpose it serves. A salad may be used as an appetizer, or it may be an accompaniment to the entrée (the main dish). It may be a main dish itself, or it may be a dessert. Fruit salads and molded gelatin salads are especially popular as desserts.

An example of a hearty salad that is both an appetizer and an accompaniment to the main dish is the Italian *antipasto* (AN ti PAS tō). The word means "before the food," or "before the main dish." An

Many of these fruits and vegetables are in the salads shown on the next page. Some of those salad ingredients aren't shown here. Can you find them?

antipasto may contain lettuce and other greens, onions, tomatoes, green and black olives, and sometimes anchovies, pepperoni, or salami, sprinkled with an oil-and-vinegar dressing. It is a varied and lively complement (something that completes) for a simple, one-dish pasta meal of lasagna, ravioli, or spaghetti with meat sauce.

Generally, the more variety you have in the rest of the meal, the less you need in the salad. For instance, let's take an elaborate meal with an appetizer, soup, bread or rolls, meat, two or three vegetables, beverage, dessert, and after-dinner mints. A simple salad of lettuce wedges and Russian dressing would be plenty. But for a simple menu of steak and baked potato, with no other vegetable, it would be nice to have a tossed salad with lettuce or spinach, tomatoes, onions, and some other crunchy raw vegetables, such as cauliflower, radishes, or cucumbers. Spice it all up with a garlic dressing.

How do you know what kind of dressing to put on different salads?

The dressing you choose depends, of course, on your own taste. At restaurants, you're usually offered two or three kinds, and the choice is entirely up to you. Sometimes it's hard to tell what to order, however, because the names given to various dressings can be very confusing.

Salad dressings

In American restaurants, "French" dressing may be red, orange, or white, and either clear or creamy. "Russian" dressing may be made from French dressing or from mayonnaise. "Italian" dressing may be almost anything, as long as it has garlic. All of these dressings are

Dressings based on mayonnaise or salad dressing

Thousand Island dressing: Contains mayonnaise, plus catsup (and/or chili sauce), chopped pickles or relish, and a chopped, hard-cooked egg. May also contain chopped green pepper, onions or celery, and paprika.

Russian dressing: Usually contains mayonnaise, plus catsup (and/or chili sauce), onion, and sometimes celery, green pepper, paprika, lemon juice, and Worcestershire sauce. Similar to Thousand Island dressing, but without chopped egg and pickles.

Roquefort/blue cheese dressing: Contains mayonnaise, plus Roquefort or blue (*bleu*, in French) cheese and lemon juice or vinegar, and sometimes sugar, sour cream, and garlic. Gets a special flavor from the blue mold in the cheese.

Creamy dressing: Contains mayonnaise, plus milk, cream, or sour cream, and sometimes vinegar, lemon juice, or orange juice, and sugar. May be turned into a creamy herb dressing by adding chopped chives, chopped parsley, and other herbs.

really American, by the way. They have very little relation to dressings actually used in France, Russia, or Italy.

Mayonnaise   Most dressings used in this country are variations of three basic dressings. The first of these is mayonnaise. Mayonnaise is made of oil, egg yolks or whole eggs, vinegar or lemon juice (or both), and seasonings, such as paprika, dry mustard, or cayenne.

The egg makes it possible to create an **emulsion**, a kind of cloudy mixture, of oil and liquids that contain water (such as the vinegar and lemon juice in mayonnaise). As you probably know, oil will not normally mix with water. When you shake them up in a bottle, the oil breaks up into small droplets for a moment, but they quickly join together again and separate from the water. When eggs are added to the mixture, they give the droplets a coating that prevents them from joining together again. As a result, the droplets remain trapped throughout the liquid. Eggs are often used in cooking to create this kind of mixture, or emulsion, of oil and water.

Cooked dressing   The second basic dressing is called cooked dressing if you make it at home, and salad dressing if you buy it in a jar at the store. It looks and tastes very much like mayonnaise, but it contains less oil. In addition, it uses a kind of starchy paste and less egg. Usually, salad dressing is less expensive and has fewer calories than mayonnaise. It is used in all the ways that mayonnaise is used.

"French" dressing   The third basic dressing is called "French" dressing. In France, salad is usually served with oil and vinegar, in separate cruets (KROO əts), which are very small pitchers. In America, the oil and vinegar are usually mixed together, along with various seasonings, and often with sugar or other sweeteners. This oil-and-vinegar dressing is used as the basis for hundreds of dressings with imaginative, and sometimes confusing, names.

emulsion (i MUHL shən)

Oil and vinegar, shown in cruets, can be mixed with seasonings to create a basic "French" dressing for a tossed green salad.

If it's all so confusing, how can you tell what you're buying in the store, or which dressing to ask for in a restaurant?

Often, you simply can't tell what kind of dressing you're getting, from the name alone. When buying bottled dressings or mixes at the store, look at the list of ingredients on the label. That will give you an idea of what the dressing will taste like. In a restaurant, ask what the dressing contains, what color it is, whether it's clear or creamy, and what it tastes like—sweet, sour, spicy, mild, garlic, and so forth.

To give you an idea of what to expect, the tables on these pages describe some of the most common dressings, with some of their variations. One table lists dressings based on mayonnaise or salad dressing (or cooked dressing). The other lists a number of dressings that start with basic "French" dressing—a mixture of two or three parts of oil to one part of vinegar or lemon juice, plus seasonings.

Dressings based on "French" dressing

Russian dressing: Contains oil and vinegar, plus chili sauce, lemon juice, and chopped onion. Sometimes has sugar, water, celery seed, paprika, and catsup. Somewhat thinner and less creamy than mayonnaise-based Russian dressing.

Red (or orange) French dressing: Contains oil and vinegar or lemon juice, plus paprika and/or a tomato product such as catsup. May have sweeteners (honey or sugar), dry mustard, onion, and cayenne.

Roquefort dressing: Contains oil and vinegar, lemon juice, and Roquefort cheese. May also contain paprika, sweeteners, and Worcestershire sauce. Thinner and less creamy than mayonnaise-based Roquefort dressing.

Italian dressing (sometimes called **garlic dressing**): Contains oil and vinegar, plus garlic. May also have sugar, celery salt, dry mustard, cayenne, and hot pepper sauce.

Creamy French dressing: Contains oil, vinegar, and lemon juice, plus cream or sour cream, and sometimes egg white or yolk. May be made into a sweet herb dressing by adding sweeteners and parsley, chives, and other herbs. May be made into a creamy Italian dressing by adding garlic.

Creamy dressings may be served in small bowls with spoons. Basic "French" dressings, which are thinner, are best served in cruets.

Some of these are called "French," and some are given quite a different name.

Making your own dressing The lists of dressing variations are by no means complete. You can make your own dressings, too, by adding your favorite spices and flavors to the basic dressings. You will have a good basic "French" dressing by mixing 125 milliliters (1/2 cup) of salad oil with 60 milliliters (1/4 cup) of vinegar. Turn it into a garlic dressing with some fresh minced garlic, or 1 milliliter (1/4 teaspoon) of garlic powder. Or add a little sugar for a sweet-sour dressing. Add whatever herbs and spices you like, being sure to taste as you go along. Usually it's best to make salad dressings in advance. This gives the combination of seasonings and flavors time to develop and mellow.

How do you know which herbs and spices to put in, and how much of each one?

Once again, the herbs and spices you choose depend on your individual likes and dislikes. You can get a good idea of what a seasoning will taste like by smelling it first. Then start slowly, by putting in a little bit at a time and tasting the dressing as you go along. With many seasonings, a little bit goes a long way, so be careful not to overdo it.

Most cookbooks have salad dressing recipes that you can try out for starters. Then you can add your own variations. Some of the most popular herbs and spices for salad dressings are garlic, dill, rosemary, thyme, oregano, and basil.

"Dressing" up leftovers Salad dressings are a good way to put new life into tired leftovers, by the way. You've already seen how leftover meat can be used in a chef's salad. You can also use leftover vege-

Herbs and spices add zest to any salad dressing—especially when you make up the recipe yourself.

tables to make a nourishing salad. Take some leftover peas, green beans, corn, or carrots, add some onions and sliced cucumbers, and serve the combination cold with a flavorful salad dressing. This salad is especially good in warm weather. It turns your leftovers into a cool, refreshing treat on a hot summer day.

That sounds good. But what about winter? What do you do with leftovers then?

You can have salads in the winter, too, if you like. But many people prefer something hot on a cold winter day. In that case, you can turn your leftovers into a hearty soup instead of a salad.

Vegetable salads may include cooked and raw ingredients. What kind of texture will this salad have?

Soups

Hot soup Soup is quite easy to make. It's fun, too, because you can put in all your favorite things. If you want, you can even change it as you go along. Making soup gives you a good chance to experiment with new herbs and spices and flavor combinations. Just remember to add new flavors a little at a time and to taste the results as you go along.

The recipe on this page for homemade soup will get you started on your own delicious creations. It's a good way to use up leftovers. This soup can also be made with fresh meat, if you don't have leftovers. Just brown half a kilogram (a pound) of stew meat or ground beef along with the onions. Crumble ground beef into little pieces as you put it into the pot.

This recipe—and many others like it that call for ingredients of your own choosing—asks you to taste as you go along to see if you have added enough bouillon and seasonings to please you. To taste, use a cooking spoon to dip a spoonful of the broth (liquid) from the pot. Pour the spoonful into a cup and taste from the cup. This way, your mouth doesn't touch the spoon, which will be used to dip into the soup again.

Icebox soup

number of servings varies with amounts of ingredients

	1 or 2 onions, sliced or chopped
30 mL	**2 tbsp cooking oil**
500 mL	**2 cups leftover beef or pork, cut into bite-size pieces (add more if you want)**
500 mL	**2 cups water for each cup meat (add more if you want)**
	leftover gravy, if available
	1 can beef bouillon or 2 small packages dried bouillon, if necessary
	seasonings of your choice, to taste
	salt and pepper, to taste
	leftover and/or fresh, frozen, or canned vegetables (chopped tomatoes, celery, green peppers, carrots, potatoes, peas, or other vegetables of your choice)

Cook the onions in the oil in a large pot, over medium heat, for about 5 minutes, or until they have a glassy look.

Add the meat and water. Add more water for a thinner soup. Bring to a boil over high heat.

Add gravy, if you have it. Stir well. Reduce the heat to simmering. Taste. Add bouillon, if you think the soup needs extra flavor.

Add fresh or frozen vegetables that take a while to cook (such as carrots, potatoes, or turnips). Add the seasonings.

Simmer the soup for about 10 minutes, until the crisp vegetables just begin to turn tender. (Test with a fork.) If you wish, add tomatoes, celery, and green peppers. Taste. Add additional seasonings, if you want.

Simmer the soup for 15 to 20 minutes to let the flavors mellow. Add vegetables that cook rather quickly, such as frozen green beans or peas. Add canned or leftover vegetables last. They are already cooked and need only to be warmed up.

Simmer for 5 to 10 minutes. Add salt and pepper to taste.

Serve hot.

Icebox soup is a delicious way to serve leftovers. What seasonings would you add to this soup?

Good herb seasonings to try in this soup are garlic, oregano, basil, rosemary, and bay leaves. You may like spices, too, such as chili powder, dry mustard, or ginger. Worcestershire sauce, soy sauce, Tabasco sauce, or vinegar can also be used to perk up the soup. Seasonings may also be used to strengthen a flavor already in the soup. If you want more celery flavor without adding more celery, add some celery salt. If you want more garlic or onion flavor, you can add these in either powder or salt form. Add any seasoning a small amount at a time—about 1 milliliter (1/4 teaspoon) for most seasonings, even less for very strong ones.

I like soup for lunch, but I don't always have all the ingredients on hand. I don't have much time for cooking at lunchtime, either.

To save time and also get a head start on the ingredients, you can begin with a commercially prepared canned or dry soup. Add any additional meat, vegetables, or seasonings you like.

Or you can make your soup ahead of time, when you have time to shop and cook. Store your cooked soup in a covered container in the refrigerator. If you want to keep your soup more than a few days, you can freeze it in plastic bags or sealed containers, ready for any occasion.

By the way, don't think of soup as just something that you have for lunch, or only in cold weather. There are all kinds of soup, for all sorts of occasions. Soup can be a drink, such as bouillon (BOOL yahn), which is a clear, flavored broth, or it can be an entire meal. It

A fancy fruit soup, left, adds a touch of elegance to a meal. *Borsch*, center, also makes a meal a special occasion. The soup on the right is chilled cream of spinach, with sour cream and croutons (toast cubes). Name another cold soup.

can include meat, vegetables, cheese, and even bread. Some soups, such as New England clam chowder, are made with milk. Soups can be hot or cold.

Cold soup? Who wants to eat that?

Cold soups Many people enjoy cold soups. Cold soups are especially popular in some foreign countries. *Vichyssoise* (VISH ē SWAHZ) is a delicious chilled French soup, made with milk, cream, puréed potatoes, and leeks (a relative of the onion). *Borsch* (BORSH) is a soup popular in Russia and Eastern Europe. It's made with chopped beets and cabbage, and sometimes other vegetables as well. It can be served hot or chilled, usually with a dollop of sour cream. *Gazpacho* (gahz PAH chō) is a cold vegetable soup popular in Spain. It contains tomatoes, onions, cucumbers, and green peppers. It's spiced with lemon juice, hot pepper sauce, ground pepper, and garlic. There are even hot and cold fruit soups, served as appetizers or desserts.

With all those soups and salads to choose from, why do people eat plain old sandwiches so much for lunch?

Sandwiches have certain advantages that make them popular for lunch. They're usually easy to make, easy to carry to school or to work, and easy to eat almost anywhere. Instead of thinking of them as "plain old sandwiches," think of all the great things you can do with them. We'll talk about that some more when we discuss packing and carrying foods.

Words to understand

entrée
contrast
chop
score
emulsion

Food and equipment to know

chef's salad	antipasto
Waldorf salad	mayonnaise
iceberg lettuce	cooked dressing
Boston lettuce	salad dressing
Bibb lettuce	French dressing
Romaine lettuce	bouillon
escarole	vichyssoise
Belgian endive	borsch
chicory	gazpacho
Chinese cabbage	
cole slaw	platter
watercress	paring knife
parsley	cruet

Questions to discuss

1. What should a main dish salad include? What else do you need to make a balanced meal?
2. What is the purpose of a garnish?
3. Name four parts of a meal during which you could serve a salad. Give an example of a salad that would be good for each part.
4. What can you do to keep the cut surfaces of apples and some other fruits from turning brown?
5. Why should you wait until the last minute to add the dressing to a tossed green salad?
6. List ten different things you could put in a salad.
7. What are signs of freshness and quality to look for when you buy salad greens?
8. How should you store lettuce to keep it fresh and crisp?

9. Mayonnaise and commercial salad dressing look very much alike. What are the differences between them?

10. Why doesn't mayonnaise normally separate, the way most oil-and-vinegar dressings do?

11. Give an example of a soup that you might use as a beverage; as an appetizer; as a main dish.

12. Name three cold soups.

Things to do

1. Look through magazine articles and ads for simple ways to garnish or decorate salads (such as radish "roses"). Cut out pictures and make a small notebook of garnish ideas.

2. Set up a salad greens display. Buy samples of as many different salad greens as you can find in your area. Rinse and drain each sample, and put each on a separate plate and label it. Everyone should try each sample and make notes on how it looks, tastes, and feels in the mouth. Make a tossed green salad from the leftovers.

3. Buy a jar of mayonnaise and a jar of salad dressing that have nutrition information panels. Compare the calories and nutrient values. If the ingredients are listed, compare those. Have a blind-fold test and see if students can identify which is mayonnaise and which is salad dressing.

4. Bring in six samples of bottled dressings for salad. Everyone should look at the color and read the label of each sample and describe what the dressing will probably taste like. Taste the dressings. Did each one taste as you expected it to?

5. Break a head of lettuce into quarters. Put one section in the refrigerator, unwrapped. Rinse and drain two other sections; put each in a plastic bag. Put one bag in the refrigerator, and the other on top of the refrigerator. Store the fourth section unwrapped in the crisper drawer of the refrigerator. Check all the samples after two days. Compare the appearance and texture of each. What have you learned about storing lettuce?

6. Make an attractive salad plate. Draw a rough sketch of how it looks. Describe what you did to make it look appealing.

7. Set up a match game of herbs and spices. Make a name card with a brief description for each seasoning you use. Sprinkle a little of each seasoning on a separate saucer or in a custard cup. See if other students can match the proper names to the seasonings. Seasonings you might include are: garlic powder, onion salt, celery salt, basil, oregano, dill, rosemary, thyme, dry mustard.

8. Mix 125 milliliters (1/2 cup) of oil and 60 milliliters (1/4 cup) of vinegar. Make your own salad dressing by adding seasonings of your choice (taste as you go along). If you like a sweet dressing, try a little sugar, some corn syrup, or the syrup canned fruits come packed in.

9. Have a "super soup" contest. Divide the class into small groups. Have everyone bring in leftovers from home. Have each group create a new soup, following the basic guidelines in the icebox soup recipe in this chapter. Taste soups from other groups and vote to choose the super soup.

Careers to consider

Would you like to work in the food marketing system?

If you enjoy dealing with people and selling things, consider a career in food merchandising.

Food companies employ many **sales representatives** and **marketing specialists**. Sometimes these people sell directly to retail outlets. Sometimes they sell to someone in between, such as a **broker**, who may in turn sell to a **distributor**.

Food companies also hire **purchasing agents** to buy the ingredients they need. These agents are experts in judging quality, in estimating how much they need, and in getting the best price. Supermarket chains need purchasing agents to buy huge quantities for their stores. Restaurants also need someone (often the manager) who knows exactly where and how to buy the right amounts of supplies with the quality they want.

Sales help in retail outlets help consumers make buying decisions. This is especially true in a small shop, where the service is very personal. A supermarket has **department managers**. These people specialize in taking care of a particular department, such as the produce department. **Stockers** keep the shelves or displays stocked with goods, properly priced and neatly arranged. **Cashiers** or **checkers** work at the cash register to total up customers' purchases.

Educational requirements in food merchandising vary, depending on the job. While you're still in high school, you might get a part-time job after school as a stocker or cashier. If you want to be a marketing specialist, you'll probably need some college business courses.

The amount of money you make in sales work is often tied directly to the effort you put into the job. The more you sell, the more you make. If you are creative, you may enjoy the challenge of thinking up new ways to sell more of your product. Whatever the sales job, however, it's important to like working with people.

7

HAS THIS EVER HAPPENED TO YOU?

Craig is in the lunchroom with his friends. They're not very enthusiastic about eating, because they usually have the same thing every day. Craig peeks into his sandwich bag.

CRAIG: *Bologna again! That makes five days in a row!*

SUSAN: *Don't complain. I've had peanut butter and jelly for eight days!*

JAN: *I've had turkey salad for six days, and I know I'll have it for at least five more—or until the turkey runs out!*

SUSAN: *I'll trade you a peanut butter and jelly for a bologna.*

JAN: *I'll give you a turkey salad for your peanut butter and jelly.*

Soon, the whole table is alive with kids making deals to trade lunch.

KIM: *I'll give you an egg salad for anything! In fact, I'll give it to you for nothing!*

PHIL: *How about a "mystery trade," Craig? We'll trade lunch and not even tell each other what it is. So whatever we have, at least it will be a surprise!*

Craig makes the trade. He peeks into the bag Phil gave him.

CRAIG: *Oh, heck! I thought that bag looked familiar. I traded back to my own bologna sandwich!*

KEEPING FOOD SAFE

Exploring . . .

How to add variety to sandwiches

The causes and symptoms of food poisoning

Rules for handling food safely

Ways foods can be preserved

How to pack lunchboxes and picnic baskets

Do you ever get tired of carrying your lunch to school because it's always the same?

Yeah, it's always sandwiches. And everyone brings the same kind. You can't even trade for something new! What's so great about sandwiches, anyway? I'd rather have icebox soup or a chef's salad.

There are three very good things about sandwiches that have made them popular with busy people for over two hundred years.

Sandwiches

The first good thing about sandwiches is that most of them are easy to make. Second, they're easy to carry. Third, they're easy to eat—at school, on the job, at a picnic, or in a car, bus, train, or airplane. You can even eat them "on the go," on a hike or a walking tour.

Many people like ham and cheese on rye with lettuce and tomatoes. What are the advantages of a sandwich for lunch?

Soups and salads are fine for lunch, too. They're especially good as a change of pace from your usual thing. But they do require a little extra care and equipment for packing and carrying. They're a little more trouble to eat, too. We'll talk later about ways to carry hot and cold foods, and foods that must be eaten from a dish or container, with a fork or spoon.

Sandwiches solve most of the problems of packing and eating. They don't spill or leak. They don't need to be kept hot or cold, except to prevent spoilage. They don't need special containers for carrying them, or special utensils for eating them. They can be wrapped in paper and can be eaten with the fingers.

The Sandwich legend It was convenience that led to the creation of the sandwich in the first place. According to legend, it was invented in the 1700s by an Englishman named John Montagu, the Fourth Earl of Sandwich. ("Sandwich" was the name of his earldom, or the land he owned.) The earl liked to play cards and games so much that he refused to stop even to eat dinner. He ordered a piece of meat brought to him between two pieces of bread, to make it easier to eat. Soon, others at the table were ordering "the same thing as Sandwich," or simply "a Sandwich." We've been eating sandwiches ever since.

I feel like I've been eating sandwiches for two hundred years! I'd like something different for a change!

New sandwich ideas If you're tired of eating sandwiches, maybe what you need is a different kind of sandwich. The following taste-changing ideas for sandwich fillings should perk up your appetite.

Chop up some raisins, apricots, or other dried fruits. Mix with cream cheese, cottage cheese, or mayonnaise. Spread on whole-wheat bread.

Moisten 30 milliliters (2 table-spoons) of peanut butter with 15 milliliters (1 tablespoon) of mayonnaise. Mix in chopped raisins, bananas, dates, celery, apples, or jam.

Chop up a boiled frankfurter. Mix in 15 milliliters (1 table-spoon) mayonnaise and 1 milliliter (1/4 teaspoon) prepared mustard.

Mix cream cheese or cottage cheese with mayonnaise and chopped stuffed olives, or chopped walnuts, or both. Serve on whole-wheat or raisin bread.

Grate some American cheese. Mix in chopped sweet peppers, stuffed olives, and mayonnaise.

Combine grated Swiss cheese, chopped nuts, and mayonnaise. Spread on rye bread.

Make up your own fantastic creation!

If you get tired of the "Montagu" sandwich, made with two slices of bread, try a "McIntosh" sandwich, made with two slices of apple. The following directions make two sandwiches.

1. Cut an apple crosswise into four slices. Cut out the core. Rub the slices with lemon juice, to keep them from turning brown.

2. Spread two apple slices with peanut butter or cream cheese and chopped walnuts. Cover with the other apple slices.

3. Or, if you like, spread filling on four round party crackers. Press them "sticky-side down" over the hole in the center of each apple slice.

Is there anything else you can use for sandwiches besides bread and apple slices?

Different breads Anything that holds its shape fairly well, isn't too juicy or sticky, and doesn't spoil quickly might be used to make sandwiches. But bread products are best. Crackers, pizza, biscuits, tortillas—all might be used to hold fillings of one kind or another. Actually, you can find a lot of variety on the bakery shelf of an ordinary supermarket. Have you tried rye bread, pumpernickel, oat-meal bread, whole-wheat bread, cracked-wheat bread, raisin bread,

How many of these breads can you name? Which kind do you like in a sandwich?

French bread, Italian bread, date-nut bread, Boston brown bread, hamburger buns, or hotdog rolls? They all give a little different look, taste, and texture to "ordinary" sandwiches.

There's one other big advantage to bread, which we haven't even mentioned. This is the fact that it keeps well. With sandwiches, all you really have to worry about spoiling is the filling.

Food spoilage and food poisoning

Food spoilage is caused by **microorganisms**. These are tiny plants and animals, so small that you need a microscope to see them. They live, grow, and **multiply** (increase in number) in certain foods under certain conditions. Some of them can make you sick; those that can are often called **microbes**, or germs.

Helpful microorganisms Not all microorganisms are harmful, by the way. In fact, for every "unfriendly" microorganism there are about five thousand harmless and even "friendly" ones working for us. Some of these are absolutely necessary to us—we couldn't live without them. Some types live in our intestines and help us with digestion. Many live in soil and garbage. They break down wastes and dead plant and animal tissues so that new food plants can use them as fertilizer.

Microorganisms also help us process many of the foods we enjoy. They play an important part in turning milk into cheese, buttermilk, yogurt, and sour cream. They turn cider into vinegar, and grape juice into wine. They make our bread light and our beef tender.

Harmful microorganisms But the ones that cause trouble can cause a lot of trouble. Disease-causing microbes are always looking for a place to grow and multiply—such as the human body.

How do they get into the body?

Usually microorganisms get into the body by sneaking past its defense system. You might think of yourself as a general fighting a constant war against millions of enemy germs trying to invade the "fortress" of your body. Your skin acts as "outer defenses." The microbes can't penetrate it unless they force their way in through a cut, sore, or burn. Even so, you have a "home guard" of millions of white corpuscles in your blood to attack and swallow up the enemy. You have automatic systems that help defend you against microbes and the poisons microbes produce. You have a marvelous transportation and supply system—your bloodstream—to bring fresh troops and supplies to any area attacked through your skin. You can patch up the break, haul off the casualties, and bring in more fresh troops and

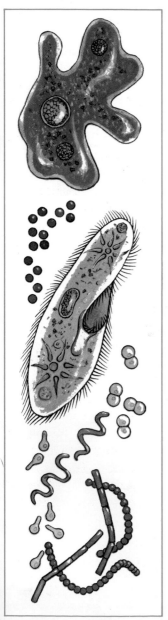

Various microorganisms

microorganisms (MĪ krō OR gə NIZ əmz)   **microbes** (MĪ krōbz)

supplies, all at the same time. Once defeated, the enemy must withdraw and wait for another lucky break—a cut or a sore—through which to penetrate the outer defenses of your skin.

But germs never have to wait to attack the body's supply lines. You cannot live without supplies of air, food, and water. And this is how most germs enter your body.

Disease germs often sneak into the body as "stowaways" in food. Whenever you take a bite or a sip from another person's hotdog, soft drink, candy bar, apple, or ice cream cone, you run the risk of picking up any **infectious** (disease-causing) germs that person may have left on the food. These germs do not actually grow and multiply until they enter your body. Other germs grow in the food itself. This is how food spoilage and food poisoning come about.

Just what is food poisoning, anyway?

Food poisoning **Food poisoning** is a general term to describe several kinds of illness. One kind is caused by poisonous plants, such as certain kinds of mushrooms. Another is caused by poisonous chemicals that plants take in from the soil or carry on their leaves and stems. **Insecticides** (poisons used to kill insects) and chemicals from polluted water are two common examples. But the kinds we will be talking about are different. They come from food that should be safe to eat. But if it is handled improperly, or left out too long at room temperature, the food is invaded by microbes that can make you sick.

These food germs can cause sickness in two ways. One way is through **food-borne infection**. In this case, microbes infect the food and grow as rapidly as they can before the food is eaten. They are then swallowed along with the food. If the germ population is large enough by the time the food is swallowed, the germs will cause illness in the stomach and intestines.

infectious (in FEK shəs)   **insecticides** (in SEK tə sīdz)
infection (in FEK shən)

The other kind of food poisoning is called **food intoxication.** The microbes themselves may be harmless in the digestive system. However, as they multiply, they produce a poisonous waste product, or **toxin,** that may cause illness or even death.

I didn't know it could be so serious! I guess we'd better find out more about food poisoning—fast!

To find out about specific kinds of food poisoning, look at the table on these pages. The table lists and describes the three most serious food poisoners—**salmonella, staphylococcus,** and **botulism.** In addition to the "big three," there are some other food poisoners even more common. They can cause nausea, diarrhea, and stomachaches. However, they are much milder in their attacks. For this reason, they cause much less alarm. They are prevented in the same ways used to keep food safe from staph and salmonella.

---

intoxication (in TAHK sə KĀ shən)   **toxin** (TAHK sən)

salmonella (SAL mə NEL ə)   **staphylococcus** (STAF ə lō KAHK əs)

botulism (BAHCH ə LIZ əm)

The "big three" food poisoners

WHAT ARE THE MOST SERIOUS KINDS OF FOOD POISONING? HOW DO YOU FEEL WHEN YOU GET ONE?	WHAT KIND OF FOOD DOES THE POISON AFFECT?
Salmonella is one of the most common food infections. The microbes attack the digestive system, causing fever, headache, diarrhea, cramps, and sometimes vomiting. This usually starts within a day, and lasts two to four days. It is seldom fatal.	Salmonella is found in raw or undercooked foods, especially meat, poultry, seafood, and eggs.
Staphylococcus ("staph") microbes produce a toxin that causes diarrhea, vomiting, and stomach cramps. This starts two to four hours after eating and lasts a day or two. Staph poisoning is rarely fatal.	Staph is found in custards, cream fillings, meat, fish, poultry, dairy products, eggs, tuna fish, and other sandwich fillings.
Botulism, though rare, is the most dangerous form of food poisoning. The microbes themselves are harmless and found almost everywhere, but the toxin they produce is a deadly poison. It attacks the nervous system, causing dizziness, double vision, and trouble in swallowing and breathing. Victims can die from suffocation. Symptoms appear 12 to 36 hours after eating.	Botulism is found in meats, fish, and poultry, and low-acid vegetables such as string beans, corn, spinach, peppers, and mushrooms. It almost always involves home-canned foods. Commercially canned products are considered safer because of the high temperatures used in canning.

Keeping food safe to eat

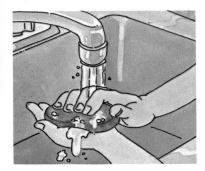

There are so many kinds of germs that there is no one simple way to kill them all. In addition, there are too many kinds of food, and too many different ways of preparing and eating those foods. For instance, you can't plan on boiling everything, since some foods are eaten raw. However, there are some good general rules. If you follow each rule, you'll have little cause for worry about food poisoning.

Cleanliness The first rule, and one of the most basic, is to practice cleanliness. Germs are everywhere. They hide in the foods you buy and in the dishes and utensils you use. They're in pots and pans, and on spoons, spatulas, can openers, and cutting boards. They lurk in the corners and play on the counter tops. They hide in the skin of your hands, especially in cuts and sores. They love spills, smudges, and greasy films. Any time food touches a dirty or **contaminated** surface (one that contains germs), it picks up some of these lurking germs. The best weapon against germs, then, is hot soapy water.

contaminated (kən TAM ə NĀ tid)

WHERE DOES THE POISON COME FROM? HOW DOES IT GROW?

Food animals carry salmonella microbes, so meat, fish, and egg products may be infected when you buy them. Pets and people may also carry these germs. They may be easily transferred from one product to another, such as from raw meat on a cutting board to another food put on the same unwashed board.

Staph microbes grow on the human body, especially on the hands, in the nose and throat, and in cuts and sores. They grow quickly in foods left out at room temperature.

Botulism microbes grow and produce toxins in places where there is no oxygen, such as in airtight containers. If any spores, from which microbes develop, are sealed into cans or jars during canning and live through the canning process, they will grow inside the can and produce the deadly toxin. *Never* eat food from bent or bulging cans, as they may be contaminated with botulism.

HOW CAN YOU PREVENT IT?

Heat kills salmonella, so cook all meat, poultry, fish, and eggs thoroughly. Wash all surfaces touched by raw meat with hot, soapy water before putting another food on the same surface. Wash your hands well before handling food, especially after touching pets or using the toilet.

To guard against staph, always wash your hands before touching food. Refrigerate foods or keep them hot—above 60 °C (140 °F). Heat kills microbes easily, but the toxin remains, even after boiling.

To prevent botulism, home canning of low-acid vegetables and meats should always be done with a pressure canner. This raises the temperature high enough to kill spores. When the can or jar is opened, the food should be boiled for 20 minutes as a precaution. (Botulism toxin can be destroyed by boiling, though the microbes cannot. This is just opposite from staph.)

Danger zone

°C   °F

Geometric growth

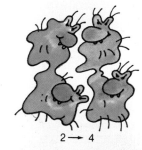

2 → 4

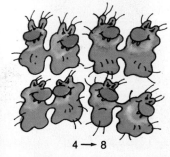

4 → 8

But germs also float through the air and "parachute" down onto food supplies that are left out in the open. To protect the food, it should be covered and refrigerated whenever possible.

Temperature   Most of the dangerous germs grow at temperatures between 5 and 60 °C (40 to 140 °F). They grow best at temperatures that are near the temperature of the human body (37 °C or 98.6 °F). To keep germs from growing in food, either keep it hot (above 60 °C or 140 °F), or else keep it cold (below 5 °C or 40 °F).

What if you can't keep food quite that cold—like on a picnic? Does just keeping it cool help any?

Anything you can do to keep the food below room temperature will slow the rate of microbe growth, even if it doesn't stop it. The cooler the food is, the slower the microbes will grow. And the slower they grow, the longer the food will stay safe to eat.

What about keeping food hot? If you can't keep it really hot, does just keeping it warm help any?

Keeping food warm doesn't keep it safe—"warm" meaning a temperature less than 50 °C (120 °F). (Anything above that temperature would feel "hot" to your skin.) Just keeping the food warm would actually increase the growth of germs. You can generally assume that if a temperature feels comfortable to you, it feels comfortable to food germs, too! And the longer the microbes are allowed to do their dirty work at temperatures they like, the worse the sabotage to your food will be.

How long does it take for food to spoil? When does it become dangerous?

Amount of contamination   Most foods will be safe at room temperatures for three or four hours if they have been handled properly from the time they left the farm. But the more germs there are in the food, the faster it spoils. Germs grow by doubling—that is, one becomes two, two become four, four become eight, and so on. If you start with a small number of germs, they grow by small numbers at first. But if you start with a large number of germs, the situation gets out of hand very quickly. For this reason, you should throw out any food that looks, smells, or tastes funny in any way. If it's not dangerous already, it probably will be dangerous very soon.

You should never eat any food that has a strange "off" taste that you can't identify. Do not even taste food that has a bad odor. Do not even open a can that is leaking, that has a broken seam or seal, or that is bulging. The bulge may be caused by gas produced by microbe growth. The same gas buildup can actually cause jars of home-canned foods to explode on the shelf.

Preservatives   One way to control microbes is to add preservatives to food. These either kill the microbes or keep them from multiplying.

But preservatives are chemicals, aren't they? Aren't chemicals bad for you?

The fact that **preservatives** are chemicals doesn't mean they'll do you any harm. Some chemicals are harmful, and some aren't. Actually, everything you eat is a chemical of one kind or another. Water is H_2O. Sugar is $C_{12}H_{22}O_{11}$. Vitamin C is $C_6H_8O_6$. The trick is to find chemicals that are bad for the microbes but not for you.

Of course, anything can be bad for you if you eat too much of it, even vitamins and minerals. Vitamin A, as we have seen, is necessary for good eyesight and healthy skin tissue. But too much of it is toxic, or poisonous. Iodine is necessary for the thyroid gland to do its job. But too much of it is toxic.

Actually, people have been using chemicals to preserve food for thousands of years. One chemical they used was ordinary salt. They either rubbed it into the food (such as meat or fish), which they then dried, or they put the food into **brine**, a mixture of salt and water.

preservatives (pri ZER və tivs)   **brine** (BRĪN)

Left: Some cucumber pickles are made with brine, some with vinegar. Right: Nowadays, bacon is usually cured, or preserved, with chemicals instead of smoke.

Other chemicals they used were acids, especially vinegar. Most germs do not grow well in foods with a high acid content. People found that by **pickling** foods in vinegar they could keep things like meat, fish, and vegetables much longer without getting sick when they ate them.

Sugar is another chemical that has been used for many years to slow down spoilage in certain kinds of foods. It is used especially in jams, jellies, and preserves. People also used smoke to make some foods last longer. Smoked fish, ham, sausage, and bacon are still popular.

All of these preserving methods were better than eating spoiled food, but they created some problems, too. Most of them changed the taste of the food. In some cases, people liked the change. But whether they liked it or not, they had to put up with it.

And, of course, eating too much of these old-fashioned preservatives would be bad for people. Too much salt, vinegar, sugar, or smoke particles is bad for anyone. For people with special illnesses or health problems, it can be especially troublesome.

The same thing can be said about our modern preservatives. Used carefully, they help reduce the risk of food spoilage. By doing this, they increase the amount and variety of nutritious food we can eat safely. But the amount of preservative, and the kind used, should be checked carefully. This is the job of the federal **Food and Drug Administration (FDA)**. The FDA runs very careful tests on the kinds and amounts of preservatives used by food processors.

It's important to eat lots of fresh foods, too. Once again, we're back to our old friend, variety. If you eat a variety of foods, chances are that they'll all be good for you.

Is that the only choice you have, though? Either eat foods that have preservatives, or foods that spoil quickly?

There are other ways of keeping foods safe for long periods without preservatives. Freezing and drying are two examples. Both methods have been around for a long time. Eskimos and other cold-climate peoples have known for a long time that frozen meat will stay wholesome for weeks and even months. Desert peoples have been drying dates, figs, and other foods for centuries. Native Americans, fur trappers, and gold prospectors in America made "jerky," a form of dried beef or buffalo meat, to carry with them on long journeys.

Freezing Freezing keeps germs from growing, but it doesn't kill them. When the food thaws. the germs that were on the food before it was frozen will start multiplying again. That's why it may be dangerous to refreeze food that has thawed. If it has stayed thawed at room temperature for too long, spoilage may already have taken place.

pickling (PIK əl ing)

I've seen signs on frozen foods warning you not to refreeze them once they've thawed. Does refreezing foods make them poisonous?

Refreezing does not make foods poisonous, but they may lose some of their quality in terms of taste and texture. Freezing and thawing tend to break the cell walls of some foods. This makes them mushy in some cases, and tough in others. This is especially true of fruits and vegetables. The amount of spoilage, however, will depend on the total time that the food, or any part of it, remained thawed and exposed to contamination.

Drying Most microbes prefer a warm, moist place in which to live. If the food is a dry product—such as nuts, grain, flour, cereal, bread, or other baked products—it usually keeps fairly well. If it has been dried out deliberately—such as dried fruits, raisins, peas, beans,

Why isn't it a good idea to refreeze vegetables?

Dry foods usually keep well. Which of these foods do you think will keep longest?

herbs and spices, or tea—it will also keep rather well. Even so, some products such as dried fruits, bread, and other baked goods sometimes have preservatives added, especially ones that keep mold from forming. You may see these preservatives listed on the package as "mold inhibitors."

The fact that bread is a fairly dry product that keeps well makes it an ideal food for pack-and-carry lunches. These lunches are often stored in dark, warm places such as lockers, desks, handbags, and briefcases until it's time to eat them. Germs love spots like these, and they breed quickly if they can find a nice, moist food that they like. The bread used in sandwiches is usually safe, but the sandwich filling can be a problem.

Packing foods to carry

Germs grow well in protein-rich foods such as meat, poultry, eggs, and tuna fish. They grow especially fast if those foods are chopped up and moistened with mayonnaise to make sandwich fillings.

How long can you keep these kinds of sandwiches?

Storage time for sandwiches Like most other foods, sandwiches can be kept for three or four hours and still be safe to eat, if the filling was not contaminated to begin with, and if the sandwiches are kept clean and are handled properly. However, if the sandwiches are

For how long will this egg salad sandwich be safe to eat?

made from foods that were left out of the refrigerator after they were cooked, germs may already have had a head start in growing. The same would be true if the sandwiches picked up germs from dirty hands, dishes, counter tops, or cutting boards.

Suppose you're eating a sandwich that someone else made? How can you tell if it's full of microbes?

Usually you can't tell whether a sandwich made by someone else is contaminated. That's why it's not a good idea to trade sandwiches with other people. You don't know when the sandwich was made, or under what conditions. You should be careful about buying sandwiches in a restaurant, too. If you have any doubts at all about when they were made, do *not* take them on a picnic or have them for lunch two hours later. Even when you make the sandwiches yourself, you should pack them so that they stay as fresh as possible. This is especially important if you plan to wait more than three hours before eating them.

How do you pack sandwiches so that they stay fresh?

Packing sandwiches First, wrap the sandwiches carefully in waxed paper, plastic wrap, foil, or sandwich bags. The longer food is left uncovered, the longer it is exposed to germs floating in the air.

If possible, refrigerate the sandwiches for an hour or so, or even freeze them. Starting them out cold reduces the time that they will be sitting around at a cozy temperature for microbes. Meat, poultry, and fish freeze quite well. Eggs, however, sometimes become tough. Lettuce will get limp in the freezer. But if you really like lettuce, you can carry a few leaves in a plastic bag and add them to the sandwich when you're ready to eat.

To keep moist fillings (including jelly) from soaking into bread and making it limp and soggy, coat the inner side of the bread with a thin film of butter or margarine.

Carry the wrapped sandwiches in a metal or plastic lunchbox. This protects the food better than a paper bag, though a bag is sometimes more convenient—you don't have to take the bag back home with you.

Put a gel-type freeze pack in the lunch box to keep foods cool. You can also freeze water in a plastic bag with an airtight seal.

Protecting sandwiches Store your lunch in as cool a place as possible. In the wintertime, keep it away from radiators. In the summertime, leave it in the shade or in an air-conditioned room.

Wash your hands before eating. Even if the food itself has not spoiled, it can provide "transportation" for germs on your hands. Remember, your hands touch hundreds of different things every day. Each touch is an opportunity to pick up infectious germs.

When possible, carry foods that do not spoil quickly. This is especially important if it will be more than three to four hours before you eat and you cannot keep foods cool in the meantime. As we have seen, meat, fish, poultry, and eggs spoil quickly. Cheese keeps a good deal better. Peanut butter and jelly can usually be eaten as long as they taste all right and show no signs of mold. Raw fruits and vegetables present little problem, though they should always be washed carefully to remove dirt and insecticides. Dried fruits, nuts, candy, and cookies also keep well.

Carrying liquids Soups and drinks should be carried in a vacuum bottle. This will keep hot things hot or cold things cold for several hours—hot or cold enough to keep bacteria from growing rapidly.

What about foods that you take on picnics? If you keep them in a covered dish, does that keep them from spoiling?

Packing picnic foods A covered dish does *not* keep foods from spoiling. In fact, a very large number of the reported cases of food poisoning come from foods kept in covered dishes, such as potato salads, macaroni salads, casseroles, and so forth. These foods are taken to picnics, family reunions, potluck suppers, and other social get-togethers. Food microbes always come to these affairs. They start eating before anyone else even sits down. They love to be left in the warm sun while the people enjoy themselves and work up an appetite by swimming, pitching horseshoes, and playing ball. By the time the people are ready to eat, the germs have already had their salad and casserole and are ready to start working on the people!

How can you keep foods from spoiling on a picnic?

On a picnic, you should use the same care that you would use in packing and carrying your lunch. Use fresh foods to begin with. Keep them clean. Pack them carefully. As much as possible, pack foods that do not spoil quickly. If possible, eat the food within three or four hours. Keep foods hot or cold, by whatever means possible. Use vacuum bottles. Pack foods with ice or freezer-gel devices. Put them in ice chests or picnic coolers with enough ice to keep them cool. Reheat foods, if possible, on a campfire or camp stove at the picnic site.

The final rule: "If in doubt, throw it out!" Remember, food bacteria don't usually go around bending tin cans and exploding glass jars to let you know they're around. They'd love for you to forget that they are there. But if you do, you may be reminded the next day by fever, headache, diarrhea, nausea, and vomiting.

Does that mean we're stuck with sandwiches if we carry our lunch to school?

What precautions should you take when packing picnic food? What foods require special care in packing?

Lunchbox variety You should pack *all* foods carefully, including sandwiches. If you want to take icebox soup to school, take it in a vacuum bottle to keep it piping hot until you're ready to eat it. If you want to take a chef's salad, pack it in a clean plastic tub. Put the tub in a large sealable plastic bag with some ice cubes.

Remember, too, that fresh, raw fruits and vegetables keep very well and add variety to your lunch. Apples, bananas, oranges, grapes, peaches, nectarines, plums, and other fruits are always delicious. Carrot sticks, celery sticks, pieces of raw cauliflower, and tomato wedges will stay safe to eat for many hours, with or without refrigeration. Of course, they will stay crisper and juicier if you keep them cool.

There are plenty of safe and appetizing foods that you can add to your pack-and-carry lunches. What you choose is up to your own taste and your own imagination.

Words to understand

microorganism	salmonella
multiply	staphylococcus ("staph")
microbe	botulism
infectious	contaminated
food poisoning	preservative
insecticide	brine
food-borne infection	pickling
food intoxication	FDA
toxin	

Equipment to know

waxed paper	freezer gel
plastic wrap	vacuum bottle
aluminum foil	ice chest
sandwich bags	picnic cooler

Questions to discuss

1. Name five or more kinds of bread that you could use to make sandwiches.
2. What causes food poisoning?
3. How can harmful microbes get into your body?

4. What are the three most serious kinds of food poisoning? Give three common symptoms of food poisoning.

5. How does cold (such as in the refrigerator) affect the growth of germs? What about heat? What kind of temperature do microbes like best?

6. List three or more rules for handling food safely.

7. Does freezing kill microbes? Why shouldn't you refreeze foods that have thawed?

8. What's the safest thing to do with a food that smells bad?

9. What should you do with a can of food that is bulging? Why?

10. Name at least four ways people kept food safe to eat before modern refrigeration and chemical preservatives.

11. Describe how to pack a lunchbox sandwich so that it stays fresh and safe to eat.

12. What can you do to keep a moist sandwich filling from making the bread soggy?

13. Name five or more foods that are especially perishable.

Things to do

1. What is your favorite sandwich? Experiment with different breads and with adding different foods to the filling. Describe three new combinations you like that add variety to your favorite sandwich.

2. Give a demonstration on how to pack a lunchbox so that the food stays fresh and safe to eat.

3. Hold a lunchbox sandwich contest. Every student should find or create a different sandwich idea that would be suitable for a lunchbox. Fix enough sandwiches so that everyone can taste a small sample cut from each. Vote to choose: the best tasting; the most unusual; the most nutritious. Make a small notebook (or a recipe box of index cards) of the sandwich ideas you liked.

4. Plan lunchbox menus for a week. Except for milk, try not to use the same food more than once.

5. Make an eye-catching "Not Wanted" poster on the "Big Three" food poisoners. You might even give them catchy names like "Sammy Salmonella," "Betty Botulism," and "Stephen Staph." Describe their favorite hangouts, how they work, what they do, and so forth. How can they be "arrested"?

6. Interview a public health inspector or a restaurant owner. Find out what is involved in a restaurant inspection. What are some of the rules restaurants must follow?

7. Make a bulletin board that illustrates rules for keeping foods safe to eat.

8. How hot is "safe"? To keep microbes from growing, food should be kept cold or kept hot (above 60 °C or 140 °F). But how hot is that?

   a. To find out, make a cup of tea or bouillon. Using a thermometer (a candy or meat thermometer will do), adjust the temperature to 65 °C (about 150 °F). Take a few sips, noting how hot the liquid feels to your lips and tongue. Now cool it to 60 °C (140 °F) and taste again.

   b. Heat another cup and see if you can guess when the liquid reaches a temperature between 60 and 65 °C (140 and 150 °F). Check your guess with the thermometer. If you guessed too low, microbes can grow!

Careers to consider

Would you like to inspect food?

If you would like to take an active part in safeguarding the quality of our food supply, consider a career in food inspection.

Government agencies such as the Food and Drug Administration (FDA), the United States Department of Agriculture (USDA), and state and local health departments send **inspectors** to food processing, food distribution, and food service locations to check on the safety and quality of the food being handled. Some of the major areas of work for food inspectors include the following.

SLAUGHTERING AND PACKING OF MEAT AND POULTRY PRODUCTS Inspectors must assure that products are wholesome, safe, and properly marked, labeled, and packaged. Animals are examined before and after slaughter to check for disease and contamination. Sanitary conditions and processing procedures are also checked.

IMPORTS AND EXPORTS OF MEAT AND OTHER FOOD PRODUCTS These inspectors must understand the rules and standards for food products in foreign countries. They must see that foods imported into this country meet our requirements. They must also see that foods produced here and exported to other countries meet the standards of those countries.

QUALITY AND GRADING OF FOODS Grade inspectors look at things such as the color, size, and texture of foods in order to assign grades (such as "prime," "choice," and "good" for meats, or "AA," "A," and "B," for eggs). Grades help buyers know exactly what quality they can expect in the foods they purchase.

PLANT AND ANIMAL PESTS This involves inspection and quarantine of plants and animals suspected to be unhealthy. Inspectors also check levels of pesticides used, in order to determine their effect on fish, wildlife, and public health.

STORAGE AND HANDLING OF FOOD IN WHOLESALE MARKETS, WAREHOUSES, AND RETAIL STORES Everywhere that food travels—from the farm or processing plant to the supermarket—people are needed to make sure it is moved and stored safely.

RESTAURANT FOOD PREPARATION AND STORAGE Local public health inspectors check food service establishments for cleanliness, safety, and health standards.

Government inspection agencies perform a variety of scientific and technical services. These include the development of standards for labels, packaging, equipment, and sanitation. Laboratory personnel include **chemists** and **medical specialists** who study diseases and epidemics, including outbreaks of food poisoning. **Microbiologists** study the behavior of tiny plants and animals that affect food. In test kitchens, **home economists** and **food technologists** examine food products to make sure they are properly labeled.

HAS THIS EVER HAPPENED TO YOU?

Brian's grandmother is ill, and his mother is staying with her for a week. His father has offered to give him an extra allowance if he will fix dinner each night while she's away.

BRIAN: *You've got a deal, Dad. First I'll fix roast pork, candied yams, and applesauce. That's my favorite dinner. There's even a pork roast in the freezer.*

The next day, Brian has basketball practice after school and is late getting home. Now he's frantically trying to get dinner ready. His younger sister Carol helps him by looking up things in the cookbook.

CAROL: *It says here that a six-pound pork roast should cook about four hours. It's not even thawed yet, so we'll probably be eating just about midnight!*

BRIAN: *You're right! And we don't even have any yams. I'm going to have to change my plans!*

CAROL: *To* what? *The only thing you ever made was when you helped fix that tuna fish salad for your photography club last year. That's* all *you know how to make.*

Later, at dinner, Brian's father comments on the meal.

FATHER: *Well, I usually thought of tuna fish salads as something for the warm-weather months, Brian—not the middle of January. But it certainly adds variety to the menu. What are you planning next?*

BRIAN: *I don't know, yet. I've got to come up with something else that's quick and easy, or we're going to get awfully tired of tuna fish!*

160

EASY SUPPERS

Exploring . . .

How to make a shopping list

Shopping decisions: what, how much, and what kind to buy

How to cook pasta

How to make stew

Managing a meal: planning, buying, storing, preparing, serving

If you're used to having meals prepared for you and set down in front of you every day, you probably don't realize the time, effort, and planning that go into getting that food ready.

BRIAN: *That's for sure! The only thing I had time to fix for my pork dinner was the applesauce!*

If you're fixing dinner and don't have much time, choose something that's fairly quick to make. And if you're a beginner in the kitchen, choose something that's fairly easy—at least to start out with. For a dinner that's both quick and easy, try a one-dish meal.

What's a one-dish meal?

You've already made one kind of one-dish meal. That's the main dish or entrée salad, such as tuna fish or chicken salad. But there are lots of other possibilities—including hot dishes. A one-dish meal is any meal that has a protein source (such as meat or cheese) cooked

A casserole makes a convenient one-dish meal. Since you can cook and serve the meal in the same dish, clean-up is easy, too.

with vegetables in one dish. Beef stew and most pasta dishes—spaghetti with meat sauce, lasagna, or macaroni and hamburger—are examples. One-dish meals that are baked in the oven are sometimes called **casseroles**.

Cooking for the whole family will be a lot quicker and easier, too, if you sit down and plan things out ahead of time. That way, you have time to check and see if you've forgotten anything. When you're sure you have everything, you can go ahead without worrying.

Planning for family meals

Menu planning   The first thing you need to do is plan a **menu**—a list of foods you want to have—for each meal. Once again, remember the Basic Four food groups. For dinner, you should have one serving from the meat group, two from the fruit and vegetable group, one from the bread and cereal group, and one from the milk group.

When you have your menus planned, it's time to do some shopping. But first, you need a list of all the things you should buy.

How do you make sure you have everything on your list?

Shopping list   First, look at your menus—the foods you plan to serve. Check the recipes for each dish and list all of the ingredients. Next, check the refrigerator, cabinets, spice rack, and so forth, to see what supplies you already have. If you see that you already have enough of a certain ingredient, you can cross it off your shopping list.

casseroles (KAS ə ˌrōlz)

You probably will notice that your kitchen already has many of the things you need—perhaps flour, sugar, oil, vinegar, spices, eggs, and so forth. These are called staple items. **Staples** are foods that are kept on hand because they are used often, in many different recipes and many different meals. They usually store well, in either the cabinet or the refrigerator. When the person who shops for groceries in your house writes up the big shopping list every week or so, he or she probably checks over the staple items to see which ones are needed. Some families keep a list handy on a bulletin board or blackboard. During the week, they write down staple items that are getting low.

It's also a good idea to look over the ads in the newspapers and the shopping reminders you get in the mail. This is especially true if you're planning to buy a lot of things. See what's on sale. See what discount coupons are available. It may be worth planning a meal around chicken if you see that it's on sale at a good price. If there are staple items that you will need soon—including cleaning supplies, paper towels, and so on—it may be worth buying them now at the special price. If you save 10 percent of a big grocery bill for a family of four by shopping for items on sale, the savings could buy a record album—or more food.

If you want to breeze through the grocery store quickly, it's worth the time to organize your final list and rewrite it. List things together that are grouped together in the store. Put all your meat items together, for instance. Do the same with your dairy foods, fresh fruits and vegetables, canned vegetables, cereals, and so forth. If you want to be really efficient, arrange the groups (meat, dairy, and so on) in the order in which they are found in the grocery store. That way, you have to go through the aisles only once, and presto—you're done!

staples (STĀ pəlz)

These staples are probably in your kitchen at home. What other staples are in your kitchen?

Wouldn't it be easier just to go up and down the aisles and pick out anything you see that you need?

Impulse buying If you shop without a list, you're always taking a chance. In fact, you're taking several chances! First, you may overlook some things you need. You may not see them as you pass by, if you're not looking for them on your list. Second, you may see things you need, but not remember that you need them. Third, you may see and buy a lot of things that you don't really need. This is called impulse buying. An impulse is a sudden, short-term wish to have something, or to do something. If you shop without a list, you are much more likely to pick up things on impulse. One more tip: never go grocery shopping when you're hungry. If you do, *everything* will wind up in the grocery cart, whether you really need it or not!

How far ahead should you plan, when you're making your list?

Buying ahead As far as staple items are concerned, you can buy a week's supply at a time, or even a month's—depending on how well the items keep. As for **perishables**—the things that will spoil within a few days—buy only what you can use within the time they will stay fresh. Meats, for example, must be refrigerated and used within a day or two. But they can be kept a month or more if frozen.

As for sale items, the amount you should buy depends on whether they're dry staples or perishables. Also think about how much room you have in your cabinets, refrigerator, and freezer compartment. If you buy twice as much as you can use, you may throw out half of it. That's the same as if you paid twice as much for the part you used.

There is often a temptation to buy something just because it's on sale. But remember: if you buy it and end up throwing it away, it was a good sale—but a very bad buy.

Okay, now I've got my list made. What happens when I get to the market? They always have ten different brands and sizes of the same thing, and I never know which one to buy.

It's often hard to decide which can or box of a certain product is the best buy. It depends on price, quality, and personal taste. As a "smart shopper," you have to think about all these things.

Using product information

Unit price sticker

Unit price Most supermarkets now have **unit pricing** to help you tell which box or can of a certain product gives you the most for your money. The unit price is usually shown on a small sticker on the shelf right below the product. It names the product and the brand name,

perishables (PER i shə bəlz)

sometimes abbreviated. It also tells the size of the package and the total price of it. This information helps you to identify the package on the shelf. Then the sticker tells you how much the product costs per unit. The unit may be a unit of weight—that is, gram or kilogram, ounce or pound. Or it may tell you the cost per unit of volume—liter or milliliter, quart or fluid ounce. Volume is the amount of space that a substance takes up in a container. A **fluid ounce** measures volume. It's not the same as an ounce of weight. There are 32 fluid ounces in a quart, but there are 16 ounces of weight in a pound.

Sometimes, unit prices simply tell you the price per item—that is, per head of lettuce, per ear of corn, or per dozen eggs. An item like paper towels is usually measured in feet and inches (meters and centimeters, in metric terms). By comparing the unit price of one package with the unit price of another, you can decide which is the best buy in terms of *quantity*. You may still have to decide for yourself which is the best buy in terms of *quality*.

Is that why some brands cost more than others—because one brand is better than another?

Brand names   A higher price does not always mean higher quality. **National brands** are sold across the whole country, and often cost more than regional brands. **Regional brands** are sold in one region, or area, of the country but not everywhere. The producers of national brands usually do a lot of advertising. They spend more money on packaging to make their products look more appealing on the shelves. They may also put recipe ideas and other helpful tips on the package. These costs are added to the price of the product.

Many large supermarket chains have their own **private label brands**. Often, these foods are made by the national brand companies. They sell enormous amounts at a discount to the supermarket chains, which then put their own labels on the products. Private label brands usually sell for less than the highly advertised brand.

Some supermarkets now carry "**no-brand**" **brands**. These labels are very plain. They tell you only what's in the package or can, such as "Green Peas," plus certain other information required by law. There are no extras. These products are usually quite a bit cheaper.

Label information   Higher price does not mean better nutritional content. Many empty-calorie snack foods are quite expensive. And many low-priced canned foods are very nutritious. To tell what a food really contains, you have to read the label.

Who reads labels? They're too confusing—a lot of numbers and abbreviations and things I can't even pronounce!

Labels may seem confusing at first—but so is anything else you're not used to. For people who can't read a blueprint, a sewing pattern, or a sheet of music, these things seem hopelessly confusing. Food labels have standard information you can learn to look for.

brand name

legal food name

net weight

list of ingredients

USRDA

company name and location

computer code (used with computer-run cash registers)

nutrition information panel

Label information

Legal food name: The legal name of the product—such as "crushed tomatoes." To use a certain name, the product must meet certain standards. For instance, if canned tomatoes are broken into pieces, they may not be described as "whole."

Company name: The name of the company that made or distributed the product, and where the company is located.

Net weight: The weight of the food itself, without the package.

Drained weight: The weight of a solid food packed in liquid after the liquid contents have been poured off.

List of ingredients: The ingredients used in preparing the product. Ingredients are listed in order, according to how much there is of each one.

Standard of identity: A federal regulation that requires specified foods to contain certain amounts of certain ingredients. The container labels of these foods do not have to list ingredients. For example, mayonnaise must contain certain amounts of oil, egg, seasonings, and so on. The name "mayonnaise" on the label tells you what the ingredients are.

Nutrition information panel: A list that must give (1) serving size; (2) the number of calories in one serving; (3) the amount of nutrients (fat, carbohydrate, and protein) in one serving.

United States Recommended Daily Allowance (USRDA): The percentage of recommended amounts that each serving contains of protein and seven vitamins and minerals. Other special nutrition information may be listed, especially on foods meant for special diet problems.

Product date Another piece of information that you will find on many food packages is a product date. **Product dating** lets you and the grocery store know which items have been there the longest, and which should be used up first.

How can you tell what product dates mean?

The date you see on most perishable foods is the pull date—the last day the product should be sold. It leaves plenty of time for you to take the food home, store it, and use it normally. Canned foods may have an expiration date instead. This date is usually a year or

Product dating is proof that the food you are buying is fresh. Dairy products show a pull date. How does a pull date differ from an expiration date?

more in the future. You can count on the food being of good quality until this date or longer.

It's therefore not necessary for you to find the package with the freshest date. As long as the date is current—that is, today's date for something you will use right away—or some time in the future, you are assured that the product is fresh.

Product dates also help you in storing foods at home. They let you know which items should be used first and which ones can be kept longer.

Products are usually safe to eat even after the date on the package has expired, although they may lose some of their original quality. The actual time that a product will stay fresh depends on the storage conditions more than the date on the package. Most foods—even staple items—should be stored in a cool, dry place.

All these information sources—unit prices, labels, product dating— can help you decide what to buy. But in the end, buying decisions are always personal decisions.

Making buying decisions

Your final buying decisions depend on your personal tastes, the money you can spend, and your life style. Your decisions should also be based on your cooking skills, how much time you have, and how much you value the convenience that a particular product offers you.

Although two cuts of meat may weigh the same, the amount of meat may vary. The boneless roast (bottom) is all meat, while the spareribs (top) have a lot of bone.

Size The cheapest product is not always the best for you. For instance, the largest package of a product often has the lowest unit price. However, it's not a good buy for you if you have to eat it every night for a week just to use it up. Also, remember your storage space. Can you store large amounts in your cabinets, refrigerator, or freezer?

Cost per serving How much does a food really cost? Think in terms of cost per serving as well as cost per unit of weight or volume. Spareribs may cost about the same per kilogram or pound as a nice boneless roast. But the ribs are almost all bone, while the roast is almost all meat. Don't buy a higher grade or quality than you need. For instance, you don't need canned whole mushrooms for a casserole. Stems and pieces will do, and they're much cheaper.

Promotions Don't be fooled by displays in the store. Check prices. Special promotions don't always mean special prices. Try the private label products. Buy fresh fruits and vegetables in season (at their harvest time) when they are best and cheapest.

Convenience **Convenience products**—foods that have had some of the preparation done for you ahead of time—cost more. If you can do the same thing yourself, it's not worth paying extra for convenience.

convenience (kən VĒ nyəns)

1 lb ground beef
1 large onion
1 green pepper
1 can (28 oz) crushed
    tomatoes
1 can (6 oz) tomato paste
1 or 2 garlic cloves
1/2 tsp salt
1/4 tsp basil
1/2 lb elbow macaroni
1/2 head of lettuce
    (or other greens)
2 or 3 tomatoes
vinegar
salad oil
garlic
sugar
salt
celery salt
dry mustard
cayenne
hot pepper sauce
French or Italian
    bread (1 loaf)
garlic salt or
    garlic powder
butter or margarine
aluminum foil
milk

There's so much to remember! Do you have to think about all these things every time you plan a meal?

It's not as complicated as it looks, because you don't have to remember everything at once. You need to think about only the things that apply to each particular situation. To see how this works in a real situation, let's take a look at a pasta supper.

Planning and shopping for a pasta supper

Making a shopping list In making out your shopping list, first write down the things you plan to have on your menu: macaroni casserole, tossed salad with dressing, garlic bread, and milk. Next, write down the ingredients you will need for each item on the menu. For the macaroni with meat sauce recipe on page 172, list the ingredients. Next, list the ingredients you need for the tossed salad. If you plan to use a homemade dressing, you should check the ingredients you will need for that. Next, see what you will need for the garlic bread. Don't forget to put milk on your list.

When you have written down everything you will need, check around the kitchen to see what supplies you already have. You can cross these things off your list. When you have finished, your list will look something like this, assuming you are using customary measures.

Finally, group the things on your list according to categories. List the items under headings such as "Meat," "Vegetables," "Dairy products," "Spices," and so on, as they are grouped in the store.

Buying ground beef The first item on the list is ground beef. When you get to the meat counter, look for bright red, fresh-looking meat. Check the date on the package. Ground beef spoils quickly if it is not handled properly. Since it is ground up into small pieces, bacteria

If the meat you buy is wrapped in butcher paper, be sure to rewrap it for storage.

can get into it easily. It should be stored in the coldest part of your refrigerator. You can store ground meat in its see-through package for about a day; be sure to loosen the ends of the package. Meat in butcher paper should be rewrapped loosely with waxed paper or plastic wrap.

The store has so many different packages of ground beef—and some of them are more expensive. What's the difference, anyway?

The price of ground beef usually depends on the fat content. No ground beef is allowed to have more than 30 percent fat. A package labeled "hamburger" or simply "ground beef" will usually have more fat, and be cheaper, than one labeled "ground chuck" or "lean ground beef." A package labeled "ground round" or "ground sirloin" comes from more expensive cuts of meat and should have less fat. The leaner ground beef is especially good for hamburger patties or a "chopped steak" dinner, but the less expensive kinds make very good meat sauces. Fat adds flavor and juiciness to meat dishes. Extra fat can always be drained or spooned off.

Unit prices are always given on packaged meats. The label will tell you the kind of meat (such as beef or pork), the part of the animal it came from (such as chuck or round), and the name of the particular cut (such as blade roast or steak). The label also tells you the price per pound and the total weight. This may be in pounds and ounces, or in pounds, to one or two decimal points—such as 1.25 pounds. (In metric, the unit is kilogram, which is a little over 2 pounds.) Finally, the label tells you the total price of the package.

Buying fresh produce   Next on your list is fresh vegetables. Tomatoes and green peppers are in season in the summer to early fall. You can buy tomatoes at other times, but the price and quality vary. If you can't find fresh green peppers, they are usually available chopped and frozen. Lettuce is available all year, though the price and quality may vary a lot from month to month and even from week to week.

A fruit bowl can serve two purposes—it can be a decorative centerpiece and a delicious dessert.

Iceberg lettuce is often shipped from the Southwest. Supplies depend on the weather in that area and the growing season.

While you are in the fresh produce section, check over the fresh fruits in season. Pasta with meat sauce is a fairly heavy meal. A bowl of fresh fruit or a fruit cocktail makes a light, refreshing dish as a dessert or an appetizer, or as a snack to have on hand.

Buying canned goods Your next item is canned crushed tomatoes. Look for private label brands and compare prices. Canned goods such as tomatoes often go on special sale. Take advantage of any sale in which canned whole tomatoes are cheaper. Cut up the tomatoes into small pieces yourself. Quality is less important when you're choosing canned tomato products for a sauce, so look for the best buy.

Buying spices and herbs When it comes to spices and herbs, such as the basil and cayenne on your list, check the product date. The longer an herb or a spice sits on the shelf, the more flavor it loses. So don't buy a large size, even if it's cheaper, unless you use a lot.

Buying pasta Next on your list is macaroni. Macaroni is a form of pasta (PAHS tə)—which comes in all kinds of shapes and sizes, with many different names. Some popular types are

spaghetti (spə GET ē)—long, thin, and round
vermicelli (VER mə SEL ē)—very thin spaghetti
rigatoni (RIG ə TŌ nē)—short, wide, ribbed tubes
ziti (ZI tē)—medium-size, smooth tubes
manicotti (MAN i KAHT ē)—large, smooth tubes that you stuff
lasagna (lə SAHN yə)—very wide, flat noodles
egg noodles—flat ribbons
elbow macaroni—small, curved tubes.

Here are different types of pasta. How many can you name?

Compare the nutrition information panels on the sides of these milk cartons. What major differences do you see between regular milk, skim milk, and lowfat milk?

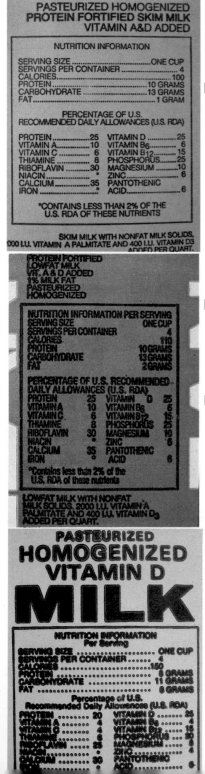

All types of pasta have one thing in common: they are made from a "paste" of flour and water that has been shaped, cut, and dried.

I love pasta, but it's so fattening! It's all starch, isn't it?

Pasta is made from flour, which has a large amount of starch. But starchy food isn't bad for you, especially if it contains other nutrients, as most flours do. Moreover, most pasta products are enriched with additional nutrients. If you look at the nutrition information panel of a pasta product, you will probably find that it contains substantial amounts of protein, thiamin, riboflavin, niacin, and iron—with only a little more than 200 calories per serving.

Buying oil and salad dressings   Salad oil comes in many different sizes, from .50 liter (a pint), or even less, up to 4 liters (a gallon), and sometimes larger. Check the unit prices to see which is most economical. But don't buy more than you can store easily and use up within a reasonable time. Oils can get rancid after a few weeks, especially in hot weather or if stored in a warm area. Some people buy olive oil because they like its distinctive flavor. However, it costs quite a bit more than regular oils. You can "stretch" olive oil by using it mixed with a less expensive oil.

If you don't have the time or desire to make your own salad dressing, you may decide to look at the bottled dressings in the store. There are also dry mixes, to which you simply add oil and vinegar.

Buying specialty breads   You will probably notice that French or Italian bread is more expensive per unit of weight than regular sandwich bread. This bread is a specialty item. You pay a higher price for its special taste and texture. To save money, use sliced white bread and make garlic toast sticks instead of garlic bread.

Buying fresh milk   In the dairy case, check the product dates and the unit prices of the different containers of milk. Milk is often cheaper when it is sold in larger containers. If you want to save on calories, buy skim milk (sometimes called "1% milk," since it has 1 percent fat or less) or lowfat milk (which has 2 percent fat content). Check the nutrition information panel to see how many calories you save.

Preparing and serving the pasta supper

Preparation time   Once you've bought everything, it's time to start cooking. The best way to figure out how long it will take you to prepare the pasta dinner is to start with the cooking time for the recipes you plan to prepare, and work backward from there.

It probably will take at least 30 minutes to cook the sauce. (See the recipe on page 172.) While the sauce is cooking, you can boil the pasta. Then the pasta and sauce should bake for about a half hour. Meanwhile, you can make the garlic bread and the salad. The combined time for the sauce, pasta, and baking is about an hour. Add

  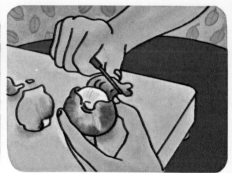

about 15 minutes for getting out pots and pans, mixing ingredients, reading directions, and so on. Add another ten minutes or so for setting the table, putting foods into serving dishes, tossing the salad, and so on. Total time for preparing this meal will be about an hour and a half.

Do-ahead steps If you don't have time to do everything before dinner, you can do a number of things ahead of time—in the morning, or even the night before. For instance, you can prepare the meat sauce and store it in the refrigerator, ready to add to the pasta the next day. You can even cook the pasta and combine it with the meat sauce in a casserole dish. Cover the dish and store it in the refrigerator, ready to put in the oven. Now the time needed to prepare the meal is simply the time needed for the whole dish to bake. (It will take a little longer to bake because it's cold.) The salad and the garlic bread can be made meanwhile. Or you can prepare the garlic bread ahead of time, wrap it in foil, and keep it in the refrigerator.

Making the sauce The first step in the casserole is to make the sauce. Get out the recipe, ingredients, and equipment you will need.

Macaroni casserole

3-4 servings

.50 kg	**1 lb ground beef**
	1 onion, chopped
	1 green pepper, chopped
	1 or 2 cloves of garlic, minced
.80 kg	**28 oz canned crushed tomatoes**
170 g	**6 oz canned tomato paste**
2 mL	**½ tsp salt**
1 mL	**¼ tsp basil**
.25 kg	**½ lb elbow macaroni**

Brown the ground beef in a large saucepan or deep skillet. Add the onion, green pepper, and garlic as the meat is browning. Add the tomatoes and tomato paste. Stir in the salt and basil.

Reduce the heat and simmer 25-30 minutes.

Cook the macaroni according to the package directions.

Pour the cooked pasta and sauce in alternate layers into a large ovenproof casserole dish, stirring gently after each layer.

Bake at 175 °C (350 °F) for 30 minutes.

CHOPPING THE ONIONS Start by chopping the onion and green pepper, so they will be ready to use. The quickest and easiest way to peel an onion is first to slice off the ends. Then cut a line down the side, from end to end, just deep enough to cut through the first layer of skin. The layer you have just cut will now slip off easily.

Now place the onion on a cutting board and cut it in half, through the stem. Place one of the halves flat-side down on the board and cut it crosswise into half-size rings. Keep the onion together as you slice.

Now turn the sliced onion and cut it the other way—across the lines you cut before. This cuts the onion into little square pieces. Do the same thing to the other half of the onion.

CHOPPING THE GREEN PEPPER Rinse the green pepper to get rid of any surface dirt. To chop the green pepper, first cut it in half, and then in quarters. Cut the stem out of each quarter, and remove the seeds and seed pods. Cut each quarter into strips. Then cut the strips crosswise into square pieces.

BROWNING THE MEAT Once the cutting is done, you're ready to brown the ground beef. Break the meat up into pieces and drop it into a large pot over medium to high heat. Stir it occasionally with a wooden spoon, breaking the meat up into smaller pieces as you do so. When the meat has begun to turn brown, add the chopped onion and green pepper. Continue cooking, stirring occasionally, until the green peppers become soft and the onions have a clear, glassy look. This is sometimes called **sautéing**. To sauté means to cook quickly, with a little fat or oil.

How can you cook the onions in fat if the recipe doesn't have any fat in the ingredients?

The ground beef provides enough fat to sauté the onions and green peppers. Cooked by themselves without any fat, they would burn.

CHOPPING FRESH GARLIC Now it's time to add the garlic. When you're using fresh garlic, you need to cut it or crush it to release the flavor

sautéing (saw TĀ ing)

juices. Pull a single clove off the bulb. With a small, sharp knife, remove the skin and cut off the pointed ends. Next, you can mince the clove with a knife or you can mash it with a sturdy dinner fork. Using a garlic press, if you have one, makes the job easier. Add one or two cloves to the sauce, depending on how much you like garlic.

ADDING THE TOMATOES By the time the onions and green peppers are ready, the meat should be completely browned. Now pour in the tomatoes and tomato paste. Use a rubber spatula to get everything out of the cans. Add the basil and salt. Let the sauce simmer (cook at low heat) for half an hour. Stir it once in a while. Don't cover the pot. The sauce should be allowed to "cook down" and thicken.

Cooking the pasta While the sauce is cooking, you can boil the macaroni. Macaroni and other pastas should be cooked in a large pot with a lot of water. This gives the pasta room to move around in the water, which keeps it from sticking together and forming clumps. It also lets the pasta cook more evenly. Before you add the pasta, the water should be boiling rapidly—that is, large bubbles should be moving and breaking vigorously. (This also helps to prevent clumping.) A tablespoon of cooking oil added to the water helps prevent the water from boiling over the sides of the pot.

Cook the pasta according to the directions on the package. Elbow macaroni usually cooks in about 12 to 15 minutes. Spaghetti is about the same. However, you can start checking after about 10 minutes, to be sure the pasta does not get too soft and mushy. Lift a piece out of the water with a fork or slotted spoon. Hold it under cold water to cool it, and then bite into it. It should be cooked through, without a white, starchy center. You may like it chewy (*al dente* in Italian—"to the tooth"). If you like it more tender, cook it a little longer.

For a casserole, pasta should stop cooking while it is still fairly chewy, since it will cook more later in the oven. Pour the pasta from the pot into a colander in the sink to let it drain.

Baking the casserole When both the pasta and the sauce are done, pour some of each into a casserole dish. Stir a little to spread the sauce. Keep adding the pasta and sauce a little at a time so that the casserole will be an even mixture. Save some sauce to put on top so all of the pasta will be covered. Otherwise, the pieces on top may dry out and even burn. Put the casserole dish, uncovered, in a 175 °C (350 °F) oven for about 30 to 40 minutes. The liquid should be bubbling gently around the sides of the casserole dish when it's done.

When do you make the garlic bread?

Baking the garlic bread If you didn't have a chance to make the garlic bread in advance, you can start on it while the casserole is cooking. Use a bread knife to cut the loaf. A bread knife has a long, narrow blade with a serrated edge. (The edge may look notched or have sawlike teeth.) However, it may not have the sharp edge of a butcher knife. When you slice a loaf of bread, use a gentle but firm sawing motion so that you don't crush the shape of the loaf. For garlic bread,

Before baking the pasta casserole, spoon a layer of sauce onto the top. Why should sauce be the last layer?

cut the loaf crosswise into slices about 2 centimeters (1 inch) thick. Do not cut quite all the way through. Leave a little bit uncut at the bottom to hold the loaf together.

The next step is to make the garlic butter. Use 60 milliliters (1/4 cup) of butter or margarine. Cut it into five or six pieces and melt it in a small saucepan over medium heat. Remove it from the heat as soon as all pieces are fully melted. Stir in 2 milliliters (1/2 teaspoon) of garlic salt. With a pastry brush, spread the mixture between the slices, being sure to brush some onto each side.

Wrap the loaf in aluminum foil and put it into the oven with the casserole during the last 15 minutes of baking. Serve the bread hot, in a bread basket covered by a napkin to hold in the heat.

If you don't have French or Italian bread, you can make garlic toast sticks. Prepare the garlic butter in the same way, but spread it on pieces of crisp toast. Cut each slice of toast into three or four sticks. Put them on a cookie sheet. Heat them in the oven for about 5 minutes before serving them, so they will be hot and tasty. You can do this during the last few minutes of baking the casserole. Serve them in a bread basket as you would the garlic bread.

Making the salad When the bread is out of the way, you can prepare the salad. Rinse the tomatoes and lettuce. Cut the tomatoes into halves, and then into quarters. Cut out the stem from each quarter. Cut the quarters into smaller wedges or into odd-shaped pieces. Tear the lettuce with your hands into bite-size pieces.

Make a French dressing out of 125 milliliters (1/2 cup) of salad oil and 60 milliliters (1/4 cup) of vinegar. Season it to suit your taste, using the ingredients for homemade dressing suggested on page 132. Try to make dressing in advance so the flavors have time to blend.

Just before you're ready to eat, toss the salad to mix the lettuce and tomatoes. At the last minute, add the dressing and toss again. (Remember, if the dressing is put on too far ahead of time, it will make the lettuce limp and soggy.) If different members of your family like different dressings, you can serve the salad plain and let everyone add a dressing at the table.

When you are having a salad with pasta, it's best to use individual salad bowls or small plates for the salad. If you put salad on the dinner plate, it will get mixed up with the meat sauce.

Serving the meal You can serve the salad in individual bowls or you can put the whole salad on the table and let people serve themselves. The same thing is true for the macaroni casserole. Serve the macaroni onto each person's plate in the kitchen, or put the whole dish on the table and let people serve themselves. (This way of serving food is called "family style," because it's the way most families eat.)

How about other pasta dishes—are they just as easy?

Other pasta dishes The cooking principles are pretty much the same for other pasta dishes. You know how to make a basic sauce, now, and how to boil the pasta. You should find it easy to follow a recipe for other dishes. Some pastas, like spaghetti, are not usually baked in a casserole. Others, like lasagna, always are. Some, like the macaroni and meat sauce, may be baked in a casserole but do not have to be. You can put the sauce directly over the boiled macaroni and serve it. But baking thickens the sauce and gives a richer flavor.

There are many pasta dishes you can try. But don't have pasta every night! There are lots of other one-dish meals that are easy to fix and great to eat. One delicious favorite is beef stew.

A beef stew supper

Almost everyone loves a beef stew. It's a good way to use leftover meat, but you can start from scratch with fresh meat, too. Look at the recipe card on page 178 for a good, basic beef stew.

Planning the menu A beef stew gives you meat and vegetables together. All you need to complete a beef stew meal is a serving from the bread group and one from the milk group. Drop biscuits would go well with this meal. You learned how to make them in Chapter 5.

Instead of buying stew-meat cubes at the store, you can save money by cutting up the meat yourself.

Serve milk with dinner, or perhaps have some ice cream for dessert. A lettuce wedge salad would add a light, crunchy texture to this meal.

When you have listed the dishes and ingredients you need, check to see which ingredients you already have. Cross these off your list.

Buying meat for stew When shopping for stew meat, you have several choices. Most stores sell stew meat already trimmed and cut up into cubes. This saves you time, and the meat has no waste. However, you usually pay a higher price for this service. Look around at the other meats. There may be something else that will do just as well, at a lower price. Thick chuck steaks and chuck roasts are usually priced lower. However, there is some waste in bone and gristle. To get .75 kilograms (1½ pounds) of stew meat, you would probably need to buy a little over 1 kilogram (2 pounds) of chuck roast. A round roast has less waste and may be easier to cut up, but it will be more expensive than chuck.

Look for special sales of meats that can be used for stew. You can use almost any cut that you can divide into bite-size pieces. You may easily save 15 percent or more. Meat is the most expensive part of the food budget. A saving of 15 percent or more can make a big difference at the end of the month.

Store meat in the coldest part of the refrigerator, loosely wrapped. (See page 169.) To keep meat longer than a day or two, wrap it tightly in freezer paper and freeze. Roasts will keep eight to twelve months, while ground or diced meat will keep two to three months.

Buying vegetables for stew When shopping for vegetables such as potatoes, carrots, and onions, look for vegetables that are clean, fresh, and firm. Potatoes and onions are usually much more economical in 5-, 10-, or 20-pound bags than when sold loose. (Potatoes are not yet sold by the kilogram.) Be sure, however, that they have no rotten spots. When you get home, take them out of the bag and check them again before you store them. Fresh, clean potatoes and onions will keep well for several weeks if they are stored in a cool, dry place. They do not need to be refrigerated.

Making the stew When you are ready to make your stew, get out the recipe and set it up where it will be easy to read while you work. Check to see that you have all the ingredients and equipment, and that you understand all the recipe terms.

Why do you need oil to brown the stew meat? You didn't need it for browning the ground beef for the pasta casserole.

BROWNING THE MEAT Stew meat is leaner than hamburger. If you don't put in a little oil, it may stick and even burn. You need oil for the onions and the other ingredients, too. The flavor gets stronger in onions and some other vegetables when they are cooked in oil, by the way. That's one reason onions and garlic are often sautéed in oil. The oil holds flavors and distributes them to other ingredients.

Easy beef stew

6 servings

.75 kg	1½ lb stew meat
30 mL	2 tbsp oil
5 mL	1 tsp Worcestershire sauce
	1 clove garlic, minced
	3 medium onions, quartered
500 mL	2 cups water
5 mL	1 tsp salt
1 mL	¼ tsp pepper
	6 carrots
	3 medium potatoes
	For gravy
60 mL	¼ cup cold water
30 mL	2 tbsp flour

Brown the meat in hot oil in a large pot.

Add the other stew ingredients except for the carrots and potatoes. Stir. Cover the pot and reduce the heat. Simmer for 1½ hours.

Peel and cut the carrots into 3-centimeter (1-inch) chunks. Peel and cut the potatoes into bite-size chunks. Add the vegetables to the stew and simmer for another half hour.

Remove the vegetables and meat from the pot with a slotted spoon, and put them into a serving bowl. Leave the broth in the pot to make a gravy.

Mix the flour and cold water together in a cup. Slowly stir the flour mixture into the hot broth. Cook about 3 minutes, stirring from time to time, until the gravy thickens and begins to bubble. (For a deeper color, you can add a teaspoon of a liquid gravy concentrate sold in the store. This kind of product also makes the flavor a little richer.)

Pour the gravy over the vegetables and meat in the serving bowl.

Once the meat is browned, it is ready for stewing. In **stewing**, you generally cover the food with liquid and cook it slowly in a covered pot. (**Braising** is similar, but you use much less liquid.)

Why do you put the carrots and potatoes in so much later?

COOKING THE VEGETABLES The meat needs a long, slow cooking period to make it tender and juicy. The carrots and potatoes cook in a fairly short time, since they're cut into pieces. If they simmered as long as the meat and onions, they'd get too mushy. Also, some of the vitamins would be destroyed by the long heating. So these vegetables are added after the other things have been cooking for a while. The vegetables should cook until they are just **fork-tender**. That means you should be able to stick a fork halfway through them with just medium pressure. They should not fall apart when you do so.

Timing is not too difficult with a one-dish meal. But it can be quite tricky in a meal where you have a lot of foods that take different cooking times. We'll take a closer look at this problem later on, when we talk about preparing a special holiday meal.

braising (BRĀ zing)

Time the addition of vegetables to stew so they will be fork-tender when the stew is done.

Making the biscuits Timing your drop biscuits with the beef stew is one problem you may have with the one-dish meal we've been discussing. As we saw in Chapter 5, the biscuits take about 12 minutes to bake. Therefore, they should be put into the oven about 10 to 12 minutes before the stew is done. If there's any doubt about whether you can make them finish cooking together, start the biscuits a little later. If the stew gets done early, you can keep it hot without any problem. That's not true for the biscuits. They're at their best when they're fresh—hot from the oven.

Making the salad The last thing to fix, while the biscuits are baking, is the salad. This is very simple. For a lettuce wedge salad, simply cut a head of lettuce in half and then slice it into wedges about 5 or 6 centimeters (2 inches) thick at the outside edge. Serve the wedges on salad plates. For this meal, you might choose a creamy dressing, such

Serve steaming beef stew with a crisp, lettuce wedge salad and hot, flaky biscuits.

as Thousand Island or Russian. Or make a quick dressing of your own by mixing mayonnaise or salad dressing with a bottled spicy dressing or catsup.

What if you don't have time to cook everything? How much of this can be done ahead of time?

Do-ahead steps The entire stew can be prepared ahead of time, cooled, covered, stored in the refrigerator and reheated. The meat and vegetables may become a little bit softer, and the flavors may blend a little more. Some people actually prefer their stew this way.

As for the salad, there is little to prepare ahead of time, except to be sure you have on hand the kind of dressing that you want. The biscuits should not be baked ahead of time. Biscuits can be warmed up, but they won't be as light and tempting as when they were fresh from the oven. If you're short on time, you can buy a can of refrigerated biscuit dough at the store. This is an example of when a convenience product may be worth the extra money to you. Follow the directions on the package. The biscuits bake in 12 to 15 minutes.

Storing leftovers If you prepare beef stew ahead of time and store it, you can put it in the refrigerator in the pot. Put plastic wrap, aluminum foil, or a close-fitting lid over the top. This keeps the stew from drying out. Leftovers can be stored the same way. In many cases, it's better to transfer leftovers from the serving dish to a plastic or glass storage dish. Many of these are much smaller than serving dishes and take up less space in the refrigerator. They often have close-fitting lids. Ovenproof dishes can go from the refrigerator to the oven to reheat leftovers. They can also be put into microwave ovens.

If you plan to freeze leftovers, wrap them in foil, freezer wrap, or plastic wrap, or put them in a plastic bag or container designed for freezer use. Put a strip of freezer tape or masking tape on the package telling what's inside and the date you put it in the freezer. Even bread can be frozen. To freshen it, wrap it in foil and put it in the oven for 5 to 10 minutes. If the bread has started to dry out, put a lettuce leaf in the package over the bread to provide a little moisture.

BEEF STEW
APRIL 20

Whether your next meal comes from your leftovers or involves a major shopping trip, a little planning and organization will make everything go much more smoothly. If you take the time to think through all the parts of the meal, it should be a delicious success.

Words to understand

casserole
menu
staples
perishables
unit pricing
fluid ounce
national brand
regional brand
private label brand
"no-brand" brand
net weight

drained weight
standard of identity
nutrition information panel
USRDA
product dating
convenience product
sauté
stew
braise
fork-tender

Food and equipment to know

chuck
round
sirloin
pasta
spaghetti
vermicelli
rigatoni
ziti
manicotti
lasagna
egg noodles
elbow macaroni
skim milk

lowfat milk

butcher paper
colander
casserole dish
wooden spoon
garlic press
slotted spoon
bread knife
bread basket
ovenproof dish
freezer tape
freezer wrap

Questions to discuss

1. Why is it important to use a shopping list? Think of at least two reasons. Describe how to make a shopping list.

2. How do you decide how much to buy? Name at least two things to consider.

3. Why are private label brands usually less expensive than national brands?

4. Why do some food labels list ingredients while others do not? How can you find out what's in foods that don't list the ingredients on the label?

5. Name three pieces of information that must appear on all food labels. List other examples of information that you *may* find that are not required by law.

6. What is the purpose of product dating? How can you use this information at home?

7. List five things to consider, in addition to price, when you make buying decisions.

8. When you get home from shopping, how should you store fresh meat? Potatoes and onions? Pasta? Oil?

9. What information should appear on a package of fresh meat?

10. Name and describe five kinds of pasta.

11. Describe how to cook pasta.

12. What's the difference between whole, skim, and lowfat milk?

13. How should you store leftovers for a day or two? What if you want to eat them two weeks later?

Things to do

1. Look through magazines for pictures of one-dish meals. Make a bulletin board with the items you find. Below each picture, indicate what you might add to make the meal complete. For example, with a macaroni and cheese casserole, you might serve a spinach and tomato salad, milk, and chocolate cupcakes.

2. Hold a recipe swap in class. Choose your family's favorite one-dish meal. Make five copies of the recipe. Bring the recipes to school and trade recipes with other students. Add the new recipes to your recipe file.

3. Plan a supper for your family. Start by figuring out the menu and collecting the recipes you need. Make a shopping list. Figure out a rough time plan for yourself, including what you could do ahead of time. Prepare the meal. Report to your class any problems you encountered and discuss how they might have been avoided.

4. Design a food label. Be sure it includes all of the things required by law. What extra information can you include that you think would be useful to consumers?

5. Compare the cost and nutritional value of several foods. Make a bulletin board or display showing the foods, the costs per serving, and the nutrition information (including the calories). For products that do not have nutrition information panels, ask your

teacher to help you find the information in tables of food values. Examples to use: milk, cola, potato chips, instant mashed potatoes, raisins, candy bar, ready-to-eat cereal, pasta.

6. Be on your toes! Sometimes the largest package does not have the lowest unit price. See if you can find three examples in your supermarket. Sometimes a larger package is a little cheaper per unit, but not enough to make it worth while. Find five examples where you think the savings aren't worth buying the extra amount. Find five examples where the savings do make it worth buying a larger package.

7. Go through your refrigerator and kitchen cabinets at home. Make a list of things your family keeps on hand as staple items. List any things you find that you would not consider staples. How did you decide which were staples and which were not?

Careers to consider

Would you like to teach others how to improve their skills in buying and using food?

If you think you would like teaching people about food, consider a career in consumer education.

Across the United States, county offices of the Department of Agriculture hire specialists in food and nutrition. These experts are **extension home economists**. Their job is to help local consumers improve their skills and management of food and nutrition. They may appear on broadcasts, hold workshops, and develop educational materials. Local clubs often invite extension home economists to speak at their meetings and to demonstrate various skills, such as how to store foods safely, or how to dry foods at home.

Utility companies also hire home economists to show consumers how to get the most from their food purchases and kitchen appliances. These home economists are sometimes called **home service representatives** or **consumer specialists**. They present educational programs to community groups or deal with consumers individually. For example, they may help someone learn to use a new microwave oven. This kind of work requires knowledge of and skill with foods, appliances, kitchen planning, and energy management.

Today many companies employ **consumer education specialists**. These, too, are usually home economists. Consumer education may mean preparing more informative packages and labels. It may mean writing educational leaflets, developing audio-visual materials, training sales people, or answering consumer mail. Some jobs involve travel to present special programs and demonstrations.

HAS THIS EVER HAPPENED TO YOU?

Steve's homework assignment for science is to find ways to save energy in the home. He and his friend, Ken have decided that a lot of energy is used in the kitchen, so they should try saving it there.

STEVE (taking notes): *Okay, first we'll cut down on the frozen foods, because it takes energy to keep them frozen.*

KEN: *We can cut down on foods that need cooking, too. We'll stick to raw fruits and vegetables and cold sandwiches as much as we can.*

STEVE: *And we'll cut down on things that need a blender or electric mixer, too. If we can't do it by hand, we'll do without it!*

KEN: *Sure. And while we're at it, let's stop using all those little appliances, like electric skillets, toasters, toaster ovens, and slow cookers. There's no reason why we can't do the things that have to be cooked on the kitchen range.*

STEVE: *We can do all the dishes by hand, too. The dishwasher uses up a lot of hot water and electricity.*

KEN: *You know, this isn't such a great idea, after all. We're cutting out half the things we like to eat, it'll take twice as long to fix what we have left, and it's all going to be cold and raw when we eat it! There's got to be a better way!*

ENERGY MANAGEMENT

Exploring . . .

Wise use of household energy

Microwave cooking

How to organize the kitchen

How to wash dishes quickly

A lot of people are trying to save energy these days. This isn't as hard as it might seem. There are lots of ways you can save energy—and time, too—with very little trouble.

But to save energy you have to stop using it, right? And how can you do that without trouble?

To save energy doesn't mean you have to stop using it. It just means you have to use it wisely. It means getting the most out of the energy you use, without wasting it.

Energy is the power or ability for action or work. When you talk about saving energy around the house, you should really talk about saving two kinds of energy. One kind is household energy, which is provided by electricity or fuels such as gas and oil. The second is personal energy—or the effort, time, or trouble it takes you to do a certain job. Many jobs in the kitchen take both kinds of energy. Sometimes, using a little more of one kind produces a large saving in the other. Sometimes it's possible to find ways to save both kinds.

Managing household energy

Ranges One kitchen appliance that uses a lot of energy is the gas or electric range. Small savings here can add up quickly. Here are some tips on how to get the most out of your range for the least energy.

Use the right-sized pot. When cooking on top of the range, select a pot that is the same size as the burner. If the pot is smaller than the burner, some of the burner surface just heats the air, instead of the pot.

Use lids, when possible. A lot of heat can be lost in the steam that rises from cooking food. Putting a lid on the pot keeps this heat in.

Don't peek into the oven. Every time you open the oven door, hot air is lost. It takes time, and extra energy, to get the oven back to the proper temperature. This can also affect the quality of the food, especially baked goods.

Use a well-insulated oven. **Insulation** in the walls of the oven keeps heat from escaping. When buying a new oven, select one with good insulation. Self-cleaning ovens have extra insulation because of the high temperature used in the cleaning process.

insulation (IN sə LĀ shən)

Save energy. *Don't* put small pots on large burners. *Do* cover pots when cooking. Allow space between oven dishes for heat circulation. Cook large amounts, and freeze leftovers.

Provide for good hot-air circulation inside the oven. When baking more than one thing at a time, space the dishes apart so that hot air can move around the food and speed the cooking. Convection ovens have a fan that helps circulate the hot air. This kind of oven cuts down on cooking time and saves household energy.

Cook large quantities and freeze the leftovers. It takes less energy to cook one large batch of food than several small ones.

Doesn't it take extra energy to freeze foods and to keep them frozen?

Freezers and refrigerators It takes a little extra energy to freeze foods, but it takes less energy to keep your freezer cold when it's full of food than when it's nearly empty. The reason is that every time you open the door, cold air spills out of the freezer. (It's the same as opening the oven door, which wastes hot air.) More food in the freezer means less cold air to escape.

A chest-type freezer, which opens from the top, uses less electricity than an upright model with doors that swing outward. When the chest-type freezer is opened, the cold air, which is heavier than the warm air in the room, stays down in the freezer. But the upright type opens from the front, which lets the cold, heavy air spill out.

Why does an upright freezer, which looks like a refrigerator, use more energy than the chest-type freezer shown here?

Of course, you should never open the freezer or refrigerator door needlessly. When you do open the door, don't leave it open longer than necessary. On the other hand, if you have several things to take out, it's better to leave the door open and get everything at once. Don't keep opening and closing the door. This causes a breeze that pulls cold air out of the refrigerator and lets warm air in.

When putting hot things into the freezer or refrigerator, you can save energy by cooling them first. Put the food into a container or sealable plastic bag and place it in cold water in the sink. Freeze or refrigerate the food when it is cool enough to hold easily in the palm of your hand.

When shopping for a new refrigerator or freezer, look for one that has good insulation. Insulation saves cold air in a refrigerator or freezer, just as it saves hot air in the oven.

Be sure to defrost your refrigerator freezer regularly. Don't let more than half a centimeter (about a quarter of an inch) of frost build up in the freezer. If you do, the refrigerator will have to work harder and use more energy. A self-defrosting refrigerator avoids the problem of frost buildup. However, it uses more energy than an ordinary refrigerator that is defrosted regularly.

To **defrost** the refrigerator freezer, first take out the ice cubes and frozen foods. If you have an insulated picnic chest, store the foods and ice cubes in it while the freezer is defrosting. Or wrap the foods in layers of newspaper to insulate them and keep them from thawing.

Turn the temperature control to "defrost" or to "off." Leave the freezer door open. Do not chip the frost off the walls of the freezer with a knife or other tool. This may damage the freezer. If you want to speed defrosting, set pans of hot water in the freezer. Change the water when it gets cool. When the freezer is defrosted, wipe out the inside of the freezer and the refrigerator section with a mixture of 5 milliliters (1 teaspoon) of baking soda to 1 liter (1 quart) of water.

Dishwashers   Another kitchen appliance that should be used wisely is the dishwasher. The dishwasher uses household energy (electricity) to save time and personal energy. This can be a good use of household energy, if the energy is used carefully and not wasted.

Don't dishwashers use a lot of hot water, as well as electricity?

People tend to use more hot water doing dishes by hand than a dishwasher uses to wash a full load of dishes. They may use hot water to rinse off the dishes before washing them. They may leave the water running to rinse the soap off the dishes when they are washed. A dishwasher, on the other hand, uses a controlled amount of water in each wash-and-rinse cycle.

To get the most out of your dishwasher, wait till it is fully loaded before running it. A half load uses just as much energy as a full load.

defrost (də FROST)

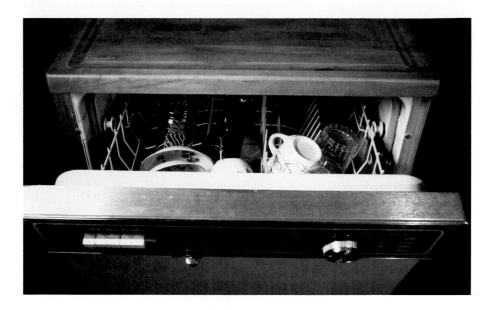

To save electricity, open the door of your dishwasher as soon as it reaches the drying cycle. What are some other energy-saving tips to remember when you use a dishwasher?

If you don't need the clean dishes right away, turn off the machine at the end of the last rinse. Open the door slightly and let the dishes air-dry instead of using the machine's drying cycle. The drying cycle uses a lot of electricity.

Small appliances   You can save additional electricity by being careful about the way you use small appliances such as the toaster, mixer, food processor, or electric skillet.

Can't you save even more energy if you just do without all those things?

You can get along without most small appliances, but you may not save any energy. In fact, you may use more, because many small appliances actually save electricity. The toaster is a good example. It can toast one or two pieces of bread quickly, with a small amount of energy. If you used the oven or broiler in the kitchen range to do the same job, it would take longer and use much more energy. Much of the energy goes toward heating the range itself. While the range is heating up and cooling down, heat energy is wasted.

Other small appliances such as toaster ovens, electric skillets, fryers, and slow cookers can save electricity in the same way. They use just enough energy to do the job for which they are intended, and no more.

Small appliances such as mixers, blenders, and food processors use electricity to save time and effort. With large jobs, this is a good use of household energy. Very small jobs can sometimes be done better by hand. It would not make sense, for instance, to set up the food processor to slice one pickle. Both personal and household energy would be wasted. But the processor would be a great help in making cole slaw for a party. The time and effort saved would be worth the household energy used.

toaster   slow cooker   electric skillet

Cooking
appliances

electric mixer   blender   food processor

Preparation
appliances

Another appliance—one that can save both personal and household energy—is the microwave oven. This is a new development in cooking equipment that has certain special advantages. It is becoming more and more common in the American home kitchen.

Microwave cooking

Microwave cooking is different from ordinary cooking in one very special way. In ordinary cooking, the stove or other appliance heats up first and then transfers the heat to the container and then to the food. This means that much of the energy goes toward heating up the appliance and container first. Only then does the food start to cook. When the food is done and is removed, the appliance and container have to cool off. The heat lost in this cooling is wasted. Microwave cooking saves energy because the oven does not heat up first. The heat is created directly in the food itself.

How does a microwave oven do that?

How microwaves work   Microwaves are something like light waves, heat waves, and radio waves. When they strike something, they may pass through it or they may be reflected or absorbed, depending on the material. Microwaves can pass through a container without heating it and go directly into the food.

To understand this process, think of a beam of light coming from a flashlight. If it hits a sheet of glass, most of the light goes on through. If it hits a bright, shiny object such as a mirror, most of the light is reflected. If it hits a dark object such as a rock or a tree, some light is reflected—but much less than with a mirror. Most of the light is absorbed.

Microwaves behave in much the same way. They pass through materials such as glass, paper, and plastic. They are reflected by metal. And they are absorbed by food. Microwaves penetrate 2 to 3 centimeters (about 1 inch) into most foods—from the top, bottom, and sides—and are absorbed by the moisture and fat molecules in food. These molecules are vibrated, or shaken up, by the microwaves. It is the motion of the molecules that creates the heat that cooks the food. Because microwaves heat the inside of the food at the same time as the outside, they cook food more quickly than ordinary ovens. Energy is thus saved in the cooking process as well as the heating-up process.

Your body is made of the same kinds of materials as the food you eat, so microwaves would affect them the same way. For this reason, microwave ovens always have a tight-fitting door with a special seal that keeps any microwaves from leaking out. There is also a special latch that makes sure the door is closed tightly before the oven will operate. You should never tamper with the latch, the door, or the seal, in any way.

What about after you take the food out of the oven? Does it still have microwaves in it?

People who don't understand microwave cooking sometimes worry about microwaves remaining in the food, as if they were some kind of radioactive fallout. This doesn't happen. Microwaves are simply the force that sets the food molecules in motion, the way a baseball bat knocks a baseball into the outfield. Once the oven is turned off, the force stops. Looking for microwaves in the cooked food is like looking for the baseball bat in a fly ball.

Container materials   Even though the microwaves heat the food molecules and not the container, the container may still get hot because it is in contact with the hot food. For this reason, most regular glassware and dinnerware should not be used for cooking. (Many dishes can be used for quickly reheating foods, however.) Ovenproof glass and ceramics are ideal for microwave cooking.

Many materials that cannot be used in an ordinary oven can go into a microwave oven. These include paper towels and napkins, waxed paper, paper or plastic-foam plates and cups, plastic wrap,

All of these materials can be used for cooking in a microwave oven. What other containers could you use?

cooking bags and storage bags, boilable plastic dishes, newspapers, and cardboard packages. For example, hot chocolate may be heated and served in the same mug. Pizza can be reheated in its original box. Coffee can be heated in a styrofoam cup. Because metal reflects microwaves, metal pots and pans and metal-trimmed dishes should not be used.

The materials used in microwave cooking can often make your job a lot easier. For example, when you cook bacon in the microwave oven, just place the strips between white paper towels and on a paper plate. Because of grease build-up, it's best not to cook more than four slices at a time. Cook the bacon for about 45 seconds per slice. Remove it from the oven and lift it off the paper towels while it is still hot, using tongs. The grease will be trapped in the paper towels and plate, making clean-up easy.

Microwave ovens are ideal for defrosting frozen foods packaged in cardboard, waxed paper, plastic wrap, sealable bags, and so forth. The penetrating action of microwaves also speeds thawing in the center of the frozen food.

The microwave oven is ideal for heating leftovers, too. Most foods can be heated right in the refrigerator dish, without removing waxed-paper or plastic-wrap covers. If the food is dry, add a spoonful of water or wrap it in a moist paper towel to freshen it up.

Cooking time and food quality Several factors affect the cooking time and quality of foods in a microwave oven. Most of these factors affect cooking in an ordinary oven, too, but they are more noticeable in microwave cooking.

One important factor is the moisture and fat content of the food. Foods with a lot of moisture (especially fat) heat much faster than dry foods. Items such as milk, cheese, and bacon cook very quickly by microwave. Another factor is density. A heavy food item like a potato takes longer to heat than a light, porous item like a dinner roll.

One important factor that affects cooking time is the amount of food being cooked. One strip of bacon takes 45 to 60 seconds to cook. Four strips take about 3 minutes. In a regular oven, cooking time changes only slightly—if at all—with the amount of food. This means that the microwave oven saves a lot of time and energy when you are cooking small amounts—but less when you cook large amounts.

As with ordinary cooking, the size and shape of the food affect cooking time. A single large piece of meat takes longer to cook than if it is cut up into small pieces. Thin pieces cook faster than thick pieces. An odd-shaped piece of food with a thin part and a thick part, such as a chicken drumstick, may cook unevenly. To help prevent this, arrange the pieces in a circle with the thick parts toward the outside of the circle and the thin parts toward the inside.

Can you cook any kind of food in a microwave oven?

In a microwave oven, it takes more time to cook four slices of bacon than to cook one slice. Would the number of bacon slices affect cooking time if you were broiling them?

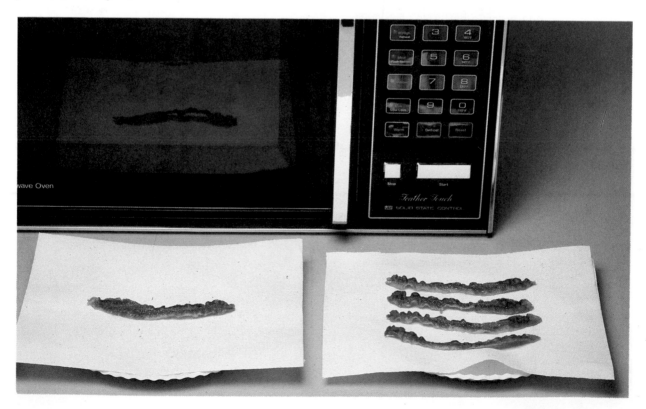

Some foods do not cook well in a microwave oven. Eggs in the shell may burst. Pancakes and breads do not develop the brown crust that people usually like. Canning requires long cooking times at high temperatures, while microwaves work best in quick cooking situations. Large quantities of food cook more efficiently in an ordinary oven. Manufacturers of microwave ovens are always looking for ways to overcome these limitations.

Other foods cook exceptionally well in a microwave oven. Fresh and frozen vegetables, fish, frozen dinners, and leftovers benefit especially from microwaves. They keep the most flavor with the least amount of cooking.

Cooking fish in a microwave oven   The quick, even heating of microwaves is ideal for cooking fish and shellfish. Fish is cooked in a matter of a few minutes. It comes out flaky but moist, tender, and full of flavor.

Many fresh fish can be cooked whole, once they have been cleaned and the inner organs removed. Shellfish can be cooked with or without their shells. Today, most people can get good frozen fish all year. Most often, you'll see fish fillets (fi LĀZ) in the supermarket—these are long, boneless pieces cut from the sides of a fish. You may also find fish steaks—thick, crosswise sections of fish. You can thaw a pound of frozen fish in about 5 minutes in a microwave oven.

Shallow glass oven dishes are perfect for cooking most fish. Since these dishes don't usually have a fitted cover, cover the dish with

How is a fish cut in order to get fillets? fish steaks?

Fish fillets with lemony-garlic sauce

4 servings

.50 kg	1 lb frozen fish fillets
60 mL	¼ cup butter or margarine
2 mL	½ tsp dry mustard
10 mL	2 tsp parsley flakes
5 mL	1 tsp garlic salt
10 mL	2 tsp lemon juice

Thaw the fish fillets in the microwave oven according to the directions that come with the model you are using. (Some have an automatic defrost cycle.)

Melt the butter or margarine in a large, rectangular glass baking dish. This takes about 30 seconds.

Add the mustard, parsley, garlic salt, and lemon juice. Stir to mix.

Dip the fish fillets in the garlic sauce, covering both sides, and arrange in the baking dish. Cover the dish with waxed paper or plastic wrap.

Cook in a microwave oven for about 5 minutes. Check for doneness. If it's not done, cook for another 2 minutes and check again.

waxed paper or plastic wrap before putting it into the microwave oven. A cover holds in the hot steam, which helps to cook the middle without drying out the edges.

Once you've used a microwave oven a few times, you'll develop the confidence to experiment with ideas of your own. All sorts of seasonings and sauces can be combined with fish. Try experimenting with lemon juice, orange juice, and other juices in cooking sauces. Chopped onions, green peppers, celery, or tomatoes can be added to many recipes, to suit your taste.

How do you know when fish is done?

Fish is done when it separates easily into flakes when you scrape it gently with a fork. The glassy look of raw fish turns to a solid color—usually white, but pink for fish such as salmon. Do not let the fish overcook. Overcooked fish is dry and tough.

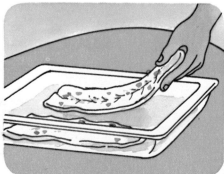

Cooking vegetables in a microwave oven   Another group of foods that cook especially well in a microwave oven is fresh and frozen vegetables. You may be amazed to find how well they keep their bright color, their flavor, and their texture during cooking.

Most vegetables are cooked with only a little water, so you don't need to drain them before serving. This cuts down on the possible loss of nutrients. It saves energy, too, because it means you have to heat less water in the cooking process. Dishes should be covered with plastic wrap or waxed paper to hold in the heat and prevent drying. Some vegetables, such as potatoes or squash, can be cooked whole, with their own skins or shells acting as a cover. Be sure to pierce the skins with a fork before cooking in any kind of oven. Without an outlet for steam, the vegetables may burst.

The cooking time depends on the amount of vegetables you are cooking. One baked potato takes only about 4 minutes, but two will probably take 7 minutes and three may take 9 or 10 minutes. The larger the quantity, the more time cooking will take.

Frozen vegetables can be thawed and cooked right in their cardboard cartons. Canned vegetables are already cooked and need only simple heating—but in an ovenproof dish, not in the can. Most people are surprised at the good quality of reheated leftover vegetables. This is another case where the microwave oven produces better quality, in less time, with less effort and less electricity.

There are other ways, too, in which you can reduce your time and effort, or personal energy, without increasing your use of household energy. In many cases, all you have to do is to organize your work.

Managing personal energy

Think about all the things you do in the kitchen. You'll find that they fall into four main types of activity. You can handle each of these activities more efficiently if you arrange your kitchen so that each activity goes on in one place.

Organizing work space   Your work in the kitchen will be easier and more efficient if you set up a **work center** for each of your various activities. Utensils, ingredients, and other materials should be stored as close as possible to the center where they will be used.

PREPARATION AND MIXING CENTER This center is usually between the refrigerator and the range. It includes the sink and as much cleared counter space as possible. Here you clean, trim, slice, chop, mix, knead, roll out, shape, and decorate. As near to this center as possible should be your staples and other ingredients—sugar, flour, spices, vinegar, refrigerated foods, and so forth. Also nearby should be your knives, peelers, measuring cups and spoons, mixing bowls, cutting boards, blender, mixer, food processor, and so forth.

COOKING AND SERVING CENTER In a well-designed kitchen, the cooking and serving center will be near the range but also within easy reach of the dining table. Near the center should be all supplies and utensils used in cooking and serving—stirring spoons, pancake turner, cooking fork, pots, pans, lids, platters, and serving dishes. Napkins, salt and pepper, placemats, tablecloths, and sugar bowl should be near the dining table.

CLEANING CENTER The most important piece of equipment in this center is the sink. The center should also include space for a draining rack and a place to scrape and stack dirty dishes. Nearby should be the supplies and equipment for scraping, washing, rinsing, and drying dishes—a rubber spatula, soap or detergent, cleanser, sponges, scouring pads, dishpan, and draining rack. Dishes are usually stored in a cabinet to the left of the sink, since dishes are most efficiently washed from right to left.

PLANNING CENTER A planning center is very nice to have, if your kitchen is large enough. It might include your cookbooks, paper and pencil, chalkboard, bulletin board, and a large planning calendar. This is a good place to keep an up-to-date grocery list of things you need.

TIPS FOR ORGANIZING WORK SPACE Here are a few other kitchen organization tips to keep in mind.

Store food near the place where it will be used.

Do not store canned goods, spices, and vegetables such as fresh potatoes and onions near heat sources (such as the range or radiators).

Use lower, easy-to-reach shelves for things you need often.

Keep counters and other work surfaces uncluttered.

Keep cabinet doors and drawers closed to avoid bumps and bruises.

If you have a lot of small appliances, don't overload electrical circuits. Don't use more than two appliances at a time. Unplug things by holding onto the plug, not the wire. Always dry your hands before touching anything electrical.

By following these suggestions you can save a great deal of time and effort on many kitchen tasks. Most jobs become much easier and more enjoyable.

Except for washing dishes! How can you possibly enjoy that?

Dishwashing by hand Perhaps the only way to make dishwashing fun is to get someone else to do it! Once again, however, you can make things go faster and easier if you organize your work.

For instance, you need to handle dishes less if you move them from right to left as you wash them (if you are right-handed). Stack the dirty dishes on your right, wash them in the sink in front of you, rinse them, and stack the clean dishes on a draining rack to your left. Even more important, though, is to have the clean dishes end up in a spot where it will be convenient to put them away. A left-handed person probably would want to organize the kitchen to work in the opposite direction. This would mean storing dishes in a different place, too.

A double sink is ideal for dishes because it allows one basin for soapy water and another for rinse water. Use rubber dishpans or padded sink mats to protect dishes from chipping.

Your dishwater will stay clean longer if you scrape dishes first with a rubber spatula. Some people like to give them a quick rinse, too. Also, scrape grease from pots, pans, and serving dishes. Soak them in water if they need it. You can even give them an early soak in a pan of soapy water as you prepare and serve the meal. As you have a few spare minutes here and there, you can go ahead and wash them in the same water, if it is still hot and soapy.

When your dishes are scraped and stacked, wash them in the order that will leave the dishwater clean as long as possible. The best order is (1) glassware; (2) flatware (knives, forks, spoons); (3) tableware (plates, cups, saucers, etc.); (4) serving dishes; (5) pots, pans, and other utensils. By the time you get to actually washing the pots, pans, and utensils, they will have soaked long enough to be fairly easy to clean.

A few extra tips:

Be extra careful of sharp knives and forks that have been soaking. They can be dangerous when they're hidden under water.

Use plastic mesh scouring pads and mild cleansing powder for the food that soaking didn't loosen. For stubborn stains, use steel wool soap pads, but be careful not to scratch cooking surfaces.

Use a cold water rinse to soak or loosen eggs, milk, cheese, rice, and oatmeal. Hot water tends to harden these foods onto dishes.

Don't soak cast-iron skillets any longer than necessary. They will rust. Don't scour them, either, or they will lose their seasoning, and foods will stick. If this happens, pour a centimeter (half an inch) of oil into the skillet and heat gently for 15 minutes to reseason the pan.

Don't soak wooden salad bowls or other wooden items in water. They may warp, crack, or lose their finish.

Dishes organized for washing. What should be different for safety?

All this may help, but I'd still rather use a dishwasher!

Using a dishwasher If you have a dishwasher, of course, the whole cleanup job will be much easier for you. The use-and-care booklet that comes with each dishwasher is the best guide for loading it. It will tell you how to get the most use from the rack space you have. A little planning is still valuable. Pots and pans may still need soaking, and in some cases scouring, before going into the dishwasher. It is often better to wash plastic and wooden bowls by hand, or to remove them from the dishwasher before the hot drying cycle begins. Some people like to give plates a quick rinse before putting them into the dishwasher (even though most models now are equipped to dispose of soft food).

All of these activities go more smoothly if you make plans about when, where, and how you are going to do them. This means that you have to organize your time, too, as well as your materials and your work space. Later on, we'll talk about how to make up a time schedule in a way that makes the most efficient use of your personal and household energy.

Words to understand

insulation
defrost
work center

Food and equipment to know

fish fillet
fish steak

gas or electric range
convection oven
upright freezer
chest-type freezer
food processor

toaster oven
slow cooker
blender
microwave oven
drain rack
flatware
tableware

Questions to discuss

1. Why does frequently opening a refrigerator or hot oven waste energy?
2. When should a freezer be defrosted?

3. Which uses more energy—a nearly full freezer or a nearly empty one? A freezer with a lot of frost built up or one with very little? A self-defrosting freezer or a regular model defrosted regularly?

4. What can you do to prevent frozen foods from thawing while you defrost the freezer?

5. What can you do to save electricity when you use a dishwasher?

6. Name four small cooking appliances that use less energy to cook than a regular range/oven.

7. Why are microwave ovens more efficient than a regular range in heating many foods?

8. Name at least three kinds of materials for containers you can use in a microwave oven for cooking foods.

9. Name three or more factors that affect how long it will take something to cook in a microwave oven.

10. How can you tell when fish is cooked enough?

11. Name the four basic work centers in a kitchen. What kinds of activities would you do at each center?

12. Give three safety rules for working with small electric appliances in the kitchen.

13. List the order in which you should wash things when you're doing the dishes.

14. What can you do to make dirty pots and pans easier to clean?

Things to do

1. Make a poster or bulletin board of ways to save energy when you're cooking. Include at least five ideas. Check with the electric or gas company in your area for additional ideas.

2. Demonstrate to your class the proper way to defrost the refrigerator in your kitchen at school. Be sure to check the use and care guide that came with the refrigerator for specific instructions. Explain briefly how to clean the inside of the freezer and refrigerator. Or, defrost your refrigerator at home and write a report on what you did.

3. Make drawings of your home kitchen. Identify the work centers. Make a list of the supplies and equipment you think should be kept at each work center. Is your home kitchen well organized? Discuss your ideas with your parents and see if there are any ways in which you might improve the organization of your kitchen.

4. Have a friend watch you wash dishes and make notes of all the steps and motions you go through. Go over the notes with your friend. Try to discover ways in which you can organize the work to cut out some of the steps and make the job easier and faster.

5. Place a medium-size potato in the microwave oven and cook it until it is fork tender. Carefully record how long it took. Do the same with a potato in the range oven, set at 175 °C (350 °F). Now do the same with eight potatoes in the microwave oven. Compare the three cooking times. What does this tell you about the advantages of microwave cooking? Peel another potato, cut it up into a dozen pieces, and wrap them in plastic wrap. Cook them in the microwave oven until fork tender, again recording the time. How did cutting up the potato affect the cooking time?

6. Place an oven thermometer in the range oven (near the front) and heat the oven to 225 °C (450 °F). Open the oven door and hold a room thermometer just outside the oven. Observe the two thermometers for 3 minutes. What happens to the heat in the oven?

Careers to consider

Would you like to represent consumer interests?

If you like analyzing issues and working out problems, consider a career in consumer affairs.

Consumer affairs specialists represent the interests of consumers in their dealings with business or government. They need to know what kinds of problems consumers have in buying or using food, equipment, or other products and services. It's important for them to be in constant contact with consumers to find out what they need and want.

Consumer specialists may deal with state legislators, members of Congress, or appointed officials (such as people in charge of various government agencies or departments). They try to influence new laws and regulations that would be helpful to consumers. Their work may also include many consumer protection services. One common service found at local levels of government is the checking of scales and other measuring devices in stores to make sure consumers are getting the amounts they pay for.

In large businesses, consumer affairs professionals may meet with consumer groups and handle consumer mail. Consumers often write to companies for information about products, for help in handling special needs, and with suggestions for improving products or services. They sometimes write with complaints that need attention. Consumer specialists can be very helpful to a company. They can alert management to changing needs and trends. They can help to develop business policies that are helpful and fair to both consumers and the company.

You can expect to see growing numbers of **consumer affairs reporters** hired by radio and TV stations, newspapers, and magazines. These people report on news of special interest to consumers. They often analyze and comment on important consumer issues. In many areas, they help solve consumer problems and alert consumers to frauds and unfair practices.

Jobs in consumer affairs generally require a college degree. Many colleges now offer study programs in consumer economics or consumer studies that would provide a good background for this kind of work.

10

HAS THIS EVER HAPPENED TO YOU?

Brenda is staying at her grandparents' lake cabin for the summer. There are six or seven kids her own age nearby. She wants to invite them over for a dinner party so she can get to know them better.

BRENDA: *Don't worry about a thing, Grandma. I'll do all the cooking myself—and the cleaning up, too.*

GRANDMOTHER: *I'm afraid you won't have much time to talk to people, Brenda. How will you get to know anyone, if you spend all your time in the kitchen, cooking?*

BRENDA: *Maybe you're right. I know! I'll get the kids to help cook! That'll keep the conversation going, too, because everyone will have something to do and talk about.*

GRANDMOTHER: *But it gets so hot in that tiny kitchen! And there's only room for one person at a time. I'm afraid you'll just have to change your plans, Brenda.*

GRANDFATHER: *Young people should be outside in the summertime, anyway! Why don't you have your party out in the yard? That way, you'll have lots of room, you won't have to worry about spilling things, and I can take a nap after dinner in peace— inside, where my snoring won't bother anyone!*

BRENDA: *A cookout! Why didn't I think of that? That's more fun, anyway. After dinner we can toast marshmallows and sing songs. We can move around—and even dance, without bumping into things. Except—what do you cook at a cookout? And how do you cook it?*

COOKING OUT

Exploring . . .

How to plan a barbecue

How to buy, store, and cut up chicken

How to make and use a fire safely

Ideas for cooking meats, vegetables, and fruits out-of-doors

Cooking out is a lot of fun. Being out-of-doors seems to make people relax and be more casual. Fresh air perks them up and adds zest to their appetite. A cookout is a special occasion, with special food. For many people, the taste (and smell) of charcoal-broiled food is a delight that can't be matched by any other method of cooking.

But even though it's informal, a cookout takes careful planning. For one thing, your dishes and kitchen utensils won't be right at hand. You'll have to figure out just what you need, and make plans for carrying things back and forth. Also, you'll have to plan your menu carefully. Some foods are especially good at a cookout, but others are difficult to fix outdoors. Don't plan to have them unless you have a kitchen nearby, or can fix them ahead of time.

What foods are good for a cookout?

Almost any tender meat can be broiled over a charcoal fire. (To broil means to cook food by exposing it to direct heat.) Hamburgers

Barbecued spareribs and kabobs make delicious and different cookout meals.

and hotdogs can be charcoal broiled. Chicken is fine for broiling, too. So are spareribs, steaks, chops, and kabobs (kə BAHBS). The name comes from the Turkish words *shish kabob*, meaning roasted meat on a skewer (SKYOO ər). Kabobs are chunks of meat or other foods stuck on a skewer. A skewer is a long, thin spike, something like a knitting needle.

Some vegetables can be grilled (broiled) over a charcoal fire. For instance, kabobs often have pieces of onion, tomato, and green pepper stuck on the skewer between the pieces of meat. Small pieces of potato can be skewered and grilled. Whole potatoes should be wrapped in foil and cooked more slowly. Most vegetables that can be baked in an oven can be wrapped in foil and roasted over a charcoal fire.

You may decide to include some foods that are easier to fix inside, in the kitchen, than outside at the cookout. These should be fairly simple foods that can be fixed ahead of time and served cold, or heated up quickly without much trouble. Potato salad is one example. Baked beans are another.

For your first cookout, a sample menu might include barbecued chicken, sweet corn, baked potatoes, tossed salad, milk or punch, and toasted marshmallows for dessert.

The first thing you have to do, then, is get the chicken.

Buying chicken

Kinds of chicken   Chicken comes in several different sizes, prices, and packages. The broiler-fryer is a young, meaty bird weighing .75 to 1.75 kilograms (1½ to 3½ pounds). It is an all-purpose chicken. It can be broiled, fried, baked, simmered, or sautéed.

The roaster (or oven roaster, or oven stuffer) is larger than the broiler-fryer, about 1.75 to 2.25 kilograms (3½ to 5 pounds). It is a little older, but still has tender meat. This chicken is best for baking in the oven.

The hen is a plump, meaty chicken, about 2.25 to 3 kilograms (4½ to 6 pounds) in weight. It is an older bird, so the meat is not as tender. It is best stewed, boiled, or cooked by other moist heat methods. It provides a lot of meat, so it's very good for soups and for recipes calling for pieces of cooked chicken.

Chicken pieces   You can buy chickens whole, or cut up. They may be cut into halves, quarters, or pieces. Generally, whole chickens are the cheapest per unit of weight. Always check the unit prices of the different forms to see which is the best buy. The most expensive form is usually separate pieces—that is, packages of breasts, thighs, legs, wings, and so forth. However, these packages may have less waste than whole chickens. Whole chickens include backs, which are mostly bone. They also have the neck, liver, and gizzard parts which you normally don't put on the grill at a cookout. If you don't have some other way to use these pieces, they add to your food cost without adding any value.

If you buy pieces, you will usually find it much cheaper to buy whole legs than separate packages of drumsticks and thighs. You can

A capon is an extra-large chicken, meant for roasting. How would you cook the others?

cut them apart yourself quite easily. Get a cutting board and a sharp knife. Hold the leg by the drumstick, with the thigh pointing downward and away from you. With your index finger, press into the joint until you find the soft spot where the drumstick and thighbone meet. It may help if you flex the thighbone up and down a little to find this point. Place the edge of the knife at that point and slice downward through the joint. (Be sure to keep your fingers out of the way!) If the knife goes between the two bones, it will cut through easily. If it hits a bone, try again. With a little practice, you should be able to find the right spot easily.

Why cut it up at all? Why not just cook the whole leg in one piece?

You can cook the whole leg in one piece, if you prefer. However, there are certain advantages to cutting it up first. Smaller pieces fit more easily onto the grill. They're easier to turn when cooking. Also, drumsticks are thinner than thighs and may cook faster. If they are in separate pieces, they can be removed sooner. Separate pieces are easier to eat than whole legs, too. Finally, separate pieces give people more choice about what to take, and how much.

How much chicken should you cook?

Serving sizes   When serving chicken, figure on at least a quarter to a half of a chicken per person, or about 350 grams (3/4 of a pound). For example, if you had six people, you would want to buy at least two broilers, cut up into quarters. Or you might get three broilers cut up into halves. If you were buying pieces, you would want about 2.25 kilograms (5 pounds). Don't be afraid to buy a little extra, by the way. Leftover barbecued chicken is delicious the next day—either warmed up or served cold.

Storing chicken   When you get the chicken home from the store, loosen the wrapping and store the chicken in the coldest part of the refrigerator. You can keep it this way for up to two days. If you plan to store it longer before cooking it, rewrap it in foil, plastic wrap, plastic bags, or moistureproof freezer wrap. Chicken can be frozen in these wrappings and stored for as long as a year. Some people like to keep chicken and other broilable meats on hand in the freezer. That

way, they can have a cookout whenever the weather is nice and the mood strikes them. If you have the right equipment on hand, you can have the fire going and be ready to cook outdoors in as little as half an hour.

Charcoal grilling

Cooking equipment   Here are some of the things you should have ready before you start your cookout.

charcoal grill or fire pit
charcoal or charcoal briquets
  (bri **KETS**)
starter fluid (or other means of
  lighting charcoal)
tongs
aluminum foil
pastry brush
paper towels

hot pads or oven mitts
barbecue sauce
salt, pepper, catsup, and other
  condiments (A **condiment** is
  any sauce, relish, or spice
  used to season food.)
water pistol (to put out flare-
  ups)

Serving equipment   You'll also need various serving dishes.

two platters or serving dishes—one to hold the uncooked chicken and one for the cooked chicken

serving dishes for vegetables and other foods

serving spoons and forks for the various foods

In addition, you'll need dishes, glasses, napkins, and silverware for the people who are eating. Paper plates and cups make clean-up easier. Keep a couple of grocery bags handy for trash. They can be used for bones and other garbage, too.

If you use paper plates, be sure they're strong enough to hold the food without bending. Or you can get metal or wicker plates that go underneath paper plates to give them support.

condiment (KAHN də mənt)

You can easily carry serving and eating equipment outdoors on large trays.

Finally, have a couple of large trays handy to put everything on. This will save you several trips back and forth to the kitchen. If you don't have a tray, use a large baking sheet or the top of a fold-up "TV" table. You may want to use this kind of table anyway. Set it up in the yard and use it to hold the things you need to have close at hand while you cook and serve the food.

Kinds of grills There are many kinds of charcoal grill designs. Portable metal grills vary from small, rectangular, fold-up models to large round grills mounted on wheels so they can be moved around easily. Some people have a brick fireplace or barbecue pit in their yard. For a makeshift barbecue, you can use a shallow hole in the ground. Surround it with bricks or stones and place an old rack from an oven over the top to hold the food. Whatever kind of grill you use, you may find it helpful to line the bottom with a double thickness of aluminum foil before you put the charcoal in. This reflects the heat upward and makes clean-up of ashes and drippings much easier.

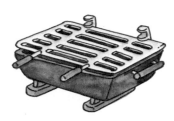

hibachi

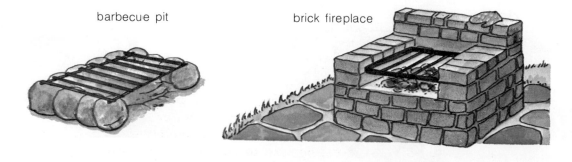

barbecue pit

brick fireplace

When should you start the fire?

Starting the fire A charcoal fire takes 30 minutes to an hour to reach the proper heat for cooking. The fire should be started well ahead of time. While the fire is catching, you can get together the other things that you will need. However, be sure that you, or someone else, will be able to check on the fire. You should never leave an open fire unwatched.

How much charcoal do you need for a good fire?

Many people use more charcoal than they really need. Then, when it all gets burning, they have a fire that is too hot to handle. To measure how much you need, first pour the charcoal onto the bottom of your grill and spread it out. If you are using briquets—the most common form of charcoal, shaped like small bricks—spread them out until there is a little space around each briquet. Spread the briquets all the way out to the edge of the grill.

Now heap the briquets into a pyramid-shaped pile. They'll catch fire better this way than if they're spread out. Use tongs to move them around. If you're using charcoal starter fluid, squirt it over the top of the pile and let it soak in. Add enough fluid so that some of the briquets get completely soaked and stay shiny with fluid. Let the fluid soak in for about 5 minutes. Then light the briquets, touching a match to each side of the pile. Do not add more fluid once the fire has started to burn. If you do, one of two things may happen. The fire may flare up immediately and perhaps even set the can of fluid on fire. Or it may not catch fire right away. In this case it will smolder with a white, smokelike vapor. When this vapor catches fire, it all burns instantly, in a kind of explosion that can singe eyebrows and set hair on fire.

After about 30 minutes, spread out the pile of burning coals with the tongs. The coals will be ready for cooking when they've turned from black to gray, in the daylight, or when they glow red at night.

You can also use an electric starter to light the charcoal. This device has a loop of metal that gets red hot when you plug it in. Simply lay the loop on top of the charcoal or bury it in the pile. After 10 or 15 minutes, unplug it and take it out. Be sure to set it down where it can cool off safely.

If you don't have starter fluid or an electric starter, you can build a small wood fire with paper and kindling and add charcoal briquets one at a time as the fire burns. Don't add too many too quickly, or they may smother the fire before they're lit.

When the coals are spread out and burning nicely, you're ready to start cooking.

Safety tips Your grill should be set up in a cleared space away from dry grass, brush, or trees. When you're finished cooking, you can let the fire burn itself out in the grill, if you're there to watch it. But if you have to leave, be sure to put the fire out first. One way to do this is to smother it with dirt or sand. Or you can scoop the coals into

When grilling indoors, why is it important to cook in a well-ventilated area?

a bucket of water. Use a garden trowel or small shovel to do this. Do not pour the water over them. This would cause them to sputter and make a shower of ashes, steam, and drops of hot water.

Indoors, charcoal should be used *only* in a fireplace with a chimney to take away the smoke, or in a very well-ventilated area. Burning charcoal makes a smoldering fire that produces carbon monoxide. As you probably know, **carbon monoxide** is a poisonous gas. It can be very dangerous in a closed area. It's the same as when a car engine is left running in a closed garage. Outside, where there is lots of air, this is not a problem. But inside, it can be very dangerous.

Grilling meats

Cooking chicken For chicken, place the grate of the charcoal grill about 10 to 15 centimeters (4 to 6 inches) above the coals. If you are cooking halves or quarters, start them out with the skin side up. **Baste** (moisten) each piece with salad oil or barbecue sauce, using a spoon or a pastry brush. Chicken can also be cooked plain, but oil or barbecue sauce helps keep it moist. Barbecue sauce also adds its own special flavor. You can buy a bottled barbecue sauce or make your own, by mixing two parts of Italian dressing with one part of catsup.

If you want an extra-special taste, you can marinate the chicken for an hour or more ahead of time. To **marinate** means to let food stand in a **marinade**—a liquid used to flavor, and sometimes tenderize, the

carbon monoxide (KAHR bən   mə NAHK sīd)
baste (BĀST)   **marinate** (MAR ə nāt)   **marinade** (MAR ə nād)

food. A good marinade for chicken is a mixture of soy sauce, white vinegar, sugar, and garlic. You can also baste the chicken with the marinade while it is cooking.

Cook the chicken slowly, turning and basting every 5 to 10 minutes, until it's tender. This should take 30 to 60 minutes. When chicken is done, it can be pierced with a fork with just medium pressure. The meat will pull away from the bone easily. It should be a toasty brown all over.

Occasionally, oil may drip down from the meat to the coals and catch fire. These flare-ups can burn the meat. To put them out, use your water pistol to squirt a little water on the coals underneath the flame. If you don't have a water pistol, a plastic squeeze bottle or pump spray bottle will also work.

Cooking red meats   Flare-ups are a common problem with beef, pork, and lamb, which have more fat than chicken. The fat melts during cooking and drips down onto the coals. In preparing these meats for the grill, it's a good idea to trim off excess fat. Leave about 1 centimeter (roughly half an inch) around the edge. Then cut gashes in this fat, and in any skin or rind around the outside of the meat, about 2 centimeters (1 inch) apart. When steaks and chops cook, they tend to curl up. Cutting gashes around the outside lets them lie flat again.

214

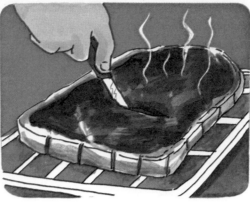

To cook the meat, place it on the grill about 7 centimeters (3 inches) above the coals. Baste it with barbecue sauce to give it extra flavor and juiciness. You can make a flavorful sauce by mixing 30 milliliters (2 tablespoons) of melted butter or margarine with 30 milliliters (2 tablespoons) of Worcestershire sauce.

How do you know when the meat is done?

Steaks and chops should be broiled until they're brown on both sides and the fat around the edge begins to have a golden look. Pork should be cooked until it's white all the way through.

Thick pieces of meat should be cooked slowly and turned often, or they may dry out and burn on the outside before they're done in the

Put the ingredients for kabobs in separate bowls so that everyone can make their own.

center. You can reduce the heat, if necessary, by raising the grate higher above the coals. To check doneness of thick pieces of meat, make a small cut in the middle and check the color.

Grilling skewered meats Another way to cook thick pieces of meat is to cut them into chunks and make kabobs. In Turkish tradition, the meat is lamb, but beef does just as well. Kabobs are handy, because you can put the whole meal on the skewer at one time, including vegetables—pieces of onion, tomato, green pepper, and even potatoes. This makes a colorful "meal on a stick." Your kabobs will be juicier and more flavorful if you marinate them ahead of time. Use the same soy-vinegar-sugar-garlic marinade that you would use for chicken, or try a French or Italian dressing.

Other ways to use a grill

Cooking foods in foil If you don't want to spend much time watching the grill, you can cook meat and other foods in foil. For instance, chicken can be grilled in foil. (See the recipe on page 216.) Many recipe books and camping guides have taste-tempting combinations of meat, vegetables, and seasonings steamed together in foil over a charcoal fire. Foil is useful in cooking many foods outdoors, with or without meat.

Many vegetables can be wrapped in foil and cooked over a charcoal fire. You can cook the corn this way. First, husk the corn, brush it with butter, and wrap each ear in a double layer of foil. Seal the

Preparing chicken for grilling.

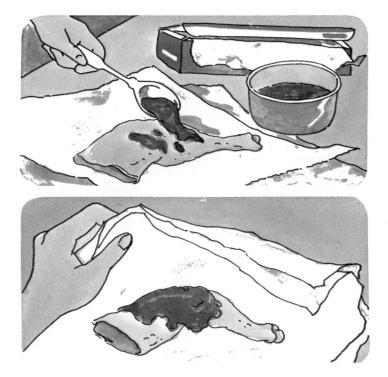

Chicken bundles

4 servings

| 1 broiler-fryer chicken, cut into quarters |
| 1 onion, sliced |
| barbecue sauce |

Place each chicken quarter on a double-thick square of foil.

Season the chicken, and spoon on barbecue sauce. Top with the onion slices.

Bring the foil up over the chicken, and seal the top and sides with a double fold.

Place the packages on the coals and cook about 45 minutes.

edges with a double fold. Place the corn on the grill or underneath, around the edges of the coals. The corn will take 10 or 15 minutes to cook.

You can also roast corn in the husks instead of foil. First, peel back the husks and remove the silk with a vegetable brush. Replace the husks and tie the ends together with a wire twist-tie. Soak the corn in cold water for half an hour before roasting it.

You can also roast potatoes in foil, the same way you do corn. Wrap unpeeled medium potatoes in foil and cook them on the grill or next to the coals, turning them now and then with the tongs. They will take about 30 minutes to an hour to cook. Check doneness by piercing them through the foil with a meat fork.

You can cook many other vegetables in foil, whether they're whole or cut up into pieces. However, foods cooked in foil do not have the roasted flavor of those that are exposed directly to the charcoal. They taste about the same as those that are cooked in the kitchen. There-

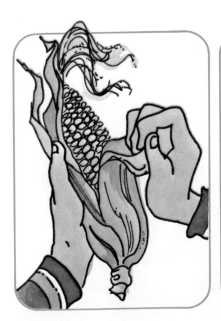

To prepare ears of corn for roasting in the husks, first loosen the husks and remove the silk. Then tie the husks and soak the ears.

fore, if space on your grill is limited, save it for meats and other foods that will get the special charcoal-broiled flavor. Cook your other foods in the kitchen.

Grilling skewered fruits and vegetables Many fruits and vegetables can be cooked on skewers, where they get the special flavor of charcoal. Firm vegetables such as potatoes, whole onions, yams, and sweet potatoes should be parboiled before being cooked this way. To **parboil** a food means to **par**tially cook it by **boil**ing. This helps the food get cooked all the way through. Otherwise, when you broil it, it might dry out and burn on the outside before it gets done in the center. Here are just a few of the ways you can cook fruits and vegetables on a skewer.

Cut unpeeled apples into quarters. Roll them in melted butter and sprinkle with brown sugar. Skewer and cook until they're fork tender. Turn once for even cooking.

Cut peeled bananas into 2-centimeter (1-inch) pieces. Skewer and dip into melted butter. Brown them on the grill and then roll them in chopped almonds.

parboil (PAHR boil)

Above: Try some of these kabob suggestions, or put together your own creative combinations. From left to right, apple kabobs, buttered potatoes, zucchini slices and tomatoes, and pineapple chunks with bacon.

Below: Ingredients for a good time: good friends, a sunny day, and a meal outdoors!

Dip orange or tangerine sections into butter and broil lightly. Serve with chicken or pork, or as a dessert.

Skewer pineapple chunks with squares of bacon between the chunks. Broil until the bacon is crisp.

Dip pieces of parboiled potatoes into butter and broil until brown. Sprinkle with minced parsley or dill.

Cut parboiled yams or sweet potatoes into cubes and skewer with chunks of pineapple. Brush with melted butter before broiling.

Cut 2-centimeter (1-inch) slices of small zucchini squash and marinate them in French dressing. Skewer and broil until tender. You can put cherry tomatoes and pieces of green pepper and onion on the same skewer.

Many cookbooks have recipes for other delicious charcoal-broiled specialties. Once you have a little experience cooking with charcoal, you'll find them easy to prepare. Then you can experiment with new combinations and sauces of your own.

Words to understand

condiment
carbon monoxide
baste

marinate
marinade
parboil

Food and equipment to know

kabob
broiler-fryer
roaster
hen
barbecue sauce

skewer
charcoal grill

barbecue pit
charcoal briquet
starter fluid
pastry brush
electric starter
tongs

Questions to discuss

1. What extra planning do you have to do for a cookout?
2. List ten foods that are suitable for cooking on a grill.
3. What are four good ways to cook a broiler-fryer chicken? What's the best way to cook a roaster? How should a hen be cooked?

4. Which kind of chicken would you buy if you needed a lot of chicken meat, such as for a chicken salad?

5. Why is it a good idea to use small pieces of chicken for a barbecue?

6. How much chicken would you buy to feed eight people?

7. Why is it dangerous to use a charcoal grill in the house?

8. Describe how you would start a charcoal fire. Why is it dangerous to add starter fluid after the fire has started burning?

9. How do you know when the coals are ready for cooking?

10. Why are foods cooked on a barbecue grill often basted?

11. What causes a charcoal fire to flare up during cooking? How can you control flare-ups?

12. How can you control the cooking temperature when you're charcoal broiling food? Should a thick piece of meat be cooked closer to the coals than a thin piece or farther away? Why?

13. Why should some foods be parboiled before they're cooked on a grill?

Things to do

1. Make a bulletin board on foods for a cookout. You might make a "fire" and a "grill" from colored construction paper. Draw, or cut from magazines, pictures of food that are good for cooking out.

2. Go to a supermarket and make a list of all the different ways chicken is sold. (Don't forget canned and frozen products!) Be sure to write down the unit prices, too. Which way (or ways) offered the best buy? Were there any of the other forms that you might choose for a special purpose? Explain your answers.

3. Make a time schedule for yourself, pretending you're going to prepare and serve the menu suggested on page 206. Be sure to include time for starting the fire!

4. Practice cutting up a whole chicken into pieces. (Ask a butcher, your teacher, a parent, or some other experienced adult for help.) Then demonstrate the cutting techniques to your class.

5. Make a poster showing the different kinds of barbecue equipment you might use.

6. Make a poster on barbecue safety. Show where you should put a fire and where you should not, how you should handle starter fluid, why you should not leave the fire unwatched, how to put the fire out, and how to avoid burns by using tongs and hot pads.

7. Ask three or more friends or relatives to describe their favorite barbecue sauce/marinade. Add these to your recipe collection. Be sure to include what foods are best prepared with each sauce.

8. You've probably heard TV commercials for barbecue sauces, steak sauces, or salad dressings that can be used as a marinade. Choose your favorite sauce recipe and write a commercial describing the taste of your sauce and explaining the advantages of using it.

9. Invent a foil dinner recipe. Use a piece of chicken or start with a hamburger patty. What vegetables could you add? What seasonings? What kind of sauce?

Careers to consider

Would you like to raise livestock, poultry, or fish?

If you like the out-of-doors and enjoy being around animals, consider a career raising animals for food.

Life on a ranch or farm has become very appealing to many people who are tired of the congestion and expense of city living. Most people who raise livestock or poultry grew up in the country and learned much about the business from experience. Many go on to college and major in agriculture to learn more about handling animal production smoothly and economically.

It's not easy to get started in ranching or farming. However, there are special low-interest loans and expert assistance available from the federal government to help people get started and stay in business. Or you might find a job on an established ranch or farm. Large ranches or farms need many **ranch/farm hands** to help in breeding, feeding, and caring for the livestock or poultry. This kind of work is sometimes called "animal husbandry." **Farm managers** are experts in handling the business and financial aspects of ranching or farming.

A farm or ranch may use the services of many kinds of specialists. Certainly a **veterinarian** (animal doctor) will be needed from time to time. **Microbiologists** and **parasitologists** are scientists who often study the diseases of animals. Other kinds of animal scientists include **zoologists** (who study animals in general) and **geneticists**, who specialize in improving species through breeding programs.

Not all farming is on land, however. "Fish farms" are farms made up of ponds, lakes, or sectioned-off areas of larger bodies of water. Here, fish or shellfish are bred and raised scientifically. Fish farming is a fast-growing industry. **Ichthyologists** and **marine biologists** are specialists in the study of fish and sea life.

11

HAS THIS EVER HAPPENED TO YOU?

Jerry wants to plan a surprise party for his parents' wedding anniversary. His brother thinks it's a great idea. But they soon realize they're going to have some problems.

JERRY: *The real problem is going to be getting everything done without Mom and Dad finding out about it.*

JEFF: *No, the real problem is going to be baking the cake without them finding out— mainly, because we don't know how to bake a cake!*

JERRY: *The problem is figuring what else to do at the party. We can't just give everybody a piece of cake and say, "Nice to see you— goodbye!"*

JEFF: *Maybe we could play some music from back when they were young. But where can we get records that old?*

JERRY: *We've also got to figure out what to say on the invitations, how many people to invite, where to put everybody, what to eat besides cake, where to get enough dishes, how much it's going to cost us, and where we're going to get the money!*

JEFF: *You know, the real problem isn't Mom and Dad finding out what we're doing. The problem is going to be us finding out what we're doing!*

222

PARTY TIME

If you've ever held a party at your house, you know there are a lot of details to take care of. Like most other things, a successful party takes careful planning.

Planning a party

It's hard to think of everything you need to do. It helps if you talk it over with someone else, and write down all the questions you can think of about the kind of party you want to have. One of the first things to decide is how many people you want to invite. Since this determines the size of your party, it affects all of your other decisions.

When you have all your questions asked, you can start finding out the answers.

Here's one question: What should you put on the invitations?

Invitations Any invitation—whether written or spoken, in person or on the telephone—should let people know when and where the party is to be held. Include the date and time, and be sure people have your name, address, and telephone number. If your house is hard to find, give directions. You might even make a simple map.

On a written invitation, it's a good idea to include the abbreviation **R.S.V.P.** at the bottom. This stands for *Répondez, s'il vous plaît* (rā PŌN dā, SĒL VOO PLĀ), which is French for "Respond, if you please"—or simply, "Please let me know if you can come." This will tell you how many people to expect, so that you can plan your party better.

If it's a special kind of party, mention that in your invitation. For example, it might be a birthday party, a Valentine's Day party, a Halloween party, or a New Year's Eve party. People also give parties to celebrate anniversaries, engagements, graduations, and other special occasions.

Your invitation can be plain or fancy. A simple handwritten note will do fine. If you feel creative, you might make a clever card with your own design and colors. Or you can buy printed invitations at a stationery store. Be sure to add any special information. For instance, if the party will include dinner, say so on the invitation. Then the guests will know not to eat beforehand. Let them know if it's to be a dress-up party. If it's to be a theme party, let them know what to wear and what to bring.

What's a theme party?

Theme parties A **theme party** is one that focuses on a central idea. For instance, a party with a "sailing" theme might have everyone dress as the crew or passengers on a yacht or cruise ship. Decorations could include cardboard portholes, travel posters, "deck chairs" (lawn furniture), fishing gear, life preservers, and so on.

A "shipwreck" party might have the theme that everyone is stranded on a desert island. Decorations might be cardboard palm

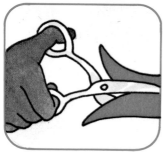

trees, pieces of driftwood, and so forth. Guests might bring some funny "prized possessions" with them that they managed to save from the sinking ship (a bird cage, a teddy bear, and so forth). For a party game, put all the items into a pile. Then have people guess who brought each one.

Here are some other ideas for themes.

The Good Old Days (1950s, Roaring Twenties, or Gay Nineties)

The Wild West

Come as You Are (dressed as you were when you got the invitation)

The World of Tomorrow (science fiction)

Teenagers of the Stone Age

Your own original idea

Entertainment   The kind of party you have, and the number of guests, will affect the kind of activity and entertainment you can plan. It's always nice to have music, whether it's on records, tapes, or the radio. If there is room, and you have a good floor for it, you might dance, too.

If you have country-and-western music, you might include a record with a square dance caller. A square dance or Virginia reel is a good way to get everyone dancing. However, you may have to brush up on the steps yourself and be ready to explain them to your guests beforehand.

For a quieter evening, you might have a game party. Card games or board games (such as Monopoly or Parcheesi) are a lot of fun. Word games and guessing games—such as Anagrams, Scrabble, Password, Twenty Questions, What's My Line? or To Tell the Truth—are popular at parties, too. Bookstores usually have a whole shelf of books with ideas for party games and entertainment.

If you like, you can give prizes to the winners of each game. Or make up first-place and second-place award medals with colored construction paper.

Space and equipment   The size of your party and the entertainment activities will affect the arrangements you need to make for space, furniture, utensils, and other necessities. Is there enough room for everyone to sit down? Do you have enough dishes? You might borrow things like records or games from your friends if there is something you need but don't have.

Give careful thought, also, to how you will serve the food, and to how people will eat it. It's easy to eat simple snacks like nuts or popcorn when you're sitting on the floor. But ice cream, cake, and a beverage would be hard to manage. A plate of food may be balanced on the lap, but it's hard to hold a glass at the same time.

Should you take the food around to everyone, or let them help themselves?

At a party, it's often easiest to put food and dishes out on a table and let people serve themselves. This is called **buffet style**. Instead of sitting at a dining table, guests take food with them to seats around the room.

The food at your party can range from a complete dinner to a few snacks or *hors d'oeuvres* (or DERVZ). These are small bits of food, or food spreads, usually served on crackers or small pieces of bread or toast. Cake is very popular at parties, too.

buffet (buh FĀ)

Punch and a variety of colorfully garnished sandwiches make an attractive buffet.

What's a birthday without a cake?

Making a cake

A cake is traditional at birthdays and weddings. It is popular at other special events, too, such as anniversaries, going-away parties, graduations, and Valentine parties. A cake can be decorated to suit almost any occasion. Cutting the cake is usually the high point of the party. It's an especially proud moment for you as the party-giver, if you make the cake yourself.

That's fine, if it's a cake you can be proud of. But how can you be sure it won't be a flop?

If you follow the recipe carefully, you can be pretty sure of a good result. If you want to make things simple and quick, there are many reliable cake mixes on the market. But most people think there is something special about a cake made "from scratch." The recipe for yellow cake on this page is dependable. Take a look at it.

Basic yellow cake

180 mL	**¾ cup butter or margarine**
375 mL	**1½ cups sugar**
	3 eggs
5 mL	**1 tsp vanilla**
560 mL	**2¼ cups cake flour, OR 500 mL (2 cups) all-purpose flour**
10 mL	**2 tsp baking powder**
2 mL	**½ tsp salt**
160 mL	**⅔ cup milk**

Cream the butter and sugar together in a large bowl, adding sugar gradually until thoroughly mixed. Add the eggs and vanilla and beat well.

Mix the dry ingredients with a fork in a separate bowl.

Add the dry ingredients and the milk to the creamed mixture in the following order, beating well after each addition: 1/3 of the dry ingredients, 1/2 of the milk, 1/3 of the dry ingredients, 1/2 of the milk, 1/3 of the dry ingredients. When all the ingredients are mixed, beat for one more minute.

Grease and flour two round baking pans measuring 23 cm (9 in) across and 4 cm (1½ in) deep. Pour in the cake batter.

Bake at 175 °C (350 °F) for 30 to 35 minutes.

Cool for 10 minutes. Remove the cakes from the pans. Cool thoroughly.

What is the difference between cake flour and all-purpose flour?

What if I don't have cake flour? Can I use regular flour?

Flour   Cake flour is a very soft flour that makes especially light, tender cakes. For this reason, many cake recipes call for it. However, you can substitute all-purpose flour. If you do, reduce the amount of flour by 1/8—or 12 milliliters for each 100 milliliters (2 tablespoons for every cup) of cake flour. For example, the yellow cake recipe calls for 560 milliliters (2¼ cups) of cake flour. If you use all-purpose flour, reduce this amount by 66 milliliters (a little over 4 tablespoons). The resulting amount of 494 milliliters is awkward to measure, though. It's all right to round it off to 500 milliliters of all-purpose flour.

What do you use to cream the butter and sugar together?

Mixing   You can cream the butter and sugar with an electric mixer, or with a mixing spoon or a large serving fork. Mash the sugar into the butter, pressing against the sides of the mixing bowl. This will be

easier to do if you cut the butter into pieces first and let it soften at room temperature for 30 minutes.

How much of the milk and dry ingredients should you put in at one time?

When you add the milk and dry ingredients, start with about a third of the dry ingredients. Stir and beat until they are thoroughly mixed into the butter mixture. Next, add about half the milk. Stir and beat again. Continue with a third of the flour, half the milk, and the final third of flour. It is important to begin and end with flour. If you don't, it will affect the texture of the cake.

What do you grease the pans with?

Filling the pan   Grease the cake pans with shortening, using a folded paper towel or napkin. Spread the shortening in a thin film over the bottom and sides of the pan. To **flour** the pans, sprinkle a spoonful of flour into each pan. Tilt the pan and tap it to make the flour fall across the greased surface. As it does so, a little will stick to the grease. Turn the pan upside down and tap it to get rid of the excess flour.

Some cooks prefer to line the bottom of each pan with waxed paper. This makes it easier to remove the cake from the pan. To do this, put the bottom of the cake pan on a sheet of waxed paper and draw around it. Cut out the circle and fit it into the bottom of the pan. Grease and flour only the sides of the pan.

When you pour the cake batter into the pans, you'll probably notice that it stays higher in the center than at the sides. It's a good idea to push the batter out toward the sides with a rubber spatula, leaving a slight dip in the center. This will fill in as the cake bakes.

The directions say to bake for 30 to 35 minutes. How do you know which time to use?

Baking   Bake the cake until it's done. When a cake is done, the sides will pull away slightly from the edges of the pan. The center should

spring back when you press it lightly with your finger. As an additional test, stick a toothpick deep into the center of the cake. It should come out clean, with no uncooked batter sticking to it.

How do you get the cake out of the pan? I baked a cake once, and it stuck. It fell apart when I tried to break it loose!

Removing cake from pan Your cake should come out of the pan in one piece if you follow the directions carefully. Cool each pan for 10 minutes on a cooling rack. The rack allows air to circulate under the bottom of the pan. Run a knife around the edge of the cake to be sure it has separated from the pan.

Next, place the cooling rack upside down on top of the cake. Flip the cake and rack over, together. Tap the bottom of the pan briskly all around with the handle of a knife. Pick the pan up (using hot pads) and jiggle it to break the cake loose.

If the cake does not come loose, try the steps again. As a last resort, turn the pan over again and pry the cake out with a plastic (or Teflon-coated) pancake turner.

If you use waxed paper to line the bottom of the cake pan, you should not have this problem. Run a knife around the edge, turn the cake out onto a cooling rack, and gently peel off the waxed paper.

When do you put the frosting on the cake?

Leave the cake on the cooling rack and let it cool thoroughly before frosting it. If it's warm, the frosting will get soft and runny. While the cake is cooling, you can make the frosting.

Creamy butter frosting

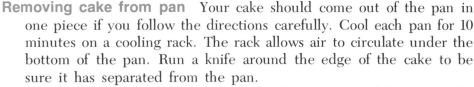

90 mL	**6 tbsp (¾ stick) butter or margarine**
.50 kg	**1 lb confectioners' sugar**
60 mL	**¼ cup milk**
7 mL	**1½ tsp vanilla**

Cream the butter in a medium-size mixing bowl, gradually adding about half the sugar. Blend well.

Beat in the vanilla and half of the milk.

Blend in the remaining sugar gradually.

Add just enough of the remaining milk to make the frosting easy to spread. It should be fairly stiff, not soft and runny.

Frosting the cake You will find recipes for many kinds of frosting in your cookbook. Some require cooking and some do not. The creamy butter frosting in the recipe on page 230 is good for icing cakes.

Before you spread the frosting on the cake, be sure to brush off any loose crumbs. Place the bottom layer upside down on the cake plate. With a knife or spatula, spread frosting over the top of the layer, almost to the edge.

Place the second layer right-side-up on top of the frosted layer. Frost the sides of the two layers next. Spread the frosting upward, from the bottom to the top. Be careful not to get crumbs on the knife or in the frosting! It can be very hard to get them out, or even to cover them up.

Finally, pile the rest of the frosting on top and spread it out to join the sides. Give the frosting some decorative swirls or dabs with the knife or spatula.

If you want, you can divide the frosting up into batches and add different food colors for the different parts of a cut-up cake.

What's a cut-up cake?

Special cake shapes A cut-up cake is one that is cut up into pieces; the pieces are then rearranged to make special shapes or designs. These cakes are excellent for theme parties. You can often create a shape that goes with the theme. For an anniversary party, you could have a "love-boat" theme, with the sailing decorations we discussed before. Instead of just a cake, you can serve—a sailboat!

SAILBOAT CAKE Start with a square cake, about 20 centimeters (8 inches) wide. Cut it across, from corner to corner, into two triangles. Cut off a strip along the base of one triangle, about 6 centimeters (2¼ inches) wide. Place the triangles on top of the strip. Spread butter cream frosting over the "sails." Frost the hull of the boat with red-colored butter frosting (use food coloring). Or use a chocolate frosting. Add candy portholes and a peppermint stick (or licorice stick) mast. If you want, fluff out the sails with a sprinkling of shredded coconut.

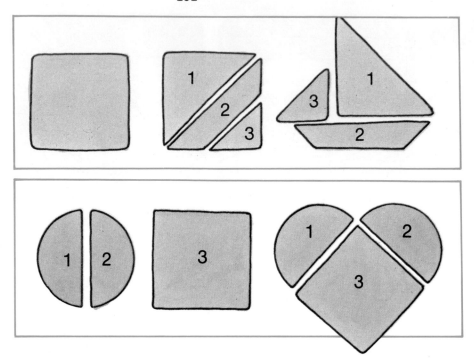

HEART-SHAPED CAKE If you prefer, you could have a valentine theme. Decorate with big red valentines cut out of construction paper, and twisted red and white crêpe-paper streamers. You can make a heart-shaped cake without using a heart-shaped cake pan. Bake two cake layers, one round and the other square. They should both be the same width. Cut the round piece in half and place the two parts along two touching sides of the square piece.

Orange-cream supreme punch

20-25 punch cup servings

.50 L	**1 pt vanilla ice cream**
1.50 L	**1½ qt orange juice**
1 L	**28-32 oz bottled lemon soda or club soda**

Scoop the ice cream into a punch bowl. Pour in the orange juice. Carefully add the soda—this makes a nice froth on top. Ladle into punch cups.

A cake is very useful in many ways. It can be the dessert for any of the meals you know how to cook now. It does fine at a picnic or barbecue party. Or it can be the food highlight of a party with snacks and *hors d'oeuvres*. See Chapter 3 for ideas for snacks at your party. You might also serve one of the beverages suggested there. Or, if you like, you can make up a fruit punch. Serve it in a large punch bowl, with individual cups or glasses.

Punch

Your cookbook probably has several punch ideas you can try. An easy but tasty one appears on this page.

The kind of party you have may suggest the kind of punch you want to serve. Hot cider would be good at Halloween; a cranberry punch would be appropriate around Thanksgiving; eggnog is tradi-

Try orange-cream supreme punch at your next party.

tional on New Year's Eve; cherry or raspberry punch would go well with the red colors of Valentine's Day. Don't be afraid to experiment with a secret formula of your own—but be sure to test it out on yourself, before you serve it to your guests!

When your food is prepared, and your arrangements have been made, and your invitations have been sent out, you've done all you can do ahead of time to make your party a success. But you aren't finished yet. As the host you have a few things to do *during* your party, too.

Directing the party

A **host** is a person (male or female) who greets, entertains, and takes care of guests. A good host can be very busy. Your first job is to greet your guests at the door when they arrive. Take their coats and show them into the room where the party is being held. Let them know you're genuinely glad they could come. Introduce them to your parents, if they haven't met them, and to any of the guests they don't know.

Who gets introduced first—and what should you say?

Introductions   Usually, you introduce a younger person to an older person, by speaking to the older person first: "Aunt Ellen, I'd like you to meet my friend, Nancy Brooks. Nancy, this is my aunt, Mrs. Butterworth."

Introduce a boy to a girl, and a man to a woman: "Alice, have you met Tom Winslow? Tom, this is Alice Harrison," or "Mrs. Cooper, I'd like you to meet Mr. Lowry. Mr. Lowry, this is Mrs. Cooper, our next-door neighbor."

If you're ever in the position of introducing someone to a very distinguished or honored person, you should address the more honored person first—that is, the person with the higher position or title: "Your Highness, may I present the ambassador from Antarctica, Dr. Penguin? Dr. Penguin, His Royal Highness, King Crab of Atlantis."

If you forget, or aren't sure, who should come first in the introduction, don't worry about it. The important thing at your party is that people meet each other in a relaxed and friendly atmosphere. Warmth and sincerity on your part are more important than formal correctness.

What if you're the person being introduced? What should you say?

When you are introduced to someone else, a simple "Hello," "How are you?" or "How do you do?" will be fine. "Hi!" is all right with young people your own age. Your host may help get you started on a conversation by telling you a little bit about each other: "Tom just moved here from Chicago," or "Judy is a volunteer candy-striper at the hospital. You won't believe some of the stories she has to tell!"

You don't have to wait to be introduced, especially if you're in a group that's all new to you. Introduce yourself by saying something like, "Hi! I don't think we've met. I'm Mary Jones. I just moved here."

Serving and other duties Between introductions and conversations, a host has to find time to take care of the food—to fill and refill the snack bowls, set out the buffet, serve the cake, and so forth. If you have a punch bowl, there should be someone to serve the punch—at first, anyway. Later in the evening, you can let guests serve themselves. There must be someone to take the dirty dishes and glasses out to the kitchen, to change the records on the record player, and to answer the telephone. (There is always someone calling about something—What should they bring? Will you mind if they're late? Is your apartment number 35 or 53?) You will also have to wipe up spills and take care of emergencies. (If he cuts his finger and she bumps her head, *you* have to go get the Band-Aids and the ice!)

Getting friends and parents to help Luckily you can get your friends to help you with many of these jobs. Look for things you can put them in charge of, such as the record player, the punch bowl, and the snack dishes. Your parents can help you with many things, too.

Speaking of parents, if it's a party for kids, do your parents have to be there all the time?

If it's a very large party, chances are you will *need* your parents' help. Also, at a large party, their presence is less noticeable. At a smaller party, you should introduce your friends to your parents when they arrive, and let your parents help you get things started. After that, you can probably manage on your own.

You might ask a friend to take charge of music for your party.

Of course, you and your friends should behave in a way that would not cause embarrassment if your parents walked in at any time. If you do, your parents can feel free to leave you to yourselves. They should stay in the house in case they're needed, but it will not be necessary for them to stay in the same room or to keep checking on you.

Directing activities Another job of the host is to try to get people to "mix" or "circulate"—to move around and meet different people and talk to them. At a teen-age party, chances are that everyone already knows everyone else. Still, little groups can form that stay unchanged all evening long. People usually enjoy themselves more at a party if they talk to a number of people instead of just one or two. This is one of the reasons for having party themes, games, and entertainment. It gets people talking and acting as a whole party instead of in little groups.

Directing these activities is one more important part you play at your party. You are the one who must set up the games, explain the dance steps, make up the teams, assign the parts, and so forth. All of this has to be done with an eye on the time, too. When should the food be served? How long should the game go on? Will there be time to dance? When should the party end?

There's one more thing you must do at your party. With all your other jobs, this may seem the hardest of all, but it's the most important: relax and enjoy it!

Words to understand

R.S.V.P.
theme party
buffet style

flouring (pan)
host

Food and equipment to know

hors d'oeuvre
cake flour
all-purpose flour
cut-up cake

cake pan
rubber spatula
punch bowl

Questions to discuss

1. What information should an invitation include?

2. How should you add the dry ingredients and milk to the creamed mixture when you're baking a cake from scratch?

3. How do you grease and flour cake pans? Explain how to make a waxed paper lining for the bottoms of the pans.

4. How can you tell when a cake is done?

5. How should a cake be cooled?

6. Describe the steps in frosting a two-layer cake.

7. Name five things you could do for entertainment at a party.

8. List five or more jobs of the host of a party.

Things to do

1. Make up three sample invitations: one for a casual get-together, one for a theme party, and one for a more formal party. (Look in an etiquette book for ideas on formal invitations.) Write a sample reply to a formal invitation.

2. Draw up a written plan for a surprise birthday party for someone. Make a list of all the arrangements you would have to make for invitations, food, entertainment, and so on.

3. Make a list of as many party theme ideas as you can think of (at least ten). Choose five of them. Describe how you might decorate the room for each party and what foods you might serve. What could you do for entertainment or activity at each type of party?

4. Collect five or more ideas for easy ways to decorate cakes. (Look in cookbooks and magazines for ideas. Make up your own, if you like.) Put the ideas in a party notebook, or file them with your recipe collection.

5. Practice making introductions. Present a demonstration to your class. Include the following situations: a new boy and another boy in class; a boy and a girl; a girl friend and your mother; a parent and a teacher; a neighbor and an aunt or uncle. How would you introduce yourself to someone?

Careers to consider

Would you like to be your own boss?

If you like to make your own decisions and don't mind taking a few chances, consider going into business for yourself.

Food products offer many opportunities for small businesses. Although supermarkets have replaced some of the small grocery stores of years ago, neighborhood delicatessens, specialty shops, and "quick-shop" stores still thrive. Many small restaurants and lunch counters start up each year. Small neighborhood bakeries often compete successfully with large baking companies. They can sell strictly fresh delicacies that are hard to bake, pack, and ship in large quantities. Roadside fruit and vegetable stands often succeed, too, by selling produce that is picked fresh daily. Supermarkets can't do this.

Small catering businesses can operate on very low overhead, or fixed expenses. They don't need a store, they don't have to keep large supplies of food on hand, and they need only part-time help.

Some food businesses are sold on a franchise basis. A large company with a well-advertised name sets up a restaurant, trains the workers, and supplies the food ingredients. The owner buys the whole operation and runs it as part of the chain. Fast-food restaurants, ice cream parlors, and hotdog stands are often run on this basis. The price of a franchise may vary greatly—from the cost of a pushcart for hotdogs to $100,000 or more for a sizable restaurant.

A college education is not necessary to go into business for yourself, but it often helps. A few business courses such as accounting, marketing, business law, and insurance are a help to the small businessperson. Even more important, however, is experience in the particular business that interests you.

People in the food business have to know how to buy good quality food in the right quantities for their needs. They must know how to store it, prepare it for sale, and display it so that it looks appealing. They have to meet public health standards for cleanliness and food handling practices. They usually work long hours and often find it hard to get away for holidays and vacations. However, most people in business for themselves will tell you they wouldn't have it any other way!

12

HAS THIS EVER HAPPENED TO YOU?

Donna's social studies class is reading about the Pilgrims. As a special project, she wants to cook a traditional Thanksgiving meal, as close as possible to what the Pilgrims ate. But she's running into problems.

DONNA: *I want it really traditional, Mom—with turkey, gravy, dressing, cranberry sauce, mashed potatoes, rolls, and pumpkin pie. I can make it all just the way the Pilgrims did, if you'll let me do the cooking in the fireplace.*

MOTHER: *It's out of the question, Donna. It would ruin all our pots and pans. And we'd never get all those things cooked and ready to serve at the same time.*

She runs into trouble with her menu, too. Her friend Ginny helps her do some research in the library.

GINNY: *It says here that the Pilgrims didn't have any sugar. How can you make a pie without sugar?*

DONNA: *And this book says their first wheat crops failed, so they used cornmeal. How can I make a piecrust and stuff a turkey with cornmeal?*

GINNY: *That's easy. The tough part is going to be catching the turkey. The turkey we eat today comes from one developed by the Aztecs in Mexico. It isn't the wild turkey the Pilgrims ate. And potatoes were developed by the Incas in Peru. The Pilgrims never even saw one!*

DONNA: *That does it! Sorry, Pilgrims, I give up! Boy, I bet they'd be mad if they could see how much their traditional meal got changed!*

A HOLIDAY MEAL

Exploring . . .

How to buy and prepare foods for a turkey dinner

How to work with yeast and pastry doughs

Time management in preparing a meal

Kitchen cleanup and storing leftovers

If you've ever tried to cook something exactly the way it was done in the past, you know that food can change a lot from one time to another. It can change from one place to another, also. In Chapter 2, we talked about the way people's food habits are influenced by climate, geography, and local growing conditions. This applies to their food traditions, too. They may change because new foods and cooking equipment become available, or because old ones are no longer available, or for both reasons.

But if you change the food, how can it still be a tradition?

The important thing about a food tradition is not always that the same food is eaten year after year without any change. The most important thing is that the food brings to mind certain ideas or memories. The food can go through changes, and often does. But if the idea lives on, the tradition lives on.

Thanksgiving dinner is an American tradition that has grown, along with the country. From simple beginnings, the meal has added new

A Thanksgiving feast

foods—just as America has added new lands, new people, and new food resources. If the Pilgrims had had a choice, they might have made the first Thanksgiving feast like the feasts they had in England. They would probably have included such dishes as roast goose, blood pudding, lentil porridge, and sweet buttered buns. But these foods weren't available. Instead, they ate wild turkey, pumpkin, squash, and corn—new foods they found in the New World. We've continued to add new foods to the meal as they've become available.

While the foods have changed somewhat, the basic tradition of Thanksgiving has not. It is still a time when American families and friends get together to give thanks for their blessings of food, health, and freedom. Today's Thanksgiving feast may include many different foods, depending on what each family likes. It tends to be a large meal, because of the number of dishes being served and because there are likely to be extra people eating.

Here's a menu you might find in many American homes.

turkey and dressing	relishes
giblet gravy	rolls and butter/margarine
mashed potatoes	pumpkin pie
green beans with butter sauce	milk, tea, coffee
cranberry sauce	

With all that stuff, Thanksgiving should be a three-day holiday— one day to cook it, one day to eat it, and one day to wash all the dishes!

Preparing and serving a holiday meal may look like an overwhelming job if you've never done it before. But if you look at each little part of the meal by itself, you'll see there's nothing that's very hard to do. The key to handling a large meal like this is *organization*. Careful planning is a must! This means thinking through each task, figuring out what to do and when to do it. It will help a lot if your kitchen is organized, too. This can save you time and steps, at moments when you can really use them.

The first step in your planning is to find out what you need to know before you tackle this meal. How should you shop for each food? How much should you buy? How long will it take to prepare each dish? How should each food be cooked? What can be done ahead of time? How do you plan everything to make sure all the dishes are ready at the right time? (This is one of the hardest things for beginning cooks, but it's no trick if you plan carefully.)

First, let's take a look at what you need to know to handle each dish on the menu.

Fixing the turkey

Buying the turkey When you go shopping for a turkey, you will find that you have quite a variety to choose from. Turkeys range in size from 2 to 12 kilograms (4 to 24 pounds), or even larger. Smaller birds may be a bit more tender than large ones. On the other hand, large turkeys have more meat in relation to bone.

You can buy a whole turkey or just turkey parts. How do you decide how much to buy?

How big a turkey should you buy?

The size of the turkey you should buy depends on how many people will be eating it, how much you think each person might eat, and whether or not you want to have leftovers.

For smaller turkeys—less than 6 kilograms (12 pounds)—plan on about half a kilogram (1 pound) per serving. With larger turkeys—over 6 kilograms (12 pounds)—plan on about 350 grams (about 3/4 pound) per person. If you want leftovers for sandwiches, salads, or casseroles, buy a larger turkey than you need for one meal.

Turkeys may be sold fresh or frozen. You can also buy turkey parts, such as legs or wings, and boneless turkey roasts. These are good for times when you don't want a whole turkey.

You can keep a fresh turkey in the refrigerator for two or three days. If you aren't going to use it in that time, freeze it as soon as you get home from the store. You can freeze it in its original plastic wrapping. (If it is wrapped in butcher paper, it should be rewrapped in moistureproof freezer paper, foil, or plastic wrap.)

Thawing a frozen bird To thaw a frozen turkey, put it in the refrigerator, on a tray to catch any leaking juices. You can leave the turkey in its wrapping. A small turkey will take a day or two to thaw in the refrigerator. A larger bird may take two to three days.

You can speed up thawing by using the cold-water method. Place the turkey in the sink (in its plastic wrapping) and cover it with cold water. Change the water now and then to speed the thawing time even more. A small turkey will thaw in three to six hours using this method. A larger turkey may take up to ten hours.

Why can't I just thaw the turkey out in the open?

The problem with thawing the turkey outside the refrigerator is that the surface of the turkey warms up while the inside is still frozen. During the thawing, the surface may soon reach a nice, cozy temperature for fast growth of microbes. This risk is less with the cold-water method because the turkey thaws quickly while you're keeping the surface cold. Even when the turkey is thawed in water, it should be cooked as soon as possible, or put immediately into the refrigerator.

When should you stuff the turkey?

Stuffing   Don't stuff the turkey until just before you put it in the oven. Or don't stuff it at all. It's easier to cook dressing separately, in a greased casserole dish. Put the dish in the oven with the turkey for the last 30 to 45 minutes of cooking. Although many families follow the tradition of stuffing the dressing into the bird, there are advantages to cooking it separately. The turkey cooks faster this way, by about half an hour. Also, it's easier and safer. The warm, dark cavity inside a cooked turkey is just the kind of place germs like. If you do stuff your turkey, wait until just before you put the turkey in the oven. And be sure to remove all the stuffing as soon as it is cooked. *Never* store leftover stuffing inside the turkey.

You can buy prepared stuffing mixes, or you can make your own. Stuffings are easy to make, usually simple combinations of bread crumbs, seasonings, and sometimes onion and celery.

Okay, that takes care of the dressing. Now, how do you cook the turkey?

Turkeys are usually roasted whole in the oven. To **roast** means to cook by dry heat, usually in an oven. It's the same as baking, but the word "roast" is used with meats or poultry cooked in an open pan.

Preparing the turkey for the oven   To get your turkey ready for the oven, first remove the small package you'll find inside the body cavity. This package contains the giblets (JIB litz)—the liver, heart, and gizzard, or stomach. The neck is also usually included in the giblet package. Rinse the turkey inside and out with running water and let it drain. Lay the turkey on its back and lift the wings up toward the neck; then twist them downward and fold them under the back. This keeps the wings flat and helps keep the bird from rolling. It also makes carving easier, later on, since the wings are folded out of the way.

Now stretch the neck skin up over the neck cavity and around to the back. Slide the skin underneath the wings and hold it to the back that way, if you can. You may need to fasten the neck skin to the back with small skewers.

Close the body cavity at the other end of the turkey by folding the skin tightly over the opening. Now push the drumsticks under the band of skin at the tail. This keeps them in close to the body, and helps hold the skin in place over the body cavity. With some birds, you may have to tie the legs and tail together with string. You may also have to hold the skin in place over the body cavity with skewers.

Next rub the skin with shortening, margarine, or salad oil. Stick a meat thermometer deep into the thigh, next to the body. Be careful not to let it touch a bone. (The bone gets hot faster than the meat and could throw off your temperature reading.)

Roasting the turkey   Put the turkey breast-side up into an open roasting pan. Cook it in the oven at 165 °C (325 °F). It will usually take about 45 to 55 minutes per kilogram (20 to 25 minutes per pound) for most turkeys.

When the turkey turns a golden color, cover it loosely with foil to help keep it from drying out. During the last hour of roasting, remove the foil and start checking for doneness.

How do you know when a turkey's done?

When the turkey is done, the drumstick will move easily up and down. The thick part of the drumstick will feel soft when you pinch it. (Be sure to protect your fingers with folded paper towels for the pinch test!) The meat thermometer should read about 90 °C (about 190 °F).

During the last half hour of cooking, use a cooking spoon or pastry brush to baste the turkey with pan drippings, cooking oil, or melted margarine. This gives it a juicy-looking shine. When the bird is done, remove it from the oven and let it cool. It will be easier to carve if it sits for 15 to 30 minutes before serving.

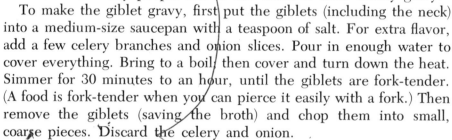

Fixing "all the trimmings"

Giblet gravy Gravy is a thickened sauce made with the drippings from meat—or poultry, in this case. The giblets are so flavorful and full of nutrition that many people like to use them in their turkey gravy.

To make the giblet gravy, first put the giblets (including the neck) into a medium-size saucepan with a teaspoon of salt. For extra flavor, add a few celery branches and onion slices. Pour in enough water to cover everything. Bring to a boil, then cover and turn down the heat. Simmer for 30 minutes to an hour, until the giblets are fork-tender. (A food is fork-tender when you can pierce it easily with a fork.) Then remove the giblets (saving the broth) and chop them into small, coarse pieces. Discard the celery and onion.

When the turkey has finished cooking, transfer it carefully to a platter. Pour the drippings from the roasting pan into a large liquid measuring cup. Let the drippings settle until the fat floats to the top. Skim off 60 milliliters (4 tablespoons, or 1/4 cup) of fat from the top of the drippings. Put this fat into a medium-size saucepan. Skim off the rest of the fat and discard it.

Now add 60 milliliters (1/4 cup) of water to the roasting pan and scrape the pan until all the brown pieces are loosened. Pour this mixture of drippings and water into the measuring cup. Add the broth that you saved from the giblets. Add extra water, if necessary, to make a total of 500 milliliters (2 cups) of liquid.

Place the saucepan containing the fat over medium heat. Stir 60 milliliters (1/4 cup) of flour into the fat until it is thoroughly blended. Gradually pour in the mixture of broth and drippings. Stir constantly and cook until the gravy is smooth and as thick as you want it. (If it gets too thick, add a little more water.) Add the chopped giblets, and salt and pepper to taste. If you don't want to use the giblets, you can make the gravy without them. Use plain water (or milk, if you prefer) instead of the giblet broth.

What do you do if the gravy gets lumps in it?

Lumps form when some of the starch in the flour doesn't get thoroughly mixed into the fat and the liquid. It's the same kind of problem as in making hot cereal. Even with constant stirring, lumps sometimes occur. There's another way to mix gravy that you may find easier. In this method, you first stir the flour and some *cold* water together thoroughly. Add the rest of the liquid you are using, and stir the whole mixture into the fat you put into the saucepan. Cook and stir until the gravy is nice and thick—the perfect topping for creamy mashed potatoes.

How do you make mashed potatoes so they're creamy—not too stiff and not too runny—and don't have any lumps in them?

Mashed potatoes There really isn't anything tricky about making mashed potatoes. To serve six people, peel six medium-size potatoes (or four large ones, or eight to ten small ones). Put them into a large saucepan in 4 centimeters (about 1½ inches) of water. Add 5 milliliters (1 teaspoon) of salt; bring to a boil over medium heat. Cover and cook for 15 to 20 minutes, or until fork-tender. If you're in a hurry, cut the potatoes into 2- to 5-centimeter (1- to 2-inch) pieces to make them cook faster.

Remove the pan from the heat. Drain off the water. Add 60 milliliters (1/4 cup) of butter or margarine. Mash the potatoes with a potato masher or electric mixer, using low speed. Gradually add 60 to 125 milliliters (1/4 to 1/2 cup) of warm milk and continue mashing until the potatoes are smooth and moist. Add salt and pepper to taste.

Mashed potatoes will be too stiff if they don't have enough milk added to them. They will be too runny if they have too much milk— so add the milk a little at a time. They will be lumpy if they aren't mashed long enough, or if the potatoes aren't thoroughly cooked. Undercooking leaves small pieces of hard, uncooked potato that cannot be mashed. On the other hand, you don't want to overcook them, either. This will make them mushy and watery.

Overcooking can be even more of a problem with the green beans. They should be cooked just to the point where they are tender, and no more.

How long does it take to cook green beans? And how do I tell when they're just right?

Green beans There's no doubt that canned green beans are the fastest to cook. They need only simple heating. But for a brighter green color and fresher flavor and texture, use fresh or frozen green beans. They take only minutes to cook.

Fresh green beans are available all year long, though the best supply is in the late spring and early summer. To prepare the beans for cooking, rinse them in cold water and snap off the ends. If you want, break them into bite-size pieces. Put the beans into a saucepan with 2 centimeters (1 inch) of boiling, lightly salted water. Cover and cook for about 10 minutes over medium heat. They're done when fork-tender.

You may find it more convenient to use frozen green beans. (They have already been trimmed and rinsed.) Cook them in basically the same way as fresh beans. Put them into a little boiling, salted water. When the water starts boiling again, cover the pot and cook for 8 to 10 minutes. For four people, use 280 grams (a 10-ounce package) of beans. For six to eight people, double the amount.

Serve the beans plain, with butter or margarine, or try this easy sauce. Melt 30 milliliters (2 tablespoons) of butter or margarine in a small skillet and add 30 milliliters (2 tablespoons) of bread crumbs (plain or seasoned). Sauté over medium heat until the bread crumbs are slightly browned—only about a minute. Spoon over the green beans once they're in the serving dish.

Cranberry sauce The tangy sweet-sour taste of cranberry sauce makes a good contrast to the rich flavor of turkey, gravy, and dressing. This traditional sauce also adds a beautiful, deep red color to your meal.

Is it hard to make cranberry sauce? Isn't it easier to buy it in a can?

Cranberry sauce may seem like a special holiday treat, but it's surprisingly simple to make. All you do is boil 500 milliliters (2 cups) of sugar and 375 milliliters (1½ cups) of water together over medium heat. Add half a kilogram (1 pound) of cranberries and return to boiling. Cover and turn down the heat. Simmer until the berries pop—about 7 minutes. The whole thing takes just about 10 minutes!

Relishes To add even more variety to your meal, put some relishes on your table. Relishes are food accents. Crisp, tangy pickles make a good contrast to smooth, creamy mashed potatoes. So do crunchy celery sticks and carrot sticks. Salty green olives with red pimento centers add even more contrast to the other foods at the table.

When it comes to pickles, you have a wide variety to choose from. There are tiny sweet-sour gherkins, long, salty dill strips, or mild

Pour cranberries into sugared, boiling water to cook a tangy, fresh cranberry sauce in minutes.

Why are relishes called food accents?

"bread-and-butter" pickle slices. Serve them all, if you like, in relish dishes, along with stuffed olives. Relish dishes have compartments that keep the pickle juice from running into the olives, the olive juice from mixing with the raw vegetables, and so forth. Other kinds of dishes will do, too. Small, shallow bowls are good for holding pickles, olives, and other relishes.

In addition to pickles and olives, your relish dishes can have flowered radishes, strips of green pepper, and little flowerets of cauliflower. Set your celery sticks and carrot sticks apart by standing them up in glasses or short mugs.

Working with yeast dough

Your Thanksgiving dinner is now a feast of flavors, colors, shapes, textures, and aromas. Just before dinner time, the rolls go into the oven, adding to the other good smells. Since you have time to plan and work ahead on your meal, you'll probably enjoy making fresh, hot dinner rolls from scratch, using yeast dough.

Yeast dough rolls Yeast is a leavening agent. That is, yeast makes dough rise. As you probably remember, quick breads such as biscuits and muffins are leavened with baking powder or baking soda. These are chemicals that produce carbon dioxide. But yeast is made up of tiny plants that give off carbon dioxide as they grow. They start to grow when the yeast is moistened and put into a mixture of flour and sugar. Yeast dough breads and rolls usually rise higher and are lighter

Yeast dough rolls

24 rolls

	1 pkg active dry yeast
80 mL	**⅓ cup warm water**
125 mL	**½ cup warm milk**
60 mL	**¼ cup sugar**
7 mL	**1½ tsp salt**
30 mL	**2 tbsp shortening**
	1 egg
625-750 mL	**2½-3 cups all-purpose flour**
	salad oil

Sprinkle the yeast into the warm water in an extra-large bowl, and stir until the yeast is dissolved.

Add the warm milk and stir in the sugar, salt, shortening, and egg, and 300 mL (1¼ cups) of the flour, mixing until smooth.

Beat for 2 minutes with an electric mixer set at medium speed, scraping the sides of the bowl occasionally. Or beat vigorously with a wooden spoon for 150 strokes.

Stir in 300 mL (1¼ cups) of the flour. Then add just enough more of the flour to make the dough soft and leave the sides of the bowl clean.

and springier than quick breads. To make yeast dough rolls, you will need the ingredients shown in the recipe on this page.

Make sure that the warm water and milk that you mix with the dry yeast is about 50 °C (120 °F). Liquids at this temperature will feel very warm, but not painfully hot to your skin.

Once your ingredients are mixed, the dough has to be kneaded so that it will be smooth, elastic, and not sticky. To knead means to handle dough in a certain way. First, you shape it into a round lump. Grab the edge farthest away from you and fold the dough toward you, across the middle. With the heels of your hands, push into the folded dough. Push it away from you with a rolling motion. Then give the dough a quarter turn, fold it toward you again, and continue kneading. Add more flour to the work surface and hands as needed to prevent sticking.

After kneading the dough, let it rest in a greased bowl, covered with a towel, in a warm place. In about one and a half hours, the dough will rise and double in size. When it has doubled, two fingers pressed lightly into it will leave a dent. Then the dough is ready to be turned out onto a floured surface so you can "punch it down." To do this, push down the center with your fist; then fold the outside edges of the dough into the dent in the center. This removes extra air in the dough due to rising.

Now cover the bowl with plastic wrap and put it into the refrigerator for two to twenty-four hours. During this time the dough will rise a little more. About two hours before you want to bake your rolls, take the dough from the refrigerator, and form it into the desired shapes.

Pan rolls For pan rolls, you will need to make twenty-four balls of dough. To do this, first pull the dough apart into halves, and then in half again. This will give you four lumps of dough. Make six balls of

Turn out onto a floured board and knead the dough until it is smooth (about 10 minutes). Shape the dough into a ball and place it in a large, greased bowl. Cover the bowl with a towel and leave it in a warm place. Let the dough rise for about 1½ hours, until doubled.

Punch down the dough and put it back into the bowl. Brush the dough lightly with salad oil, cover the bowl with plastic wrap, and place it in the refrigerator for 2 to 24 hours. About 2 hours before serving, form the dough into rolls and place them in a greased baking pan. Cover pan with towel and let it stand at room temperature for about 1½ hours, until doubled again.

Brush the tops of the rolls with melted butter or margarine, and bake them in the oven at 200 °C (400 °F) until they are golden brown. The amount of baking time will vary according to the shape of the rolls. Pan rolls, for example, take 15-20 minutes, clover leaf rolls only 10-15 minutes. Serve hot.

Mix the ingredients for rolls; then knead the dough until it is smooth, and shape it into a ball. Cover the dough, and leave it in a warm place until it doubles in volume. If the light pressure of two fingers leaves a dent, the dough has doubled. Punch it down, knead, and refrigerate; shape into rolls.

dough from each lump. They should each be about the size of a golf ball or a ping-pong ball. Place the balls into a greased, 30 cm × 20 cm baking pan (12″ × 8″). Cover the pan with a towel, and let the dough rise again for about one and a half hours. The rolls should be doubled in size.

Brush the tops of the rolls with butter or margarine and place the pan in the preheated oven. Bake until the rolls are golden brown.

Cloverleaf rolls To give your rolls a little different look, make cloverleaf rolls. Each roll is made from three small balls of dough. The yeast dough recipe here will make two dozen cloverleaf rolls.

That means I'll need 72 little dough balls! How can I tell how big each piece should be, to make all 72 pieces equal?

To make your pieces equal, first pull the dough apart into quarters. Then roll each quarter into a rope with your hands. Now pull dough off in pieces about the size of large grapes and shape the pieces into balls.

Grease twenty-four muffin-pan cups and place three dough balls into each cup. Cover the pan with a towel and let the dough rise until doubled, about 1 to 1½ hours.

Brush the tops of the rolls with melted butter or margarine. Bake them until golden.

As you can imagine, your oven is going to be very busy on Thanksgiving Day. The turkey will take about five to six hours. The rolls go in at the last minute, so they can be brought to the table fresh and piping hot. This means that the pie has to be baked first, before the turkey goes into the oven.

Making a pie

Basic pie dough The secret to a good pie is good piecrust. And the secret to a good piecrust is working quickly, with as little handling as possible, especially after water has been added to the flour. For a one-crust pie (one that does not have a crust on top), you will need the ingredients listed in the recipe for pie dough on this page. (For a two-crust pie, double the ingredients.)

To cut the shortening into the flour, use a pastry blender, a large fork, or two knives used scissors-style. You can tell that the shortening is all cut in when there are no more large clumps of shortening and no loose flour.

To check that the dough is moist enough, gather it together in your hands and shape it into a ball. If it doesn't hold together well, you may need to add another 5 milliliters or so (a teaspoon or two) of water.

Roll the dough with a lightly floured rolling pin on a sheet of waxed paper. Or roll it on a lightly floured surface. Start at the center and roll outward, in all directions. Flatten the dough out a little at a time, pressing a little harder in the center than at the edges. Keep the outside shape as close to a circle as you can. If the

Basic pie dough

250 mL	**1 cup all-purpose flour**
2 mL	**½ tsp salt**
90 mL	**⅜ cup, or ¼ cup + 2 tbsp shortening**
30 to 45 mL	**2 to 3 tbsp cold water**

Mix the flour and salt together. Cut in the shortening, until you have an even mixture of small, flour-covered bits of shortening.

Sprinkle the water into the mixture, a little at a time. After each spoonful, mix lightly with a fork until the dough is just moist enough to hold together.

Roll out the dough until it is about 2 centimeters (1 inch) larger all around than the pie pan. Trim off the ragged edges with a knife. Leave about 1 centimeter (½ inch) all the way around.

Transfer the dough to the pie pan, and press it gently into the pan. Trim and decorate the edges.

Store the covered, unbaked piecrust in the refrigerator until you're ready to use it.

dough breaks at the edges, pinch it together right away. To check the size of the circle, place the pie pan upside down on the dough.

If you've rolled the dough on waxed paper, it's easy to get it into the pie pan. Center the pie pan upside down on the dough. Holding the waxed paper and the dough with both hands, quickly flip them over. Gently peel off the waxed paper. Carefully adjust the dough to fit the pan evenly.

If you haven't used waxed paper, you can pick up the dough by rolling it lightly around the rolling pin and then unrolling it into the pie pan. Or you can fold the dough in half, and then in quarters. Pick it up, put it into the pan, and unfold it.

When you are pressing the dough to fit the pan, press it from the rim of the pan toward the center to avoid stretching it in the center. Stretching will cause shrinking during baking.

An easy and good-looking decoration for the edge of the crust can be made with a fork. First, fold under the dough that sticks out beyond the rim of the pan, to make a double thickness around the edge. Press around the edge with the tines (sharp points) of a fork to pinch the double thickness of crust together and to decorate.

This pie crust has been decorated by pinching the edge between the thumb and forefinger. The top of the pie is sprinkled with cinnamon.

Pumpkin pie filling Many families have a favorite recipe for pumpkin pie filling. If you want to try a new recipe, look in general cookbooks, in magazines around holiday time, or on the label of a can of pumpkin. The filling is very easy to make. Usually, it's a simple mixture of canned pumpkin, milk, eggs, sugar, and various spices.

If you're in a hurry, or don't have all the needed ingredients, you can buy pumpkin pie filling that includes everything. Simply pour it into the piecrust and bake.

On the other hand, if you have plenty of time and want to do everything from scratch, you can use your own fresh pumpkin instead of canned. Cut the pumpkin in halves or quarters. Scrape out the seeds and stringy parts and throw them away. (Or wash the seeds, dry them, and eat them like sunflower seeds.) Cut the pumpkin shell into cubes and peel off the rind. Put the pieces into a saucepan over medium heat, in 3 centimeters (1 inch) of salted water. Cover the pan and cook the pumpkin for 25 to 30 minutes. Drain and mash the cooked pumpkin. Use 500 milliliters (2 cups) of cooked pumpkin to replace the canned pumpkin in your pie filling recipe.

Bake the pie according to the directions in your recipe. Pumpkin pies are usually baked in a hot oven (200 °C, or 400 °F) for about 50 minutes. You can check doneness by sticking a knife halfway between the edge and center of the pie and pulling it out. It should come out clean.

Pumpkin pies are delicious served warm or cool. Many people like to top the pie with whipped cream before serving.

With the pie, now, that makes nine different things I'm fixing. How can I do all that at one time?

Organizing your time

Listing things to do Obviously, you're going to run into some trouble getting everything done unless you organize your time carefully. To do this, first list all the steps for each thing you plan to fix. Then write down the amount of time each step takes.

Planning what to do in advance You can begin to see that some of these things are going to overlap. So the next thing you should do is to figure out what can be done in advance. Many foods can be prepared, covered, and refrigerated ahead of time.

Even when you plan and work ahead, you're going to end up with a few occasions when you have to do two things at the same time. Doing two things at once is called **dovetailing**. For example, while the green beans are cooking, you can mash the potatoes. Or while the rolls are baking, you can make the gravy. It's helpful to use a

dovetailing (DUHV tāl ing)

List all the steps for preparing each item on your menu and the time each step will take.

Turkey
- Thaw turkey – 3 days in refrigerator
- Prepare to cook – ½ hour
- Cook – 5 to 6 hours
- Cool – 30 minutes

Gravy
- Cook giblets – 1 hour
- Cut up giblets – 5 minutes
- Mix & cook gravy – 10 minutes

Cranberry Sauce
- Boil cranberries with sugar – 10 minutes

Stuffing
- Cut & mix – 15 minutes
- Cook – 45 minutes

Mashed Potatoes
- Peel – 10 minutes
- Cook – 20 minutes
- Mash – 5 minutes

Green Beans (Frozen)
- Cook beans – 15 minutes
- Make sauce – 2 to 3 minutes

Pumpkin Pie
- Filling – 15 minutes
- Piecrust – 15 minutes
- Baking pie – 50 minutes

Relish Dishes
- Carrot & celery sticks – 20 minutes
- Radish flowers – 10 minutes
- Pickles & olives – no preparation
- Cauliflowerets – 10 minutes
- Green peppers – 5 minutes

Pan Rolls
- Mix – 15 minutes
- Knead – 10 minutes
- Let rise – 1½ hours
- Refrigerate – overnight
- Shape dough – 10 minutes
- Put in pan & let rise – 1 hour
- Bake – 15 to 20 minutes

Setting Table – 10 minutes
Serving – 10 minutes

List the things you can do in advance.

Day Before
- Mix bread dough
- Make cranberry sauce (it's better chilled, anyway)

Morning
- Prepare relish dishes
- Bake pie
- Make stuffing
- Prepare turkey & put in oven
- Set table
- Cook & cut up giblets

kitchen timer to keep track of the cooking time for one item while you work on something else.

Making a schedule The next thing to do is to list all of the preparation and cooking times on a schedule. Start with the time you want to eat and work backward from there. The last hour on your schedule will be very crowded, so it will help if you break it down into 5-minute intervals.

Let's say you want to sit down to eat at 4:00 in the afternoon. Allow yourself 10 minutes to put things into serving dishes and carry them to the table. That means everything should be done at 3:50, except for the rolls, which should go straight from oven to table.

When you put everything together, your schedule for that last hour will look something like this.

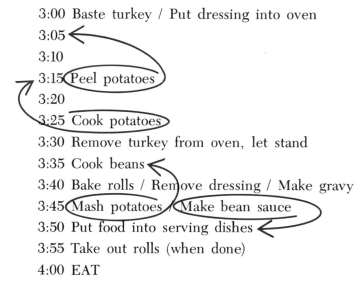

3:00 Baste turkey / Put dressing into oven

3:05

3:10

3:15 Peel potatoes

3:20

3:25 Cook potatoes

3:30 Remove turkey from oven, let stand

3:35 Cook beans

3:40 Bake rolls / Remove dressing / Make gravy

3:45 Mash potatoes / Make bean sauce

3:50 Put food into serving dishes

3:55 Take out rolls (when done)

4:00 EAT

Why are there arrows on the potatoes and the bean sauce?

Your schedule has pointed out a major problem at 3:45. There are three things you have to do at the same time, which won't dovetail. You should be making gravy (which you started at 3:40), mashing potatoes, and making sauce for the beans, all at the same time. But each one of these things needs your direct attention. You can't leave one of them while you turn to another. This means you'll have to find an empty time slot when you *can* do each one.

The solution shown here is to reschedule the mashed potatoes. You can mash them a little earlier, just after you put the beans on to cook, before you start making the gravy. When the potatoes are mashed, set the dish on top of the range, where the heat rising from the oven will help keep the potatoes warm until dinner time. Of course, this means you will have to peel and cook the potatoes earlier, too.

You have to reschedule the bean sauce, also. This sauce takes a very short time to make. You can safely postpone it until the gravy is finished, and crowd it into the last 10 minutes.

Table service

Setting the table Your last few minutes will be less frantic if you've set the table ahead of time. It should be set with the tablecloth, napkins, plates, silverware, glasses, bread plates, salt and pepper shakers, and any flowers, candles, or other decorations you plan to have. Be sure to reserve spaces for the turkey and all the serving dishes that will come later.

Serving For a large meal like this, you may want to cut down on the number of foods that are passed around the table. The turkey, especially, will be very hard to pass (unless the meat is cut off and put on a separate plate). An easier way might be to serve the food **English style**. Here, the food is dished onto the plates by the host, and then it is passed to the guests. Or you might serve the turkey this way, but serve the rest of the dishes **family style**. In family style, the serving dishes are passed to the guests, who help themselves.

Clearing the table When everyone has finished eating the main course, the table should be cleared before serving dessert. Remove all the serving dishes first. Then take away the plates, silverware, and glasses. Everything but the glasses should be removed on the person's left side. Also, leave any forks and spoons needed for dessert or coffee. Use a large tray when removing dishes from the dining table. It will take fewer trips that way. A tray helps when you're setting the table, too.

Do not stack the dishes at the table. Take as many as you can carry easily at one time and carry them to the kitchen. Quickly scrape and stack the dishes there. Put away the leftovers if you have time, or put the serving dishes in the refrigerator for the time being. Do not keep your guests waiting any longer than necessary. When the table has

been cleared, bring out the dessert dishes. As soon as dessert is finished, excuse yourself and go back to the kitchen to finish putting away the food. The dishes can wait, because you can wash the germs off later. But you can't do that with leftover food.

Storing leftovers Leftovers should be stored in as small a dish as possible, so they will take up less space in the refrigerator. Cover them with a lid or foil or plastic wrap to keep them from drying out. If possible, use an ovenproof dish for easy reheating later.

Any food that will not be eaten within three or four days should be frozen. Put the food in a freezer container or wrap it in foil, plastic wrap, or freezer paper. Label the package with the contents and date so you won't forget what it is, or when you froze it.

With the food safely put away, and the dishes stacked, you can rejoin your guests for awhile. The dishes can wait until later. Thanksgiving is a time for people to enjoy themselves. That includes the people who prepare the dinner, as well as those who eat it!

I never realized that one meal could take so much planning!

Most meals don't take this much planning. But when you want to have a big meal with a lot of different dishes, you should be ready to handle it. A little planning can make any meal, large or small, a big success—and a time for thanksgiving!

Words to understand

roast English-style service
dovetailing family-style service

Food and equipment to know

giblets roasting pan
gravy meat thermometer
relishes potato masher
pan rolls pie pan
clover leaf rolls kitchen timer

Questions to discuss

1. How would you figure out how much turkey to buy for a holiday meal?
2. What's the safest way to thaw a turkey? What's wrong with thawing it out in the open on the table?

3. How can you cook dressing without stuffing it into the turkey? Discuss two advantages of cooking the turkey and dressing separately.

4. Why is a meat thermometer useful when cooking a turkey? Where should it be placed?

5. What might cause lumps in gravy? How can you prevent them?

6. What is the purpose of relishes? Name five things you could serve as relishes.

7. Describe two ways to get pie dough into the pie pan after you have rolled it out flat.

8. Explain the steps in making a time schedule for a meal.

9. Give two examples of things which you might dovetail in fixing a meal.

10. Why is English-style service a good way to serve a large meal?

11. Explain how to clear the table before serving dessert.

Things to do

1. Look through magazines and cookbooks for ideas for decorating the tops of pies (especially fruit pies). Look for lattice tops, double-crust pies, pastry cutouts, and ideas for handling the edge. In your notebook or recipe file, sketch ideas you might want to try.

2. Plan a Thanksgiving menu you might serve your family. Then make a grocery list for the meal. Indicate how much you would buy of each food and in what form you would buy it (fresh, frozen, dried, canned).

3. Make a batch of yeast roll dough. Experiment with shaping the dough into different types of rolls, such as pan rolls, cloverleaf rolls, crescent rolls, and Parker House rolls. Look through cookbooks for ideas on shaping these and other kinds of yeast rolls.

4. Plan a menu for a dinner you would serve to five of your friends, plus yourself. Collect the recipes you would use. Make a time schedule for preparing this meal, following the example given in this chapter.

5. Discover why each step is important in making yeast roll dough. Make a batch of dough and try the following experiments.

   a. Pull off a golf-ball-size piece of dough before you knead the rest of the dough. Shape it into a roll and bake it with the other rolls.

   b. Pull off another piece of dough after you've kneaded the dough, but let it rise without punching it down. Bake it along with the other rolls.

c. Set aside one of the rolls from the dough that has been kneaded and punched down. Bake it along with the other rolls, but do not brush the top with melted butter or margarine.

Compare the experimental rolls with the others. What does this show you about the effects of kneading, punching down, and brushing with melted fat?

Careers to consider

Would you like to make predictions about the future?

If you like to study events and trends in the present in order to decide how they will affect the future, consider a career in food economics.

Many government agencies need information about the supply and price of food in the future. This greatly affects the cost of living, which affects many planning decisions. International agencies, too, want to know whether there will be enough food to feed the world, and where shortages are likely to be most severe. Banks and other financial institutions advise their customers about food commodities they think would be good investments.

These and other organizations employ **analysts** to collect information and evaluate it. The future price of wheat, for instance, may be affected by the amount on hand in granaries at present, the number of new acres planted, the chances of drought or flood, losses to insects and disease, labor strikes, and crop failures in other parts of the world.

Many of the people who study this information are **economists**. They are experts in the many things that affect business and trade. **Statisticians** are hired to make calculations and discover trends in the facts and figures. Economists and statisticians usually have a college degree in economics or business administration. They often have graduate degrees in specialized business areas. **Secretaries, typists, file clerks, computer programmers,** and **librarians** are all needed to handle the large amounts of information required for this work.

If you like excitement, you might enjoy working in a commodity exchange. Here, **brokers** buy and sell "futures" for their clients. A "future" is a contract to deliver a certain amount of a commodity (such as wheat) at a certain time in the future, for a certain price.

The broker's client may be a **speculator**. This is a person who buys, for example, a wheat contract on the chance that the price will go up and he can sell the contract later for a profit. Or the broker's customer may be a **buyer** or **purchasing agent** for a large food company. The company likes to be able to buy commodities at a known price in the future. This means they can make plans for the future, without having their plans upset by sudden price changes.

13

HAS THIS EVER HAPPENED TO YOU?

Greg is baby-sitting with the Robinson children—Michael (three months old), Jane (two years), and Tommy (five years). He's brought his sister, Jennifer, along to help him, especially at feeding time.

JENNIFER: *I don't know what's wrong, Greg. Michael keeps pushing the bottle away and crying like he's mad or something.*

GREG: *I can't help you now, Jen. I'm busy in the kitchen. How do you reheat green beans without burning them? Tommy—get away from that stove!*

TOMMY: *I don't like green beans. Neither does Jane. She doesn't like anything.*

At the dinner table, their problems continue. Jane refuses to eat.

GREG: *Come on, Jane, at least have some French fries. Look—Tommy ate all his French fries. In fact, he's had three helpings. Tommy, you've got to eat something besides just French fries!*

TOMMY: *I don't want to. I'm not hungry anymore. Look! Jane dropped her French fries in her milk. Can I have them?*

JENNIFER: *I give up! Were we like this when we were little, Greg? If we were, how did Mom and Dad ever get us to eat enough to stay alive?*

FEEDING CHILDREN

Exploring . . .

Tips on handling eating problems

How to fix foods with child-appeal

How to heat up leftovers and canned foods

How and what to feed babies

Kitchen safety and handling emergencies

Getting small children to eat—especially getting them to eat the right things—can sometimes be a problem.

GREG: *It sure can! Jane wouldn't even eat her dessert. And then she was fussy all evening, just like Michael!*

There are many different reasons why children don't eat. Most of them are not serious. The solution usually is to remain calm and take a relaxed approach to the problem. A little "mealtime psychology" may help, too.

Mealtime psychology

Psychology isn't anything mysterious. It can best be described as "the science of human nature," or simply understanding why people do what they do. In the case of children who are problem eaters, it means understanding what they think and how they feel at that age and at that moment in their lives.

You may have noticed that two-year-olds, for example, are curious. They're always getting into things—touching them, tasting them, and sometimes breaking them to see what they are made of. Two-year-olds can also be stubborn. They don't like to be told what they can and cannot do. You may have noticed, too, that the things they like and don't like often change from day to day. The game they liked yesterday is boring to them today. The doll they threw in the corner last week is their favorite one today. Put these three things together—curiosity, stubbornness, and changing interests—and you have some things to think about in planning your "mealtime psychology" for young children.

What should we have done with Jane? Every time we told her to eat something, she said "No!"

Encouraging children to eat   Children often get stubborn if you try to force them to eat. Forcing them usually creates more problems than it solves. A better approach is to let their natural curiosity take over. If they see something on the table, chances are they will want to try it, especially if they see others eating it. Children like to imitate others. And they like to try "grown-up" things, or things that older children like.

The important thing is that they keep trying new foods. They will grow to like many of them—remember, their interests and their

Greg can encourage Jane and Tommy to eat by eating his own meal. How does this method work?

If children fill up on empty-calorie snacks such as these, they won't be able to finish their meals. What are some good snacks?

tastes change from day to day. But they should not be forced to eat large portions of a food before they are ready for it. If they are forced, they may develop bad feelings and memories about the food that will keep them from *ever* liking it.

Okay, but what if they still won't eat anything? Is it okay to let them starve?

Children's appetites   Healthy children will not starve themselves. Sooner or later, they will get hungry and eat. A child who does not eat anything at all for more than a day may be ill and should be taken to see a doctor.

Of course, even healthy children may refuse to eat at mealtimes if they've filled up on the wrong things between meals. This is where firm control may be needed. Children who don't eat nutritious foods at mealtimes should not be allowed to have desserts or empty-calorie snacks (high in calories, low in other nutrients) between meals. Their appetites should be saved for nutritious foods, first. Only then can they afford to eat other things.

Babies' appetites   New babies usually have very good appetites. Most babies double their birth weight in their first six months and triple it in twelve months. This means that a baby who weighs 7 pounds at birth will probably weigh 14 pounds after six months and 21 pounds when it's a year old. All this growth gives most young babies a very healthy appetite.

After the first year, however, the growth rate slows down. Babies may actually eat less than they did at the end of the first year!

Parents should be aware of this decrease in babies' appetites and not try to make them eat as much.

There's one thing you do have to remember, however. Even if the baby is hungry, there may be something else wrong that keeps it from eating. Since it can't tell you what's wrong, you may have to guess. The baby may be wet and need to have its diaper changed before it thinks about eating. Or the bottle may be too hot, or too cold. It may have a clogged nipple, so that nothing comes through. (Rinse the nipple under running water and push a toothpick through the opening.) The baby may have a gas bubble in its stomach and need to be "burped."

Sometimes babies are too tired and cranky to eat. They may need to be held, rocked, jiggled, or sung to, before they will relax enough to eat. Parents usually know what works best for their own child, so be sure to ask them before they leave for the evening.

What if kids play with their food at the table? Does that mean they're not hungry?

Playing with food   Older babies and toddlers often play with their food as part of their natural curiosity. It's their way of exploring and examining it. Children love to get attention. If they can get it by playing with their food, they will keep doing so. If they can't, they will usually get tired of playing and settle down to eating. Remember, they are hungry, and hungry children will eat sooner or later. Rather than making a scene when children play with food, and forcing them to eat, it's better to depend on a healthy appetite and good mealtime habits to encourage eating.

How do you get them to form good mealtime habits?

Children's eating habits are greatly affected by the approach you take in feeding them. This approach should be based on what you know about child psychology plus a little basic information about nutrition. Combine this with a serious but relaxed attitude toward eating. You will then have a good basis for making wise choices about what to serve and how to serve it.

How to feed children

Table service   Here are some simple guidelines for happy mealtimes. Serve meals at a reasonably regular time, when children will be hungry. If the meal is delayed too long, the child's healthy appetite may turn into a growling, upset stomach. Serve the meal at the same place each day, so children will get used to eating when they sit down there. Make sure that everyone is seated at a comfortable height in relation to the table. Make sure that the things young children should have are within reach. Make sure that things they should *not* have are *out* of reach! This includes sharp knives, hot dishes, and anything they might knock over or spill.

Why is it a good idea to let children serve themselves?

New foods should be given to children one at a time. Each one should be served along with other foods that they already like. Show the child that you like the new food, but don't make a big fuss about it. Small children can be very clever. If they see you doing too big a "sales job" on the food, they may decide that it must be pretty bad!

Whenever possible, it's a good idea to let children serve themselves. Children like to take part in making decisions, and should be encouraged to do so. Let them help set the table if they are old enough. Give them small, child-size plates that are just right for child-size portions. Let them take as much as they want of each food, including at least a "taste" of any new foods. If they want more, they can ask for seconds. This is always better than serving them too much in the first place, and getting into a fight with them to "clean their plates."

What about table manners for kids? Is that important?

Table manners   Table manners depend on the age of the child. Picking up peas with the fingers might be all right for a two-year-old, but it looks silly for an eight-year-old. The most important rule is simply to behave in a way that will make the meal a pleasant occasion for everyone. Set a good example in your own table manners and attitude toward food. Young children imitate the behavior of the older people around them.

Make a general rule that people should not leave the table (unless there is an important reason) until they have finished eating what they want. Set a reasonable length of time for eating. It should be long enough that children can enjoy their food and chew it properly without gulping it down. But it should not be too long a time. That could encourage children to dawdle and play games while their food gets cold and tasteless.

At the table, let children take part in the conversation. Don't plead with them to eat, or threaten them, or try to bribe them. When they are finished eating, simply remove their plates or let them take them to the kitchen themselves. They should understand that if they haven't eaten enough nutritious food they may not have any high-calorie desserts, sweets, or other snacks.

Food games Parents sometimes use games to get small children to eat. The spoon becomes a "choo-choo train" and the child's mouth is a "tunnel." While this game may work, it usually isn't necessary. What's more, it encourages children to think of mealtime as a time to play games rather than as a time to eat. A little pleasant conversation is always nice at the table, but too much laughing, shouting, or game-playing should be avoided. It's hard to eat at the same time.

Preparing food for children

Heating foods When feeding older children, you will often find that parents have prepared the meal ahead of time. However, you may have to heat some things up or do a little simple cooking. Precooked meats and vegetables can be heated simply by putting them into a covered pot and placing them on the range over medium heat. If there is no liquid with the food, add a little water to prevent burning

Panbroiled hamburgers make a quick and easy dinner dish.

and sticking. This also creates steam, which helps to heat the food on all sides. Stir the food now and then, and check to see how hot it is. It should be ready when the liquid has simmered for 2 to 5 minutes. If you're not sure, lift out some food with a clean spoon and taste it.

Foods can also be reheated quickly and easily in a microwave oven. If the container is ovenproof, put it directly into the microwave oven, with a lid or piece of plastic wrap or waxed paper over the top. You can also put ovenproof dishes into a regular oven (but do not use plastic wrap or waxed paper). When you do this, however, it takes longer because you have to heat the whole oven first.

It may add to your abilities as a baby sitter if you can cook a few favorite foods of children, such as hamburgers and other simple meats. These do not taste as good when they're warmed over. They're at their juicy best when fresh. One of the simplest ways to cook hamburgers and other tender meats is to panbroil them.

How do you panbroil meat?

Panbroiling hamburgers Panbroiling is very easy. Simply place the meat in a heavy frying pan or on a griddle. A heavy pan distributes the heat more evenly than a light one. Turn the burner on to medium heat. The pan does not need to be preheated.

Do not add fat. This is what makes panbroiling different from frying. When you fry foods, you are cooking them in hot oil or fat. Most meats have enough fat to keep them from sticking when you panbroil. If the meat is very lean, you may need to brush the pan lightly with oil or use a spray-type cooking oil. Do not cover the pan.

Cook slowly. Turn the meat over occasionally. To brown evenly, the meat needs to cook more than once on each side. Pour off (or spoon out) extra fat as it cooks out of the meat. Do not overcook, or the meat will become tough.

When hamburgers are done, they are firm and can be turned easily without falling apart. There should be no red meat left showing. However, they should still be tender and juicy, not hard and rubbery, when you press them in the center. If you're not sure how well done they are, make a small cut in the center and take a look at the inside. A medium-rare hamburger will be pink inside.

Panbroiling can be done with small steaks, chops, and other tender cuts of meat that are less than 3 centimeters (1 inch) thick. Larger cuts cannot be cooked this way, because the meat usually gets dry and burned on the outside before it gets done on the inside.

Kids eat hamburgers all the time. What could I do that would make a meal more special?

Making meals special Most children enjoy having a baby sitter—it's a special occasion for them. What you do to make it special helps make up for the fact that their parents are not home. Often their parents have gone out to a party or other special event themselves. Children don't need to have a party every day, but once in awhile is nice. There are many things you can do to give their meals a party flavor.

Left: Cookie cutter shapes. Right: Smiling pancakes.

You can use cookie cutters to create interesting shapes in bread, cheese, and other flat, soft foods. You can make flowers, animals, diamonds, cloverleaves, and so forth. You might cut a shape out of a slice of white bread and then cut the same shape out of a slice of brown bread. Put the brown cutout back into the white slice, and the white cutout into the brown slice. Use the two slices to make a peanut butter and jelly sandwich.

It's also easy to make "smiling pancakes." Make pancake batter the way you learned in Chapter 5. Pour out 60 milliliters (1/4 cup) into a small pitcher. Mix in 15 milliliters (1 tablespoon) of maple syrup. Dribble two eyes, a nose, and a smiling mouth onto the hot griddle and let the face brown. Then pour a round pancake over it. Let it cook until bubbles form. When you turn the pancake over, be sure to smile—because it will be smiling back at you!

You can create faces, designs, letters, and words on other foods with melted cheese, chocolate syrup, frosting, raisins, nuts, seeds,

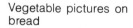

Vegetable pictures on bread

and so forth. A tradition among some families is to print letters on cookies or other favorite foods of children. The children must learn to say the letters before they may eat the foods.

Variety There are many simple ways to give children's foods appealing variety in tastes and textures. Spread creamy peanut butter in the groove of a stalk of crisp celery. Combine chewy hamburger, juicy tomatoes, crunchy lettuce, and creamy cheese in a crisp shell for a meal with real appeal—a *taco!*

Look for variety in color, as well as taste and texture. Fruits and vegetables come in the brightest of colors—red, yellow, green, orange, blue, and purple. Most children like fruits. Make a "fruit kabob" by sticking pieces of apple, melon, peaches, grapes, and cherries on a toothpick.

Many children like crisp, raw vegetables better than cooked ones. Give them bowls of round, sliced cucumbers and radishes, long strips of green pepper, curly shaved carrots and crumbly grated carrots, and stringy shredded cabbage or lettuce. Then give them a slice of bread spread with cream cheese. Let them create their own design, face, or picture on the bread with the various vegetable shapes and colors. The result is sure to be a brand new experience in taste, texture, shape, color, and fun!

What about things with a lot of sugar in them? Can kids have those, too?

Sweet foods Most children like sweet things, such as cake, cookies, pies, puddings, and ice cream. These things add to the enjoyment of eating. This is fine, as long as it does not interfere with good nutrition, or add too many calories to the diet. Actually, many desserts and party foods contain milk, fruits, nuts, seeds, and whole grains, which are nutritious. Carrot cakes, oatmeal cookies, peanut butter cookies, fruit pies, and fruit puddings contain valuable nutrients in addition to sugar.

The Basic Four For children to get the nutrients they need, they must get at least two-thirds of their calories from nutritious meals and snacks. The Basic Four food groups are a good guide to nutrition planning for young children as well as for older children and adults. The main difference is that for a young child, a serving of each food is about half what it would be for an adult—except for milk. Children should have more milk than adults—from .50 to .75 liter (2 to 3 cups) a day, compared to .50 liter (2 cups) daily for adults.

How can you tell a baby who can't even talk yet how to eat and what to eat?

The rules for feeding infants (children who are not yet one year old) must be a little bit different, of course. But your basic attitude and approach should be the same. Be relaxed but businesslike about feeding. Let the baby decide how much it wants to eat.

Feeding babies

Newborn infants can get along quite well on just mother's milk or formula. Formula is a balanced mixture of milk and essential nutrients. After the first few months, babies usually need extra iron. They are born with stored supplies of iron, but these are soon used up. Then they need foods such as egg yolks, meats, fortified cereal, or formula fortified with extra iron. You can see that variety in foods and nutrients is important early in the baby's life.

Fixing bottles Most formula is packaged in one of three ways: ready-to-use, liquid concentrate, or powder. Each kind has directions on the can telling you how to prepare it. The ready-to-use formula is a liquid and needs nothing added. Simply shake the can, open it, and pour the formula into the baby bottle. The concentrate is also a liquid, but it must be **diluted** (mixed with water to make it weaker). Usually, one can of concentrate is diluted with one can of water. The powdered form is mixed according to the directions on the package.

The directions may also include rather complicated instructions for sterilizing the formula and the bottles. Sterilizing (killing dangerous microbes by boiling) is not as common as it was years ago. Whether the bottles are sterilized or not, cleanliness is very important. Be sure to wash your hands before handling food or feeding equipment. Make sure bottles, nipples, and bottle liners (if used) are clean. Before opening the can, rinse off the can and the can opener.

Often the parents will have the formula already mixed and stored in the refrigerator. They may have poured it into bottles waiting for you to use. If the baby is very young, you may have to heat the bottle. You may be able to heat it in a pan of hot water in the sink, if the water from the faucet is hot enough. If not, place the bottle in a pan of water on the stove and heat the water to simmering. Check the temperature of the formula by shaking a few drops on the underside of your wrist. The skin there is more sensitive to hot and cold. The formula should feel neither cold nor warm to your skin.

Bottle feeding When taking a bottle, most babies like to be cradled in your arms. Hold the baby's head up just a little. Tip the bottle so that the nipple is filled with liquid, not air. Stop the feeding after 50 milliliters or so (an ounce or two) to burp the baby. To do this, lean the baby forward in a sitting position and rub its back until it burps. Or hold the baby upright against your chest, with its head just above your shoulder. Gently rub or pat its back. Be sure to place a cloth on your shoulder, just under the baby's mouth, because it may spit up some milk when it burps. Babies who are four months old or over may be able to hold the bottle themselves. They may not need to be held in your arms, but most still enjoy it.

diluted (di LOO tid)

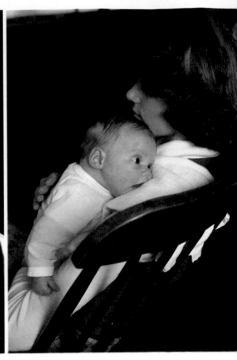

Left: When Jennifer feeds Michael from a nursing bottle, she holds his head up slightly as he drinks. Center: To burp Michael, Jennifer can move him into a sitting position and rub his back. Right: Or she can hold Michael upright, with his head just above her shoulder, and then pat his back.

What about babies who are starting on solid foods?

A baby may also have fruit juice and some strained solid foods. Up until the age of three months, solid foods are given in small "taster" amounts, to get the baby used to solid foods.

Solid foods   From three months to a year, solid foods supply more and more of the baby's nutritional needs. These foods will usually be puréed and strained. **Puréed** food is cooked and forced through a sieve or food mill, or chopped up in a blender, to make a smooth paste. It may be strained to remove excess fiber.

Between six months and one year, babies usually begin eating unstrained meats and vegetables along with their other foods. These may be commercially prepared "junior foods" or foods that have been mashed or ground up in a food blender.

You can heat solid baby food by putting it into an electric feeding dish or a small bowl set in a pan of hot water. Or you can warm the bowl of food in a microwave oven for a few seconds. Be careful that it doesn't get too hot. "Warm" to a baby means body temperature. Vegetables, meats, and cereals are usually served warm. Fruits are usually served cold, or at room temperature.

puréed (pyor ĀD)

Don't spoon the food directly from the jar unless you expect the baby to finish all of it. Taking food out of the refrigerator, letting it stand at room temperature during feeding, and then putting it back increases the chance of spoilage. Also, the baby's saliva may be carried by the spoon to the food in the jar. It will start to "digest" some of the starch in the food, making it runny. It's better to spoon out what you need and put the container back in the refrigerator.

From one year on, babies can chew up many of the same foods that the rest of the family eats—if cut into finger foods. These are foods that little fingers can pick up and handle easily. They include tiny sandwiches, green beans or French fries cut into small pieces, and whole-kernel corn. The amount depends on the baby's appetite. Start with small portions and give seconds and thirds if the child wants them.

How do you give a baby solid foods without making a mess of the baby and the kitchen—and you?

Spoon feeding During spoon feeding, the baby should be in a sitting position on your lap or in a high chair or feeding table. Place the spoon well back in the baby's mouth. You can wipe the spoon gently against the baby's upper lip as you take it out, to get all the food off. Give the baby time to swallow, but be ready with another spoonful quickly. If you're not ready, the baby may start crying for the food, which makes feeding difficult. If the baby is hungry, it will probably

Which of these finger foods would be easy for a toddler to eat? Which of them wouldn't you give to a toddler? Why?

be as eager to eat as you are to feed! Babies can start taking a few sips from a cup at four or five months, but it may be several more months before they will drink a full serving.

Self-feeding   At around one year, babies usually begin to try to feed themselves—with a spoon, with their fingers, or by putting the whole dish into their mouths. At first, it may seem that more food goes onto the table and the floor than into the baby's mouth. Once again, don't panic. Don't let the baby think that throwing food around is cute, but don't shout or scold, either.

> *My biggest problem in baby-sitting is—when I'm trying to fix food, the kids are running around getting into things. I never know what to pay attention to first.*

Whenever you baby-sit, your most important responsibility is to look after the children. This means, when you're cooking, that you have to keep one eye on the stove and one eye on the children. Don't start working in the kitchen until babies are safely settled in their crib or playpen.

Never leave a child unattended. If something happens, you must be there to take care of it. It won't help later for you to say that you were "only gone for a minute." Small children can come up with lots of ways to hurt themselves in the kitchen. This makes kitchen safety more important than ever.

A playpen will keep a toddler safe while you are working in the kitchen.

Kitchen safety

Hot things   One of the most important rules in the kitchen is to keep children away from hot things and hot things away from children. Remember, small children love to reach for things and pull them down. This might be the handle of a pot of soup on the stove. Turn all pot handles inward so that children cannot reach them. Don't let electrical cords dangle where children can reach them. Keep table-cloths out of reach, too, especially if dishes, which children might pull down with the cloth, are set on the table. Keep hot dishes well back from the edge of the kitchen counter. Don't carry hot liquids across the room if children are standing in the way. Just a little spill might splash a child in the eyes or face.

Sharp things   Be careful of knives and other sharp or pointed tools. The kitchen is full of them. Many of them are bright and shiny—just the sort of things that children like to reach for. Be careful of things that children can break, especially glassware. Don't let children crawl or walk barefoot where glass has broken until the floor has been thoroughly vacuumed to pick up tiny slivers.

Falling   Do not let children climb up on counters or shelves where they might fall and hurt themselves. Most children are not really naughty or troublesome, but they are adventurous. They depend on parents and baby sitters to tell them what they can safely do and what they cannot. Be sure to wipe up spills immediately. Just a little water or grease may cause a serious slip on a hard kitchen floor.

Choking   Do not let children play with plastic wrap or bags. They may cover their faces with them, so that they cannot breathe; or they may bite off small pieces and get them caught in their throats.

Be careful of all things that children might swallow, for example small, hard foods such as dried beans, peas, corn, or dry pet food. Things can get caught in a child's windpipe and cause suffocation.

What should you do if a child gets something caught in its windpipe?

If a child has swallowed a dangerous object, but can still breathe, call an adult (preferably a parent) and call a doctor. If the child is choking and cannot breathe, you will need to act at once. Hold the infant or small child in your lap and over your knees, so that the head is down. Use the palm of your hand to strike several quick blows between the child's shoulder blades. This should force out enough air to clear the object out of the windpipe. Repeat until the object is dislodged. If the child is too big to hold in your lap, stand behind him or her, holding the child over your arm so that the head is down. Strike the blows between the shoulder blades with your free hand.

In an older child, if the object is firmly stuck and the child cannot breathe any air into the lungs, the following method may be neces-

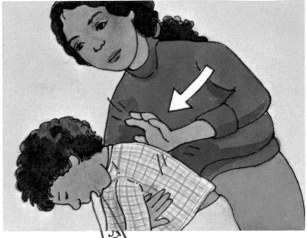

To relieve choking, give several quick blows between the shoulder blades to clear the object from the windpipe. Use the method of pressing into the midriff only if the child cannot breathe at all. *Never* use that method on infants—it may cause serious injury.

sary. (Do not use this technique on infants or very small children, as it could cause serious injury.) Stand behind the child, placing your arms around the chest. Put the thumb side of your fist against the stomach, just below the ribs. Grasp your fist with the other hand and press into the midriff with several quick, upward thrusts. This forces air out of the lungs to dislodge the object. Be sure to adjust the strength of your thrust to the child's size.

For most coughing fits, such forceful measures aren't necessary. What usually happens is that a small bit of food or liquid goes down the child's windpipe, which causes coughing. If the child gasps air in, the material is only pulled deeper into the windpipe. Try to get the child to hold his or her breath to control the cough. Then tell the child to breathe in slowly through the nose. When the child's lungs are full of air, tell him or her to cough once or twice to clear the windpipe. Naturally, it is difficult to explain all this to a small child who is choking. You may have to help out with a slap on the back.

What if kids swallow something they shouldn't, like poison or something sharp?

Poisons Small children often swallow things that you wouldn't even put into your mouth, like cleaning supplies, rat or roach poison, even garbage. If you are baby-sitting and you think a child has swallowed something poisonous, immediately call responsible adults—the child's parents, your parents, or neighbors. You can also call a poison control center for advice. There should be a number listed on the inside cover of the phone book. If the child is unconscious and cannot be wakened, immediately call the fire department or the police department. Check to see if the child is breathing. Hold a small strip of bathroom tissue to the nostrils and see if there is enough breath to make it move. If the tissue doesn't move, give the child mouth-to-mouth resuscitation.

When you are baby-sitting with small children for just a few hours in the evening, you probably won't have to worry much about kitchen safety. Quite likely, the children will have eaten dinner already, and you won't even have to go into the kitchen.

What's the point of knowing so much about feeding kids, if you usually don't have to do it anyway?

Even if parents leave you detailed instructions, they can't cover everything. You have to be able to fill the gaps. The more you know about feeding and caring for children, the better you can follow directions properly—without difficulty and without misunderstanding.

There may be times, on weekends or during the summer, when you will take care of children all day long. You may then have much more responsibility than just planning and serving meals and snacks.

Other baby-sitting tips

When you baby-sit, make sure you know the phone number where parents can be reached. Put it near the phone. What other phone numbers should you have for emergencies?

As a baby sitter, you should try to learn as much as you can about the care of children—including the basic techniques of feeding, dressing, changing, bathing, and amusing them. In addition, you should know the basic rules of safety and what to do in an emergency.

Parents' instructions   If you are baby-sitting in the evening, at dinner time, the parents will often have the children's food ready, with specific directions about how, when, and how much to feed them. If they do not leave instructions, you should make a point of asking for them. Whatever instructions parents leave, you should follow them as carefully as you can.

Emergency phone numbers   It is always a good idea to ask the child's parents what they would like you to do in any emergency situations. Get the phone number where the parents can be reached. Get the numbers of their doctor, and of the fire department, police department, poison control center, and neighbors, friends, or relatives to be contacted if the parents cannot be reached. This does not mean that you expect something to happen. It just means you want to be prepared if anything does.

House tour   Have the parents take you on a tour of the house. Find out where the child's clothing, bed, and food are located. Also check where first aid supplies, fire extinguisher, and exits are, in case of emergency.

Family customs   Ask for special instructions about bedtime rules, family customs, watching television, snacks, and so forth. Does the child have a favorite bedtime toy or blanket? What should you do if the child wakes up at night? Should you give him or her a bottle, or a drink of water? Should you rock the child to sleep? Should you change its diaper? Should you turn on a night light?

Getting experience Our discussion has centered on feeding children. It has not covered all the things you need to know and do as a baby sitter. You can learn more by taking care of younger brothers and sisters at home, under your parents' guidance. You may find additional child care instruction available through your home economics classes, or through organizations such as 4-H, Scouts, Camp Fire Girls, Y-teens, the Red Cross, or church- or community-sponsored classes.

Words to understand

panbroil
dilute
purée

Food and equipment to know

finger food
formula
junior food
strained baby food

Questions to discuss

1. What's a good way to introduce a new food to a young child? What might happen if you force children to eat a large portion of something they don't like?
2. What are some things that might make a baby fussy while you are trying to feed it?
3. What's wrong with playing games to get children to eat?
4. List five tips for helping children form good mealtime habits.
5. How would you heat canned foods or leftovers? What can you do to prevent burning and sticking?
6. Describe how to panbroil hamburgers. How do you know when they're done?
7. Describe two or three ideas for making a meal special for children.
8. How can you warm up a baby bottle? How should you check the temperature?

9. How do you burp a baby?

10. Describe briefly how a baby's diet gradually expands to include more variety during the first year or so of life.

11. Why should you not feed a baby a portion of food directly from the jar?

12. Name four or more examples of finger foods for toddlers.

13. List five or more tips for kitchen safety when you're cooking with young children around.

14. What emergency phone numbers should you have handy when you're caring for children?

Things to do

1. Observe a group of preschool children in a nursery school, day care center, or similar setting. Take notes on what they like and don't like to do. Observe them eating. Describe some of the eating habits you saw. Did older children have different habits from younger children?

2. Invite three or four parents to your class to discuss baby-sitting. The topics might include: what they look for in a baby sitter, how to handle small problems, what to do in emergencies, discipline, kitchen safety.

3. Invite a small group of experienced baby sitters to your class to discuss feeding children. What problems have they run into? How did they handle them? Make a list of useful tips they have to offer.

4. Make a bulletin board on feeding young children. Cut out pictures from magazines of children eating and of foods with child-appeal. Focus on key ideas, such as colors, textures, imagination, easy-to-eat foods.

5. Ask a group of young children to draw pictures of their favorite foods. Label the drawings with the children's first names and ages. Decorate your classroom with the drawings. Discuss in class which foods are common favorites. Why are those foods so appealing?

6. Hospitals often sponsor classes for new parents on the care and feeding of infants. Ask at your local hospital whether they have these classes. Invite one of the teachers to visit your class and demonstrate feeding techniques. They might also cover how to prepare a bottle, how to hold and burp a baby during feeding, and tips on feeding solid foods.

7. Ask a doctor, nurse, or Red Cross volunteer to demonstrate what to do if a child is choking. If time permits, also cover other emergencies—such as burns, cuts, and poisons.

Careers to consider

Would you like to write about food?

If you're good at writing and enjoy thinking about and working with food ideas, consider a career as a food writer.

Dozens of magazines and hundreds of newspapers across the country employ **food editors** to plan, write, and edit their food sections. On the food pages, you might find information about new foods, tips on shopping or cooking, diet articles, general news about food (such as price trends or shortages), or illustrated articles full of recipe ideas. On large publications, the food editor is likely to have one or more **assistant** or **associate editors** and sometimes other staff members to share the work load.

Where do food editors get their information and ideas? Some of it comes from news releases prepared by **publicity writers** working for food companies and public relations agencies. These writers must be very creative about thinking of new ways to interest people in using the products they represent.

If working for yourself appeals to you, you might try to become a **free-lance writer**. This kind of writer is hired by companies for special projects or by a publication to write a specific article. **Authors** of cookbooks and other kinds of food books also work for themselves. They usually get paid a percentage of the book sales (called a royalty). To work as a book author or a free-lance writer, you usually need a lot of experience both in writing and in working with food.

The hardest thing about becoming a food writer is getting started. The first job you get probably won't be the job of your dreams. It takes time and experience to build a reputation. It is definitely helpful to get a college education with several courses in journalism and foods. If you're interested in writing textbooks or other educational materials, you'll find education courses and teaching experience helpful, too.

14

HAS THIS EVER HAPPENED TO YOU?

Arthur has saved up his money to take his date to an expensive restaurant. It's his first time there, and he's trying hard not to let it show.

ARTHUR: *The service here is really excellent! (Aside: I wonder if I was supposed to tip the guy in the tuxedo, who brought us to the table and gave us the menus.)*

NANCY: *It certainly is. And I hear the food is marvelous! (Aside: Why don't they write it in English? He'll think I'm a real dummy when I try to order—I can't even pronounce anything!)*

ARTHUR: *I really like the way the room is decorated. (Aside: At least it's dark, so no one can see if I use the wrong fork!)*

NANCY: *And everyone is dressed so elegantly. (Aside: Maybe I should have left my coat at the checkroom. Did that woman over there keep hers with her, or not? It's so dark, I can't tell!)*

ARTHUR: *The prices are really very reasonable, considering what they give you. (Aside: What do they give you? I can't tell what's included and what costs extra. I hope I brought enough money. If I didn't, I'll really look like a fool—she'll never go out with me again!)*

WAITER: *Good evening. Are you ready to order?*

NANCY: *It all looks so good, I just don't know what to order! (Aside: I sure don't! I wish he'd order first. Then I could just get the same thing. If I make a fool of myself, he'll never ask me out again!)*

EATING OUT

It's unfortunate that eating can sometimes make us nervous and upset. Eating is a time when people should be able to relax and enjoy themselves.

How can you relax when you've got a dozen people watching you to see if you make a mistake?

Sometimes it does seem as if everyone's watching you. Actually, other people have better things to do than watch you all the time. What's really important is not which fork you use. What matters is that you act in a polite and considerate way that does not disturb the dining pleasure of other people. This attitude, plus a basic understanding of how restaurants work and how to eat in company, will get you through any meal smoothly and enjoyably.

Arthur gives his coat to the checkroom attendant and receives a numbered ticket. When he leaves the restaurant, Arthur will use the ticket to identify and pick up his coat.

How restaurants work

You already know a lot about eating in public. If you don't think so, watch a two-year-old in a restaurant sometime, and you'll see that you've come a long way. Once in a while, of course, you may see a teen-ager in a restaurant who is noisy, plays with the food, bangs the silverware, demands attention, and leaves the table in a mess, like a two-year-old. This person has *not* come very far—but you probably don't put yourself in that class. What you need is simply a little information about restaurant procedures and customs.

One thing I'd like to know is: what do all those people in a big restaurant do?

Employees Depending on the size and type of restaurant, you may meet the following employees.

The **checkroom attendant** takes coats, umbrellas, and packages that would be awkward to take with you to the table. Men check their coats. Women often do not, especially if they have light wraps. A bulky, wet, or snowy coat should be checked. The **captain** (sometimes called *maître d'hôtel*, or host) meets you at the entrance to the dining room, checks your reservation (if you've made one), and takes you to your table. Restaurants often require a reservation, especially during their busy hours. A **reservation** holds, or reserves, a table for

You can be sure of having a table at a restaurant at the time you want it by calling ahead for a reservation.

maître d'hôtel (MĀ trə dō TEL)

you. To make one, call the restaurant ahead of time. Let them know what time you plan to arrive and how many will be in your party.

A **waiter** or **waitress** takes your order, brings your food, clears the dishes, and brings you the bill. A **dining room attendant** may clear the used dishes from the table, and perhaps pour the water before the meal. Cafeterias also have these employees, who remove dirty dishes. A **cafeteria** is a less expensive restaurant where people pick up a tray and walk past the food items, picking out what they want as they go.

I'll take the cafeteria. At least you can see what you're getting. But on a menu—how can you tell what it all means?

Menus Menus are sometimes confusing because they have words that are unfamiliar to you. Many of these come from French. Here is a list of some of the French terms you may run into in almost any restaurant.

à la mode
(ah lə MŌD)
"in the current style"; in the United States, it usually describes pie and means "with ice cream"

amandine
(AH mən DĒN)
with almonds

au gratin
(ō GRAH tən)
prepared with a topping of grated cheese and fine bread crumbs

au jus
(ō ZHOOS)
"with juice"; usually describes meat served in its own juices

bouillon
(BOOL yahn)
a clear broth

Some desserts that you may see on a restaurant menu include (clockwise from upper left) chocolate mousse, strawberry parfait, and cherry pie à la mode.

consommé (KAHN sə mā)	a condensed bouillon
crêpe (KREP)	a thin pancake
demitasse (DEM i TAS)	a small cup (usually of coffee)
entrée (AHN trā)	main course (usually a meat, fish, or other protein dish)
filet mignon (fi LĀ min YAHN)	a small, tender, round piece of steak
garni (gahr NĒ)	garnished or decorated
julienne (JOO lē EN)	cut into thin slivers or sticks, as meat, vegetables, or cheese
mousse (MOOS)	a light, frothy, molded dish
parfait (pahr FĀ)	a dessert made of layers of ice cream, fruit, and syrup, usually served in a tall, narrow glass
pois (PWAH)	peas; *petits pois* (PE tē PWAH) are tiny peas
potage (pō TAHZH)	soup (usually a hearty type)
ragoût (ra GOO)	stew
soupe du jour (SOOP də ZHOOR)	featured soup for that day
vin (VAN)	wine
vinaigrette (VIN ə GRET)	a sauce (usually a salad dressing) containing vinegar

Even if you know all these words, how can you tell what's included with each thing, and what costs extra?

Menus are usually organized into different sections from which you can order. The **à la carte** menu (a French phrase, meaning "from the list") lists individual items with a price next to each one. It may be divided into different sections, such as appetizers, soups, entrées, vegetables, salads, desserts, and beverages. There may be a separate

à la carte (ah lə CAHRT)

This Scandinavian smorgasbord has an assortment of foods, including cold fish dishes, cold meats, and salads. The term *smorgasbord* comes from Sweden.

section for seafood and perhaps for sandwiches. To find out how much your meal will cost, simply add up the prices of all the things you want to order.

You will probably get more for your money by ordering from the section called "dinner menu" (or "complete dinner"). This method of ordering is sometimes called **table d'hôte** (another French phrase, meaning "table of the host"). The price of the entrée, or main course, usually includes an appetizer or soup, salad with choice of dressing, bread or rolls, the main dish, and a choice of two vegetables. Dessert and beverage may or may not be included. Any other items are ordered *à la carte* and cost extra. If you're not sure what the dinner includes, don't hesitate to ask the waitress/waiter. Also feel free to ask them to describe a particular dish if you're not sure what it is.

If a young man has invited a young woman out to dinner, and she's not sure how much he can afford to spend, she might ask him what he plans to order. She is probably safe ordering anything around the same price or in the price range of anything he suggests she would like. If they have agreed to split the check, it is convenient if they both order things in the same general price range. That way, they can simply divide the bill in half, and avoid figuring out who owes what for each item ordered.

Should one person do all the ordering, or should you each order for yourself?

Ordering In some restaurants, the waiter/waitress may expect the man at the table to order for the woman as well as for himself. If this is not convenient, the man may say something like: "Have you decided what you'd like, Sue?" and let her answer by ordering for herself. By custom, the woman's order is taken first.

Some restaurants have a **smorgasbord**, or buffet table. Here, diners pick up a plate and take as much as they want of each item on the

table d'hôte (TAH bəl DŌT)   smorgasbord (SMOR gəs BORD)

table. Usually, you are allowed to go back as many times as you want. Pick up a clean plate each time you do so. A server or dining room attendant will remove the used plates from your table.

Sometimes restaurants combine a smorgasbord for appetizers and table service for main dishes. Others may have a salad bar where you make up your own salad. Often, you are allowed to go back for salad as many times as you wish.

Restaurants are usually happy to explain these special features to you on the telephone, along with their price range for sample entrée items. However, remember that these prices do not include all of your costs for the evening.

Paying and tipping

It's quite possible that your total cost will be as much as 40 percent more than the price of entrée items ordered on the dinner menu. Dessert and beverage may be extra. State and local taxes may add 3 to 10 percent, and you still haven't added the tip.

Inexpensive restaurants often have a cashier located somewhere near the entrance. When you're ready to leave, take your check with you and pay the cashier on the way out. Leave your tip on the table as you get up to go—or, if you need change, you can return to the table with the tip after you've paid the cashier.

In many restaurants, especially more expensive ones, you pay the waitress/waiter. When you're ready to leave, ask for the check. Don't snap your fingers or clink your silverware to get your server's attention. Simply catch his or her eye and raise your hand slightly. Or wait until your server passes nearby and call politely, "Waiter," or "Waitress," to gain attention. In a large restaurant, it's a good idea to note carefully at the start what your server looks like. This can save you the embarrassment of calling to the wrong person later on.

Your server will total your check and bring it to you, often on a little tray or plate. Place your payment on the tray along with the check. The server will bring your change back on the same tray. It's customary for you then to leave your tip on the tray.

If two or more people are splitting a check, the easiest method is for one person to collect the money and pay the server. You should round off the amounts each person owes. Don't try to figure it out to the last penny. This creates a great deal of confusion and inconvenience. If you want separate checks, be sure to ask for them in advance—not after you've already ordered.

How much should you tip?

A **tip** (sometimes called a gratuity) is a gift of money given to someone as a way of saying "Thank you for your service." Most of the income of a waiter or waitress comes from tips.

At a good restaurant, you should tip the server 15 to 20 percent of the bill. To figure 15 percent quickly, first get 10 percent by moving the decimal point one place to the left. Then add half of that amount again. For example, 10 percent of $12.00 is $1.20. Half of that is $.60. So 15 percent would be $1.20 + $.60 = $1.80. To get 20 percent, first figure 10 percent ($1.20), and then double the amount ($1.20 × 2 = $2.40).

Dining room attendants at a cafeteria or fast-food restaurant are not tipped. Neither is the captain at an expensive restaurant. Checkroom attendants are tipped from 25 to 50 cents for each check stub—or whatever amount is suggested at the window.

Okay, now I know how to order food and how to pay for it. Is there anything special I need to know about eating it?

Most table manners are a mixture of common sense and common courtesy, together with a few special rules and customs. They are worth learning because they make eating with other people a less awkward, more gracious, and more pleasant experience.

Table manners

Flatware One of the problems young people often run into is the question of flatware. What do you do when you are faced with more than one knife, fork, or spoon?

One solution, of course, is to wait and see what other people do—assuming they know more about it than you do. In a private home, where the hosts are seated at the table, this can be a good rule to follow whenever you are unsure of what to do in a particular situation. Just do things the way the hosts do.

However, you will feel more confident and at ease if you know what to do without copying others. The simplest rule to remember about flatware is that knives, forks, and spoons should be laid out in the order in which they are to be used. Start at the outside and work

Identify this flatware from the descriptions on the next page.

inward. For instance, if you are at a formal banquet and the first thing served is a fruit cocktail, the spoon on the outside should be the proper one to use. If you are served soup first, the soup spoon should be on the outside. Here are a few other tips.

The largest spoon is usually a soup spoon.

The largest knife and the largest fork are the dinner (or meat) knife and fork.

A small, blunt knife is a butter spreader. It is usually placed on the bread and butter plate.

A small (but not tiny) fork is a salad fork or a dessert fork. Dessert forks and spoons are often served with the dessert itself.

A tiny fork is an oyster or cocktail fork, used for eating oysters, shrimp, or other appetizers.

American style of eating   There are two ways to use a knife and fork together: the European style and the American style. Both are considered proper for this country.

To cut meat in either style, hold the fork in your left hand (if you are right-handed) with the prongs, or tines, pointing downward. Brace your index finger against the back of the fork. Stick the fork into the meat to hold it. Hold the knife in your right hand, with your index finger pointing along the back of the knife, and cut across the meat. Never hold a knife or fork in your fist.

In the American style, you now slide the meat off the fork with your knife. Cut only one or two bites at a time. Lay the knife down on your plate. Switch the fork to your right hand. Hold the fork like a pencil, with the tines upward. Stick the fork into the piece of meat or slide it under the meat to lift it up to your mouth.

European style of eating   In the European style, you leave the fork in your left hand, tines downward, and lift the piece of meat to your mouth as soon as it is cut. You don't have to put the knife down. This saves a lot of time and avoids a lot of clanking flatware, but it takes a little practice in using your left hand.

You can also eat vegetables using this style, with your fork in your left hand. You may hold it the same way as before, or with the tines

up. You may use the knife to push the vegetables onto your fork, if you like.

When you are through eating (using either style), lay your knife and fork together on your plate so that they will not fall off when the plate is removed.

Do you ever use your fingers to eat anything?

Finger foods　Many foods are considered finger foods (foods you can eat with your fingers), even at formal occasions. Breads and rolls, of course, are eaten with your fingers. First put a piece on your bread plate, if there is one (on your dinner plate otherwise). Put butter to the side, on the plate. (Be sure to take the butter from the butter dish to your bread plate with the knife that comes with the butter. Do not use your own knife for this.) Break off small pieces and butter them as you eat, rather than buttering the whole thing at once. However, if the rolls or bread are hot from the oven, it's all right to butter the whole piece at once, so that the butter will melt. Break off small pieces as you eat.

Celery, carrot sticks, radishes, pickles, olives, most raw fruits, nuts, cookies, and small cakes are also eaten with your fingers. Corn on the cob is held with the fingers, too. Butter and season only a small portion to eat at one time.

Chicken is usually eaten with a knife and fork. You may use your fingers in casual situations such as picnics, barbecues, or at a fast-food

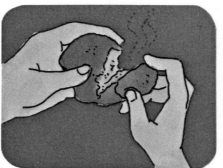

restaurant, where the chicken is dry and crisp. French fries, too, may be eaten with your fingers, if served with hamburgers, crisp chicken, or other finger foods. But if you are eating a steak or other food with a knife and fork, use the fork for your French fries, too. Cut them into bite-size pieces before putting them into your mouth.

Soup   You may pick up a mug or cup of clear soup and drink it if you wish. A soup with chunks of meat or vegetables, or any soup in a bowl, should be eaten with a spoon. Dip the soup spoon quietly into the bowl or cup. Fill it a little less than completely full, so the soup won't drip as you lift it to your mouth. Do not blow on it to cool it. Sip the soup quietly from the side of the spoon. You may tip the bowl or cup slightly to take up the last few spoonfuls.

Spaghetti   Your spaghetti may be served with a large spoon as well as the fork. Hold the spoon in one hand and then twirl a few strands of spaghetti against it with your fork. This winds the spaghetti around the tines of the fork and makes a neat package that you can lift to your mouth. You can also twirl the spaghetti against the plate, without using the spoon.

Baked potato   Fix the potato the way you enjoy eating it most. You may cut a single slit across the top and season it with butter, salt, and pepper. Or cut an X and crush the corners, creating a flower effect. This breaks up the flesh of the potato so that the butter seeps through evenly. If you prefer, cut the potato up into pieces as you eat. You may eat the skin or not, as you prefer.

If the potatoes are cooked in foil, the foil is usually removed before the potatoes are served. If it is not, you may simply peel it back. Or you may remove it, pinch it into a wad, and set it on the side of your plate.

What if you get a piece of the foil in your mouth? Should you spit it out, or go ahead and swallow it?

Removing things from your mouth   If you get something in your mouth that you can't or shouldn't swallow, remove it from your mouth with as little fuss as possible and put it on the side of your plate. If you can do so gracefully, use your fork to get the object out of your mouth and put it on your plate. If you can't, use your fingers. It's better to use your fingers than to sit there sputtering, trying to get the thing onto your fork. Little bone chips, fish bones, gristle, shells, or bits of foil or paper wrappings are best removed with your fingers for this reason. Pits from stewed fruits—such as plums, prunes, or apricots—should be taken from your mouth with your spoon, since it is easy and natural to do so. Pits from raw fruits that you eat out of hand can be removed with your fingers.

If you are not sure how to handle a particular situation, ask yourself: "What would cause the least fuss and the least annoyance to other people?" Chances are that your behavior will then be proper. **Rules of table manners are not designed to trick or torment you.**

They are intended to help you and everyone else at the table enjoy the meal and each other's company.

What about talking with your mouth full? How can you enjoy each other's company if you can't even talk?

Talking with food in your mouth If you're going to have pleasant dinner conversation, there will be times when you have to talk with food in your mouth. However, you should not talk with your mouth so full that it slurs or muffles your speech. Never talk with so much in your mouth that bits of food fly out when you speak. Don't stuff your mouth so full that people can see what you're chewing. Nobody wants to see—or hear—your food after it goes into your mouth. For this reason, you should chew with your mouth closed and not slurp, blow, or lick your food, or smack your lips as you eat.

What if you accidentally spill something? What should you do?

Accidents Accidents happen sometimes, even if you're careful. If you spill something on the tablecloth and can easily pick it up, do so. For instance, a glob of jelly or butter can be scraped up with your knife and put neatly on the edge of your plate. If there's nothing you can do about the spill, make a simple apology and let it go. If you upset a glass, surround the liquid with your napkin quickly, before it flows into someone's lap. If you spill something on a person, apologize and offer your napkin.

The rules of good table manners help prevent accidents. For instance, you should not put your elbows on the table during the meal, when the table is crowded with dishes. This increases the chance that you will knock something over or drag your sleeve in the food. You can, however, rest your hands and forearms on the table.

Nancy rests her forearm on the table during dinner. Is this considered good table manners?

You should not reach over other people's plates or across the table to get a serving dish. This increases the chances of an accident as well as being annoying to others. Ask the person nearest the dish to pass it. (Don't forget to say "Please" and "Thank you.")

When passing foods to others, turn the dish so that the other person can take it by the handle. If the dish is hot, and you need to hold the handle yourself, set it down near the person and turn the handle around for him. If there is no place to put down a serving dish, offer to hold it while the other person spoons out a portion. Then he or she can pass the dish on to the next person.

What if they pass something you don't like? Do you have to take it?

Foods you don't like or can't eat   It's nice to take at least a little of each food, if you can—just for the variety, if nothing else. It's especially courteous at a small gathering where the host chose and prepared the food. However, if you're allergic to something, pass the dish on. If the food is already served on your plate, you do not have to eat it.

When is it okay to start eating?

When to start eating   At a large party or banquet, you may start eating when several people near you have been served. At a small gathering, it's polite to wait until everyone has been served. However, if there is a delay, you do not have to wait until your food gets cold.

At a dinner party, it is customary to follow the lead of the host(s). They will show people where to sit. Wait for them to sit down, unless they ask you to be seated first.

When the host picks up his or her napkin, you may unfold yours and lay it across your lap. At a restaurant, pick up your napkin when everyone has been seated. When you leave the table, place your napkin back to the left of your plate, loosely doubled (but not re-folded).

What if they have seconds on something you like? Should you take it?

Seconds   If you're offered a second helping of something you like, by all means take it. This is a compliment to your hosts—it shows that you really enjoyed the food.

Thanking your host   Don't be shy about complimenting your host(s) on anything you enjoyed about the meal—the food, the table decorations, or anything else. Be sure to thank them, before you leave, for inviting you and for a pleasant evening. If everyone has acted courteously and thoughtfully—which is what good manners are all about—it should have been a very pleasant evening for everyone.

Words to understand

checkroom attendant

captain

maître d'hôtel

reservation

waiter/waitress

dining room attendant

cafeteria

à la carte

table d'hôte

smorgasbord

tip

Equipment to know

soup spoon

dinner knife

dinner fork

butter spreader/knife

salad/dessert fork

oyster/cocktail fork

Questions to discuss

1. How would you make a dinner reservation at a restaurant? Why is a reservation important?
2. What should you do if you don't understand the names of some dishes on the menu?
3. How much money should you leave for a tip? What should you do if you don't have enough change?
4. Why are table manners important?
5. If you've got a number of pieces of silverware at your place setting, how can you figure out which to use for what?
6. Where should you put your knife and fork when you've finished eating?
7. How is the European style of eating different from the American style?
8. Describe the proper way to eat a dinner roll.
9. Name six foods that you can eat with your fingers, even at formal occasions.

10. How would you remove a small bone from a mouthful of food?

11. What should you do if you spill something at the table?

12. Explain how to pass a dish of food to another person.

13. At a small dinner party, when should you start eating?

14. Suppose you are in a group of eight people at a restaurant. You are each going to pay for your own meal. How would you handle it?

15. How much tip would you leave for a dinner bill that added up to (a) $6; (b) $10; (c) $12.50; (d) $15; (e) $16.20? Figure out *about* how much 15 percent *and* 20 percent would be for each bill, rounding off to the nearest dime.

Things to do

1. Make up a skit in which you and your date go into an expensive restaurant. Include players for the checkroom attendant, *maître d'hôtel* or host, waiter or waitress, and dining room attendant. Include ordering, calling for the check, paying, and tipping.

2. Describe what you think the following dishes would be like.

fillet of sole *amandine*	asparagus *vinaigrette*
broccoli *au gratin*	chocolate *mousse*
apple pie *à la mode*	strawberry *parfait*
prime ribs of beef *au jus*	lamb *ragoût*
carrots *julienne*	jellied *consommé*

3. Go to several restaurants in your area and ask for a copy of their menu. (Explain that it is for your class; most restaurants will be glad to cooperate.) Discuss the menus with a group of your classmates. What would each item be like? What would you order if you could spend as much money as you wanted? If you were on a tight budget?

4. Study some menus from actual restaurants. Play the part of a waiter serving a group of your classmates who have come into your restaurant. Bring them the menus and answer their questions about the items listed.

5. Keep a list of foreign food terms and dishes, including non-French words. Start by defining or describing the following:

borsch	*strudel*
flan	*tempura*
parmigiana	*teriyaki*
pilaf	*subgum*
Wiener schnitzel	*won ton*

6. Imagine that you're going to start a restaurant of your own. What dishes would you serve? Design a menu for your restaurant. Include all the side dishes and beverages as well as the entrées.

7. Make up a bulletin board with some of the "dos and don'ts" of good table manners. Illustrate your rules with stick figures or cartoon characters.

Careers to consider

Would you like to serve food to others?

If you enjoy meeting new people—and helping them enjoy themselves—consider a career in food service.

People are eating away from home more often than ever before. This means there's a steady need for workers to serve those meals and to help make eating out an enjoyable experience.

Waiters and **waitresses** work in restaurants, where they take orders and serve meals to customers seated at tables, in booths, or at the counter. In a cafeteria, people choose what they want to eat from a counter display. Their selections are usually dished out by **cafeteria servers**, but the customers carry their own food to their tables. School lunchrooms often serve food cafeteria-style. In carry-out restaurants, the emphasis is on portable foods served quickly. **Counter attendants** take orders and serve the food in disposable packaging that can be taken out. Some fast-food restaurants offer both carry-out service and limited table service. An office canteen offers beverages and portable luncheon items to people working in a particular company.

Many people find work in food service very satisfying because they enjoy meeting and serving a variety of people. They like helping customers choose food they will enjoy eating. A friendly, courteous personality is essential in this kind of work.

Working in food service has several advantages. Hours are varied and sometimes may be flexible. Often you can get free meals during working hours. Since most food service workers wear uniforms, you can save money on clothes. Jobs are available all over the country, so you can live almost anywhere.

Wages for waiting on tables may seem low. Actually, most of the money you can make comes from tips. The more you put into your job, the more you're likely to carry out in tips!

15

HAS THIS EVER HAPPENED TO YOU?

Tony's social studies class is discussing food as a topic in current events. They've each brought in a headline in which food is the main issue.

TONY: *My article says that more and more people are going hungry.*

JERRY: *Mine says that the food supply is increasing!*

DIANE: *Mine says our food today is full of poison.*

PHIL: *Oh, yeah? Mine says that it's safer than ever.*

RENÉE: *This one says we eat too much meat.*

SUSAN: *But this one says we don't get enough protein.*

JACK: *This one says artificial sweeteners are bad for you.*

MARIA: *Well, this one says that sugar is even worse!*

JOEY: *This book says you should take large doses of vitamins.*

ALICE: *This article says large doses are poisonous!*

TONY: *I don't get it. These articles can't all be true. But if they aren't true, how do they get printed? How do you know what to believe?*

298

FOOD IS NEWS

Exploring . . .

Guides for evaluating what you read and hear

Outlook for the world's food supplies

The cost of food

How to analyze diets and food claims

New foods for the future

Food is news. Pick up almost any newspaper or magazine and you'll see an article that has something to do with food. The trouble is, the articles often seem to disagree with each other. One article says one thing and the next one seems to say the exact opposite.

That means one of them is wrong, doesn't it? How can it get printed if it isn't true?

The government is not allowed to regulate the publication of books, magazines, and newspapers. The First Amendment to the Constitution guarantees everyone the right of free speech—which is good. But this also means that people are free to say things that may not be true, or not completely accurate.

Advertising claims can be regulated to some extent by the **Federal Trade Commission (FTC)**. It's the FTC's job to keep an eye on business practices and stop those which are illegal. For instance, let's say a certain manufacturer claims that using his jump rope will improve your hearing. The FTC can order him to stop making a false or misleading claim in order to sell a product. However, the FTC is not able to check into every claim made by every company in the country. You often have to decide for yourself whether a certain statement is completely true or not.

The FTC has no power at all to regulate statements made in books or in newspaper and magazine articles. If a certain author claims that drinking extra water—or eating pickles, or doing push-ups—will improve your hearing, the government can't do anything about it. The author has not made the statement in order to sell water, or pickles, or push-ups. Remember, though, that the author *is* trying to sell *books*. If he can sell more books by saying things that sound unusual and exciting, he may be tempted to do so.

Okay, so how can *you tell what to believe?*

You have to evaluate each statement for yourself. Here are some questions you can ask that will help you judge the accuracy of the articles you read:

What are the author's motives? Does he or she have something to gain by convincing you of something? (If so, that would discourage telling you "the whole truth and nothing but the truth.")

What are the author's qualifications? Is the person an expert on the subject?

Where was the article published? Articles in scientific and professional magazines, or in textbooks and good reference books, are checked by experts in the field. Articles in general magazines and newspapers usually are not—except to make sure that the author was quoted correctly.

Does the article tell both sides of the issue, or is it biased? An article is biased if it picks out facts to support one point

Irrigation makes it possible to grow crops on land that normally would be too dry. Name some places in this country where irrigation is used.

of view, without telling all the other facts.

What do other experts say about the issue? Sometimes you can't judge whether a report is true or not until you read several other reports on the same subject.

Does the information fit well with what you already know? Chances are, if you can find *some* things that you know are wrong, there are *other* things wrong, too.

Does the article make wild, fantastic claims? Claims for miracle cures and "unbelievable results" are usually just what they say—"unbelievable."

Is the method scientific? Did the author study a large number of cases? Was there a carefully controlled experiment? Was the experiment repeated by someone else with the same results?

Is the logic (reasoning) correct, and is the conclusion justified? It would be quite easy, for instance, to run a study that found very few cases of rheumatism among people who drink baby formula. But this does not mean that drinking baby formula prevents rheumatism. Rheumatism is a disease that mainly strikes older people. Baby formula is drunk mainly by babies.

There is a lot of controversy about food today. It needs a lot of clear, careful thinking. These questions will help you in deciding what to believe about the various issues.

Okay, what I want to know is—will there be enough food for everyone in the future? My article says there won't.

Some people are very gloomy about our future food supplies. Others are very hopeful. Often, this is because they base their studies on different facts and assumptions.

World food supplies

WORLD FAMINE PREDICTED

The Food and Agricultural Society of the World has released a report on the

People have been concerned about the world food supply for a long time. About 200 years ago, a British philosopher named Thomas Malthus predicted that the world would soon have more people than it could feed. However, a lot of things have happened since then to increase the amount of food the world can produce.

The **Food and Agricultural Organization (FAO)**, a part of the United Nations, is one of many groups working to improve food supplies and farm methods in the world today. Improved farm practices have increased the amount that can be grown, and have kept the soil from wearing out so quickly. Increased use of farm machinery has meant that each farmer can get more work done. Irrigation and water-saving methods have increased the amount of land that can be used for farming.

Chemical fertilizers have raised harvests in America by over 50 percent in the last twenty-five years. In some parts of the world, they

Bags of rice are waiting for shipment. Rice is a basic food in many countries. What factors could affect the production of rice? How might a shortage of rice affect its price?

could increase food production by two to five times. Better control of pests such as weeds, plant diseases, and insects have also helped. About a third of the world's food crops are still lost to these pests each year. Improved pest control in the future will make more food available for people.

One of the most dramatic developments in recent years has been the **green revolution**—the development of new, high-yielding plant varieties. These plants grow faster, produce more food, and resist disease better than the old plants. New breeds of animals have also increased the amount of meat and poultry available to the world.

In the past, people in less developed countries have often starved because emergency food supplies could not be distributed to them in time. Improved storage and transportation facilities have helped correct this problem. Advances in food processing and handling have reduced spoilage and loss to rodents and insects. When these improvements are made available in more parts of the world, much more food can be saved.

Our supply of fish and other seafood may be greatly increased by adding more "fish farms" along our shores and streams. High-protein algae and other foods from the sea can also be grown and used for animal feed.

Although these factors have all helped to increase the food supply, world population has also been increasing. At an increase of only 2 percent a year, the population doubles every thirty-five years. Food production has not been able to keep up with the demand.

As a result, you may see reports that there is not enough food being produced to feed everyone properly. This is certainly true. You may also see reports that food production has increased greatly, and could be increased even more. This is also true. But we are finding out more and more that the world's resources are limited. Food production cannot catch up with and stay ahead of the population if the number of people continues to increase as it has in the past.

What makes the cost of food keep going up?

Many things affect the price of food. Some of them can be controlled, but some cannot.

High cost of food

FOOD PRICES UP AGAIN

The wholesale price index for food rose again last month for the

For many years, increases in farm production in the United States actually made food prices go down, compared to other products. Americans spend about 18 percent of their income, after taxes, on food. In most countries the percentage is much higher than this. There is no doubt, however, that food prices have been going up lately.

Part of the reason is that the farmer's costs are rising rapidly. For one thing, the cost of oil has risen tremendously. Farms need gasoline, which is made from oil, to run tractors and other machinery. Oil is also used as a raw material for chemical fertilizers and insecticides (insect killers). The costs of land, machinery, and other equipment have also gone up. Farmers have to borrow money to pay for these things, but interest rates on the money they borrow have gone up, too.

In the past, chemical fertilizers and insecticides greatly increased crop yields, which helped reduce the cost of food. However, this has created pollution problems in some cases, so their use has been reduced. This has added to the increased cost of producing food.

For most food products, the price paid to the farmer is only a small percentage of the price in the food store. A large part goes to pay for **processing**—cleaning, trimming, cooking, canning, freezing, grinding,

These workers are sorting and packing tomatoes for shipment. What are some other processes in marketing foods? How do they add to the cost of food products?

Grain is being loaded onto a ship for export. How do exports affect the cost of food at home? Why do we export foods?

baking, and packaging. Much of it goes for storage and transportation, usually by truck or freight car. **Marketing expenses** are also added. These are the costs of distribution (the process of getting foods to the consumer, which includes advertising and selling in retail stores). Inflation has raised all of these costs in recent years. These increases all get passed on to you, the consumer, in the price you have to pay for food.

In recent years, the international situation has also tended to push food prices up. Increased world population has created a need for more food, which means that people are willing to pay more to get food. This pushes up the price on the world market. If we sell food on the world market, it also increases the price at home.

Some people say we should not sell food on the world market if it increases our food prices at home. Others say we should, because it will help pay for all the things we have to import, especially oil. If we import much more than we export, it adds to inflation, which increases the cost of everything.

What about dieting? How do you know what really works and what doesn't?

There are hundreds of diets around that promise to "melt away" pounds of fat without effort. A few basic facts will help you judge how much they're worth.

Weight-loss diets

People who are trying to lose weight would love to think they could do it without effort or will power. There are plenty of people around who are ready to promise that they can. Most of them, of course, are eager to sell a product, a service, a magazine, or a book.

Many of these "magic" diet plans seem to work very well for the first week or so. After that, the results are less impressive. You may even find yourself gaining back the weight you "lost," even though

LOSE 10 POUNDS IN ONE WEEK

An amazing new diet discovery lets you eat as much as you want and still lose over 10 pounds your very first

you stick to the diet. The reason is usually that the diet disturbs your body's normal chemical balance. This results in a weight loss—but of water, not fat. Water is lost easily and gained back easily. Fat is gained slowly but is also lost very slowly.

A kilogram of fat represents about 7,700 calories. (That means a pound of fat is worth about 3,500 calories.) A 55-kilogram (120-pound) woman uses up about 2,100 calories a day. Let's say she gets shipwrecked on a desert island and has absolutely nothing to eat or drink for a week, except water. If she continues her normal level of activity, she will lose only about 2 kilograms (a little over 4 pounds) of fat in that week. Any other weight loss will be water loss.

Good diets are not starvation diets, so they should not promise a loss of 2 kilograms (4 pounds) a week. Safe, reliable diets usually produce about .50 to 1 kilogram (2 pounds or less) of real fat loss per week.

Be careful of any diet that limits you to only a few foods, or that cuts out an entire food or nutrient group, such as meat, breads and cereals, or carbohydrates. The key to good health is still balanced meals. Weight loss should come about through reduced portion size (smaller amounts), rather than reduced variety.

How about the way foods are grown? Aren't natural foods better for you than foods that are grown with a lot of chemicals?

The "health food" market has turned into a big business. Sales estimates for 1980 run as high as $4 billion. Whether or not these foods are better for you is a controversial issue.

Quality of our food supply

NEW HEALTH FOOD STORE OPENS

Organically grown tomatoes, brown rice, whole grain flour, sunflower seeds, and ginseng root are just a few of the

Science and agriculture, working together, have greatly increased the amount and variety of food available to the American people. Some people believe that the quality of our food has also improved, but others feel it has gone down. Some think that all food should be grown **organically**. This is a rather loose term meaning that no chemical pesticides (pest killers) should be used, and that all fertilizers should come from natural organic sources—that is, from plants and animals. This would include leaves, grass, stalks, and animal manure.

Most reliable scientific studies show little or no difference between the nutritional content of foods grown organically and those grown with chemical fertilizers. However, there are some advantages to organic farming. It reduces the problem of having chemical fertilizers wash out into streams and lakes, which increases the growth of algae. (**Algae** are tiny green plants which darken the water and keep other

organically (or GAN ik lē)   **algae** (AL jē)

things from growing in it.) Organically farmed soil absorbs and holds water better, too. It also helps to recycle waste materials. The biggest disadvantage of organic farming is that it takes much more time and work than regular farming. This makes it more expensive. If we tried to produce all of our food organically it would raise the cost of food greatly. We would also have trouble growing enough food to feed everyone in this country.

Some health food enthusiasts claim that natural vitamins are better for you than synthetic vitamins, made in a laboratory. Actually, they are both chemicals with exactly the same molecular structure no matter where they come from. Health food stores sell a large number of vitamin products and other nutrition supplements. Critics of these products argue that there is no need for supplements among normal people who eat a balanced diet. They are also concerned that large doses of many nutrients may actually be harmful. If you think you have a real nutrition problem—such as a vitamin deficiency—see your doctor.

Products in health food stores are often much more expensive than foods in the supermarket. Many of them are exotic items not found anywhere else. Some of these foods may have a special taste or texture which makes them worth the price to you. But don't buy them on the basis of fancy health claims until you have good reason to believe the claims are true.

Aren't a lot of junk things put into food these days, just to make you think you're getting more?

Food scientists are constantly developing new food resources. Some of them may seem strange at first, but they promise new hope for the future.

Legumes and grains in bulk (not packaged) for sale in a health food store. Why are health foods often more expensive than those in supermarkets?

COTTON SEEDS ADDED TO WHEAT FLOUR

The next time you bite into a "ham on rye," you may be surprised to find out that it's really "ham on cotton seed." Food scientists have recently developed a new method for

New foods from technology

We may see many new foods in the future. Although they should all be carefully tested, we should not reject any of them simply because they are new and unfamiliar. Many of them may add to the quality of our food as well as the quantity.

Scientists have known for a long time, for instance, that cotton seeds contain a lot of vegetable protein. But there were problems involved in getting at the parts that would be useful in human food. Recently, these problems have been overcome. Cotton seeds can now be used safely to boost the protein content of many foods, particularly baked goods. This is good news for Americans—but it is especially good news for the developing countries of the world that are poor in protein resources.

Protein can also be obtained from tiny plants such as algae, yeasts, and fungi. These plants grow very quickly. They can double their weight in as little as two hours. (Chickens take two to four weeks; and cattle take one to two months.) These plants can grow on gar-

Soybeans contain protein and provide food for animals and human beings.

bage, sewage, and animal wastes. They can then be processed into fertilizer, animal feed, or protein supplements. This means that they can help solve the pollution problem at the same time they contribute to the food supply.

Soybeans and other plant foods can also be used to make **textured vegetable protein (TVP)**. This is vegetable protein that is made to look, taste, and "chew" like meat. It is often used as a meat "extender," and as a meat substitute, it is a valuable source of protein in vegetarian diets.

I see lots of articles about additives in food. How can you tell what's safe and what isn't?

Most Americans eat food that has been grown, processed, and shipped by others. Some people worry about what goes into that food before it reaches them.

Safety of additives

An **additive** is an ingredient added to a product for some specific reason. Some additives contribute color or flavor. Some are important to texture. Others are preservatives—that is, they help to prevent spoilage or the growth of harmful microbes. Vitamins and minerals are considered additives, too, when added to a food.

The Food and Drug Administration (FDA) runs careful experiments to find out whether each substance added to food is safe to eat,

NITRITES LINKED TO CANCER

A four-year study commissioned by the government has concluded that

additive (AD ə tiv)

This orange drink contains saccharin. The label calls attention to possible danger from its use. Why does the government permit the sale of additives that may be dangerous to health? What are some other additives?

and how much can be added without harmful effects. These tests are very strict. They use very large doses of the substance in order to detect the slightest harmful effect. Some people even think that the doses used are too large. For instance, in one study, rats were fed large amounts of nitrite to find out whether this substance, which is used as a preservative, could lead to cancer. To get an equal percentage of nitrite into the body, a human being would have had to eat 7,000 hotdogs a day!

The decision about whether to use additives or not can be very complicated. Sometimes, the dangers of using the additive are less than the dangers of *not* using it. Nitrites, for instance, are added to meats and certain other processed foods to prevent botulism, which is a deadly form of food poisoning. Many food scientists feel that the risk of botulism *without* nitrite is greater than the risk of cancer *with* it. Tests on saccharin, an artificial sweetener, suggest that using very large amounts may increase the chances of cancer. However, people with diabetes can't use natural sweeteners such as sugar or honey. Natural sweeteners also add extra calories and thus extra weight, which can be a health hazard to people with heart trouble or high blood pressure.

Very often, the chemicals used as food additives occur naturally, too. It would be impossible to eliminate them entirely. Nitrites, for instance, are found in spinach and other leafy vegetables. They are

An FDA inspector is grading and inspecting meat. What else does the FDA do?

even manufactured by our bodies from our own saliva! Only about 20 percent of the nitrite in the body comes from processed foods.

Artificial flavorings often contain the same flavor chemicals found in natural foods. However, there are often many different chemicals involved in the natural flavor. It may be too difficult or expensive to produce all of them. As a result, the artificial flavoring may be just as safe, but perhaps not as tasty, as the natural one.

It is good for people to be concerned about the quality of our food supply, and to take an active interest in maintaining it. No one would want to return to the conditions of a hundred years ago. At that time, there were no laws to prevent the sale of spoiled or adulterated food. (A food is **adulterated** if it is made impure by adding harmful or poor-quality ingredients.) To correct this situation, Congress passed the **Pure Food and Drug Act** in 1906. This law set up the FDA as a watchdog agency to maintain high standards of quality in the food industry. Most experts agree that, as a result, our food today is safer and better than ever before.

adulterated (ə DUHL tə RĀ tid)

Words to understand

FTC
FAO
green revolution
food processing
marketing expense
organic farming

algae
TVP
additive
adulterated
Pure Food and Drug Act

Questions to discuss

1. What federal agency would handle a deceptive advertising claim?

2. Why are articles printed in scientific or professional magazines more reliable than those in general magazines?

3. What clues might warn you that an article may not be accurate? (Describe at least three.)

4. Describe three or more things that have increased the amount of food produced in the world during the past fifty or so years.

5. How does the cost of food in the United States compare with the costs in most parts of the world?

6. Name four or more things that are part of the price we pay for food.

7. What does a growing world population have to do with the cost of food in the United States?

8. How can you judge if a diet for losing weight is a good one?

9. Is natural vitamin C from a product such as rose hips better for you than vitamin C found in a vitamin pill? Why or why not?

10. What federal agency checks on the safety of food additives?

11. How is textured vegetable protein (TVP) used in our food supply? Give at least two examples.

Things to do

1. Make up a "Food Is News" bulletin board. Bring in food-related articles and arrange them on the bulletin board. Discuss the articles in class. Why is each one important? Do you think the information is accurate? What makes you think so (or not)?

2. Bring in the label from a food product with several additives, or bring in the whole package. Write to the manufacturer and ask for a description of each ingredient. Ask why it is added and what the product would be like without the ingredient. Report your findings to the class.

3. Make up a "Food News" newspaper (or magazine). Have each member of your group write a short article on some food-related issue. Type the articles in columns in a newspaper form. You might run it off on the mimeograph or spirit duplicating machine and distribute it to other classes.

4. Bring in a diet article and report on it to the class. Is it a sensible diet? How many calories does it include? Does it provide variety and balanced nutrition? Does it promise realistic results?

5. Make a poster (such as a bar graph) illustrating the percentage of personal income that is spent on food in various countries. Ask your librarian for sources of information, or write to the U.S. Department of Agriculture or the Food and Agricultural Organization of the United Nations (your librarian can give you the addresses).

Careers to consider

Would you like to be involved in developing new foods?

If you are good at science and enjoy working with laboratory equipment, consider a career in food science and technology.

Food scientists work with the chemical make-up of foods. Some work on developing new forms for old foods. Products similar to mayonnaise or ice cream but made from yogurt are an example. Scientists have also found ways to make some perishable foods keep longer. In fact, there are now some milk products that are processed so they won't need cold storage.

Other food scientists may develop synthetic foods from various compounds. Synthetic vitamins and artificial flavorings, for example, have been used for years. Special foods can be developed to meet specific diet needs, such as infant formula or special foods for hospital use. Some food research aims to develop new products that imitate old, familiar ones. Often the new products offer advantages such as less fat or fewer calories. Sometimes they cost less. Textured vegetable protein is often used to make imitation meats, products which look, taste, and "chew" almost like real meats.

Some food scientists look for new plant and animal food sources. Examples are fish meal, krill (tiny shrimplike creatures), and microscopic plants such as yeast and algae. Technologists are busy developing these sources into food products or food supplements for people, or as feed for animals.

Food scientists include **chemists, physicists, biologists, engineers,** and **home economists**. Plant and animal **geneticists** also improve the food supply by developing new breeds of animals or varieties of plants that are healthier, grow quicker, and produce more food.

Food scientists may work at a university, for the government, or in the research and development department of a large food company. The pay is good, but the educational requirements are high. Food scientists need at least four years of college, and very often have advanced degrees. Some assistant technician jobs are available to graduates of junior (two-year) colleges.

Pronunciation key

This key will help you correctly pronounce words in this text that you may not know. Look at the pronunciation for *contaminated*:

> kən TAM ə NĀ tid

Find the sound of each letter in the key. The capital letters tell you which syllables are stressed, or said with the most force. The syllable in LARGE CAPITAL LETTERS is stressed most. Syllables in SMALL CAPITAL LETTERS are stressed a little less, but more than the rest of the syllables. Now pronounce kən TAM ə NĀ tid.

a	act, lap	yoo	use, cure, few	n	nap, noon
ā	age, late	u	book, put	p	play, top
ah	star, father, not	uh	cup	r	ran, steer
aw	law, all	ə	along, moment,	s	sit, yes
e	end, met		modify, protect,	t	tip, hat
ē	see, even		circus	v	very, wave
er	learn, fur	b	big, job	w	wide, always
i	is, hit	d	do, red	y	yellow, onion
ī	ice, mile	f	fair, if	z	zebra, freeze, bees
ir	ear, deer	g	go, dig	ch	chill, reach
ō	open, no	h	head, behave	sh	sharp, crash
oi	foil, boy	j	joke, bridge	th	three, both
or	horn, door	k	king, kick	th	then, breathe
ow	flower, out	l	light, bell	zh	treasure
oo	hoot, rule	m	meet, him	ng	bring, think

Glossary

Words in heavy type within a definition are also defined in the glossary. Cooking terms are keyed with a ■, and their page numbers are given.

additive (AD ə tiv): an ingredient put into food, which may add color, flavor, texture, or **nutrients,** or act as a **preservative.**

adulterated (ə DUHL tə RĀ tid): made impure by the adding of harmful or poor-quality ingredients.

à la carte (ah lə CAHRT): **menu** items listed and priced separately.

algae (AL jē): tiny, green plants that grow in water.

amino acids (ə MĒ nō AS ids): small units that make up **protein.** Essential amino acids are those the body needs but can't make and must get from food.

anemia (ə NĒ mē ə): a physical condition caused by a lack of iron. Symptoms include tiredness and a pale appearance. See also **mineral.**

aroma (ə RŌ mə): a smell or odor. The aroma of food adds to its flavor.

assimilated (ə SIM ə LĀ tid): absorbed into the bloodstream. See also **metabolism.**

■ **bake:** to cook by dry heat in an oven. *p. 65*

baking powder: a **leavening agent** used in baked goods such as quick breads and cakes.

baking soda: a **leavening agent** used in baked goods such as quick breads and cakes.

Basic Four: a guide to good **nutrition.** The four food groups are the Milk Group, the Fruit and Vegetable Group, the Meat Group, and the Bread and Cereal Group.

■ **baste** (BĀST): to moisten a **roasting** or **broiling** food with oil, barbecue sauce, or **marinade,** using a pastry brush or spoon. *p. 212*

■ **beat:** to mix, with a quick, regular motion that lifts the mixture up and over itself, using a spoon or electric mixer. *p. 67*

bland: mild; relatively flavorless.

■ **blend:** to mix two or more ingredients thoroughly and evenly by **beating** or **stirring.** *p. 67*

■ **boil:** to cook in liquid at boiling temperature (100 °C; 212 °F). The boiling point has been reached when bubbles form and break in the liquid. *p. 100*

botulism (BAHCH ə LIZ əm): one of the most dangerous of all types of **food poisoning.**

■ **braise** (BRĀZ): to cook meat slowly in a small amount of water or other liquid, or in its own steam, in a covered pan. *p. 178*

bran: the outer covering of the whole grain kernel. It is rich in **vitamins, minerals,** and fiber.

brine (BRĪN): a **preservative** mixture of salt and water that also flavors the food placed in it.

■ **broil:** to cook by exposing food directly to a source of heat, such as an oven broiler unit or charcoal grill. *p. 107*

buffet (buh FĀ) **style:** a method of serving a meal in which food and dishes are set out on a table and people help themselves.

cafeteria: a relatively inexpensive restaurant where customers use trays and pick up the food items from a counter.

calorie (KAL ə rē): a measurement unit for food **energy.**

captain: also called **maître d'hôtel** or **host,** this restaurant employee greets guests, checks **reservations,** and seats customers.

carbohydrate (CAHR bə HĪ drāt): a source of food **energy.** Sugars and starches are carbohydrates.

carbon monoxide (KAHR bən mə NAHK sīd): a poisonous gas. It is given off, for instance, when charcoal burns.

casserole (KAS ə rōl): a one-dish meal **baked** in the oven.

chalaza (kə LĀ zə): a ropelike strand of thick **protein** in an egg that holds the **yolk** in place.

checkroom attendant: a restaurant employee who takes care of customers' coats, umbrellas, and packages.

■ **chop:** to cut into small pieces. *p. 120*

complement (KAHM plə MENT): to add to; or to complete.

condiment (KAHN də mənt): any sauce, relish, or spice used to season food—salt, pepper, or mustard, for example.

consistency (kən SIS tən sē): **texture** and thickness.

contaminated (kən TAM ə NĀ tid): infected; containing **microbes.**

contrast (KAHN trast): difference.

convenience (kən VĒ nyəns) **product:** food that has been processed and packaged so that less work or preparation time is needed.

■ **cream:** to combine, soften, and beat until smooth a fat, or shortening, with a sugar, using a spoon or electric mixer. *p. 67*

■ **cut in:** to blend shortening with flour or other dry ingredients until large crumbs form, using a fork or pastry blender. *p. 114*

deficiency (di FISH ən sē): lack; shortage.

defrost (də FROST): to remove ice build-up from a refrigerator or freezer.

diet: the foods that a person eats; also, a special plan for eating.

digest (dī JEST): to break down food in the stomach and intestines into small, simple units that the body can use.

digestion (dī JES jən): the act of digesting.

■ **dilute** (di LOOT): to thin out **consistency** by adding liquid. *p. 272*

dining room attendant: the restaurant employee who pours water before a meal and clears used dishes from the table; sometimes called busboy or busgirl.

dovetailing (DUHV tāl ing): doing two or more things in the same time period.

drained weight: the weight of a solid food packed in liquid after the liquid has been poured off.

empty calorie: a unit of food energy that is high in **fats** and **carbohydrates,** but low in **vitamins, minerals,** and **proteins.**

emulsion (i MUHL shən): a cloudy mixture in

which oil is suspended in small droplets in a liquid.

endosperm (EN dō SPERM): the starchy part of the grain kernel that remains after milling.

energy: the power to do work. Household energy is the energy used in running a home, usually supplied by electricity or fuels such as gas and oil. Personal energy is a person's power or ability for action or work, supplied by food.

English-style service: a method of serving a meal in which food is put onto plates at the table by the **host** and passed to the guests.

enriched (in RICHT): a term describing processed food which has had certain amounts of iron and three of the B **vitamins** (thiamin, riboflavin, and niacin) added to it.

entrée (AHN trā): the main course.

family-style service: a method of serving a meal at the table in which food dishes are passed to the guests, who serve themselves.

FAO: Food and Agricultural Organization. A United Nations group whose purpose is to improve the farming methods and food supplies of the world.

fasting: going without food.

fat: (1) a type of **nutrient** that supplies concentrated **energy**; (2) a stored form of **energy** in the body; (3) oil, butter, etc., used in cooking.

FDA: Food and Drug Administration. A federal agency that watches over and maintains standards of safety and quality in the food industry.

■ **flour** (pan): to coat a greased pan with flour. *p. 229*

fluid ounce: a customary measurement unit for liquid volume. There are 32 fluid ounces in one quart.

food-borne infection (in FEK shən): illness caused by food **contaminated** with **microbes**. When contaminated food is eaten, the microbes infect the body and cause stomach upset or illness.

food intoxication (in TAHK sə KĀ shən): illness caused by eating food that contains **toxin**, or poison, produced when certain **microbes multiply** in the food.

food poisoning: a general term used to describe illness caused by eating **contaminated** food, or by eating poisonous plants or chemicals.

food processing: the cleaning, trimming, grinding, mixing, cooking, baking, canning, freezing, and/or packaging of foods.

fork-tender: a test for doneness of cooked food. The food is soft enough so that a fork can easily be stuck into it.

fortified (FOR tə fīd): a term describing processed food that has had extra **nutrients** (that may not have been in the unprocessed food) added to it.

■ **fry:** to cook quickly in an uncovered pan with a small amount of **fat**. See **sauté**. *p. 94*

FTC: Federal Trade Commission. A U.S. government agency that watches over advertising and other business practices to protect consumers.

garnish (GAHR nish): to decorate.

germ: (1) the inner part of a grain kernel that has a nutty flavor and is rich in **vitamins**, **minerals**, and oil; (2) a **microbe**.

glucose (GLOO kōs): a sugar produced when the body breaks down food. It is used to provide **energy** for the body.

glycogen (GLĪ kə jən): a form of starch into which the body changes **glucose** for storage. It can be changed back to glucose when needed for **energy**.

green revolution: the development of new, high-yielding plant varieties.

habit: routine action. Eating habits include the kinds of foods a person usually eats, as well as how, when, and where the foods are eaten.

host: the person (male or female) who greets, entertains, and takes care of guests.

infectious (in FEK shəs): likely to cause disease or infection.

in season: a term that refers to the time of year when a certain fruit or vegetable is harvested.

insecticide (in SEK tə sīd): a substance that kills insects.

insulation (IN sə LĀ shən): a protective layer that helps prevent heat loss (as in an oven) or loss of cold air (as in a freezer).

■ **knead** (NĒD): to fold and press dough repeatedly to develop a springy **texture**. *pp. 114; 250*

leavening agent (LEV ən ing Ā jənt): an ingredient that produces carbon dioxide, which makes a food rise. See **baking powder, baking soda,** and **yeast.**

life style: the way a person lives.

maître d'hôtel (MĀ tre dō TEL): See **captain.**

marinade (MAR ə nād): a mixture into which food is placed to add flavor and/or to tenderize.

■ **marinate** (MAR ə nāt): to let food stand in a **marinade.** *p. 212*

marketing expenses: food industry costs of bringing food to consumers. They include the money paid for distribution, advertising, sales people, and so on.

mature (mə CHUR): fully grown.

menu: a list of foods served at a meal or available in a restaurant.

metabolism (mə TAB ə LIZ əm): all of the body's processes involved in using food for **energy** and for cell growth and repair.

metric system: a decimal system of measurement. The basic unit for weight is the gram, the basic unit for length is the meter, and the basic unit for volume is the liter.

microbe (MĪ krōb): a **microorganism** that causes disease or infection. It is sometimes called a **germ**.

microorganism (MĪ krō OR gə NIZ əm): a tiny plant or animal that can be seen only through a microscope.

mineral (MIN ər əl): an element; the most basic kind of matter. Some of the minerals important to nutrition are calcium, iron, iodine, and fluorine.

muffin method: a technique for mixing ingredients. Dry ingredients are mixed together in one bowl and liquid ingredients are mixed in another. Then the liquid is added to the dry and briefly mixed.

multiply: to increase in number.

national brand: a brand of food found for sale across the country.

net weight: the weight of packaged food without the package.

no-brand brand: a brand of food with a plain label that gives only the product name and information required by law.

nutrient (NOO trē ənt): a substance that the body needs in order to live and grow. **Carbohydrates**, **fats**, **proteins**, **vitamins**, **minerals** and water are nutrients.

nutrition (noo TRISH ən): the study of **nutrients** and how the body uses them.

nutrition information panel: the section of a food package label that lists the main **nutrients** found in that product.

organic (or GAN ik) **farming:** a method of farming in which only natural fertilizers, and no manufactured **insecticides** or fertilizers, are used.

■ **panbroil:** to cook in a pan or griddle with little or no **fat**. *p. 269*

■ **parboil:** (PAHR boil): to partially cook a food by **boiling** it. *p. 217*

perishable (PER i shə bəl): describes a food that will not stay fresh long.

pickling (PIK əl ing): a method of preserving food by keeping it in an acid liquid, such as vinegar, or in **brine**.

preservative (pri ZER və tiv): a substance added to food to kill **microbes** or to prevent them from growing.

private label brand: a brand of food that carries the name of a supermarket chain and is sold only in those supermarkets.

product dating: the system of marking a date on a food product. A pull date gives the last date it should be sold. An expiration date tells how long the food will be good.

proportion (prə POR shən): relationship between amounts of various items.

protein (PRŌ tēn): a **nutrient** needed to build and maintain living cells. It can also be used for **energy**. Complete protein is protein that contains all the essential **amino acids**. Incomplete protein lacks one or more of the essential amino acids.

Pure Food and Drug Act: a law passed by Congress in 1906 that banned the adulteration of food.

■ **purée** (pyor Ā): to make a smooth paste by forcing cooked food through a sieve or **chopping** it finely in a food mill or blender. *p. 273*

regional brand: a brand of food sold in only one region of the country.

reservation: an arrangment by which a table in a restaurant is saved, or reserved, for a customer.

restored: (ri STORD): a term used on processed food labels which states that **nutrients** lost during food processing have been replaced.

■ **roast:** to cook by dry heat. Usually meat is roasted in an oven, but vegetables may be roasted in foil on a grill, for instance. *p. 245*

R.S.V.P.: Abbreviation for "*Répondez, s'il vous plaît*" (rā PŌN dā, sēl voo plā), French for "Please reply." It is often written at the bottom of an invitation.

salmonella (SAL mə NEL ə): one of the most serious types of **food poisoning**.

■ **sauté** (saw TĀ): to cook quickly in an uncovered pan with a small amount of fat. See **fry**. *p. 173*

■ **score:** to make shallow slits or gashes with fork tines or a knife. *p. 121*

seasoned pan: a pan that has a built-up, smooth surface of oil.

■ **simmer:** to cook in liquid, just under the boiling point, so that small bubbles form at the bottom of the pan. *p. 100*

smorgasbord (SMOR gəs BORD): a Swedish term for a **buffet** table.

standard of identity: the legal definition of a product, based on its ingredients.

staphylococcus (STAF ə lō KAHK əs): one of the most serious types of **food poisoning**. Its name is sometimes shortened to staph.

staple (STĀ pəl): a food, such as flour, sugar, or oil, that is kept on hand in the kitchen because it is used often.

■ **stew:** to cook food slowly in a large amount of liquid in a covered pot. *p. 178*

■ **stir:** to move ingredients in a circular motion in order to **blend** them, to keep them smooth, to keep solids from settling, or to distribute heat evenly. *p. 67*

table d'hôte (TAH bəl DŌT): a restaurant menu that lists prices for complete dinners, rather than for individual food items.

taste buds: the parts of the tongue that sense sweet, sour, bitter, and salty tastes.

texture (TEKS cher): the feel of food in the mouth —crisp, soggy, tender, chewy, and so on.

theme party: a party where decorations, food, costumes, and so on focus on a central idea.

tip: a gift of money given to restaurant employees as thanks for a certain service; also called a gratuity.

toxin (TAHK sən): a poison.

TVP: textured vegetable protein. It is used as a meat substitute or a meat extender.

unit pricing: a system in which stickers on store shelves give costs per unit of weight or per quantity for each product. From unit prices you can tell which product gives most for the money.

U.S. customary system: the traditional system of measurement in the United States. The basic units for weight are the ounce and the pound, the basic units for length are the inch and the foot, and the basic units for volume are the cup and the quart.

USDA: United States Department of Agriculture. This government department works to keep a wholesome food supply available and to improve food production and distribution.

USRDA: United States Recommended Daily Allowance—the amounts of **nutrients** that a person needs each day, according to federal standards.

vitamin (VĪ tə min): a type of **nutrient**. Vitamins A, B, C, D, E, and K are among those known to be needed by the body.

waiter/waitress: a restaurant employee who takes your order, serves the meal, and brings the bill.

whole-grain foods: products made from whole kernels of grain. See **bran, endosperm,** and **germ.**

work center: an area set up in the kitchen for doing a certain kind of task in the most efficient way.

yeast: a microscopic plant that acts as a **leavening agent** for baked goods such as bread.

yolk: the yellow part of an egg—the cell that develops into a chick.

Equivalents: U.S. Customary and metric measurements

The metric equivalents in this table and the text are approximate. For easy measurement, metric units have been rounded off to the nearest 5.

VOLUME	Customary	Metric	
tsp	1/8 teaspoon	.5 milliliters	mL
	1/4 teaspoon	1 milliliter	
	1/3 teaspoon	1.5 milliliters	
	1/2 teaspoon	2 milliliters	
	2/3 teaspoon	3 milliliters	
	3/4 teaspoon	4 milliliters	
	1 teaspoon	5 milliliters	
tbsp	1 tablespoon	15 milliliters	
cup	1/4 cup	60 milliliters	
	1/3 cup	80 milliliters	
	1/2 cup	125 milliliters	
	2/3 cup	160 milliliters	
	3/4 cup	180 milliliters	
	1 cup	250 milliliters	
qt	1 quart	1 liter	L

WEIGHT	Customary	Metric	
oz	1 ounce	28 grams	g
lb	1 pound	.5 kilograms	kg

LENGTH			
in	1 inch	2.5 centimeters	cm

TEMPERATURE			
°F	degrees Fahrenheit	degrees Celsuis	°C

To change °F to °C, multiply by 5/9, after subtracting 32

Index

PHOTO CREDITS

Page 1: J. Viles/Shostal **2-3**: L. Harmon/Shostal **5**: Sigrid Owen/DPI **7** *left top*: J. Gerard Smith *left center and bottom*: Oscar Mayer & Co. *right top*: John Manno *right bottom*: W. Stegemeyer/Shostal **12**: Landon's, Miami **14**: Sam Falk/Monkmeyer **15**: USDA **16**: Martin M. Rotker/ Taurus **19**: Cynara **20** *top*: Photo Media *bottom*: B. Helms/Shostal **23** *top*: G. de Steinheil/Shostal *bottom*: General Mills, Inc. (Betty Crocker's Cookbook) **24**: E. S. Beckwith **25**: Photo Media **27**: Sigrid Owen/DPI **29**: J. Gerard Smith **30**: B. Helms/Shostal **34**: Tom Rowe **37**: J. Gerard Smith **38** *right*: C. F. Mueller *left*: Sigrid Owen/DPI **39** *top*: B. Helms/ Shostal *bottom*: Anthony Howarth/ Woodfin Camp **40** *top*: Frances Laping/ DPI *bottom*: Eric Carle/Shostal **41**: Hal McKusick/DPI **42**: Wil Blanche/DPI **44** *top*: J. Gerard Smith *bottom*: William R. Wright/ Leo DeWys, Inc. **45**: Photo Media **46**: J. Alex Langley/DPI **47**: Paul Conklin/Monkmeyer **50**: Ann Hagen Griffiths/DPI **55, 62, 63, 64,69**: J. Gerard Smith **74, 76**: Jack McConnell **79**: E. S. Beckwith **80**: USDA **81**: J. Gerard Smith **84**: Shostal Associates **85**: Cynara **87**: John Manno **92**: Mimi Forsyth/Monkmeyer **102**: A. Ippolito/Shostal **104, 106**: USDA **107**: J. Gerard Smith **110**: Oscar Mayer & Co. **114**: J. Gerard Smith **118**: Mimi Forsyth/ Monkmeyer **123**: John Manno **124** *left*: Del Monte Corporation *right*: J. Cunningham/Shostal **128-129** *left*: L. Harmon/Shostal **129** *right*: J. Viles/Shostal **131**: L. Willinger/ Shostal **132**: E. S. Beckwith **133** *top*: Photo Media *bottom*: Green Giant Company **135**: John Manno **136**: B. Helms/Shostal **140**: Jack McConnell **142**: Oscar Mayer & Co. **143**: B. Helms/Shostal **149** *left*: Photo Media *right*: Oscar Mayer & Co. **151**: J. Gerard Smith **152**: E. S. Beckwith **155**: J. Gerard Smith **160**: John Hopkins/Nancy Palmer **162**: Pepperidge Farm, Inc. **163**: J. Gerard Smith **167** *top*: D. W. Clark *bottom*: John Manno **168**: J. Gerard Smith **169**: W. Stegemeyer/Shostal **170**: J. Gerard Smith **171**: Cynara **175**: John Manno **177**: J. Gerard Smith **179**: John Manno **184**: Jack McConnell **187**: White/Westinghouse Appliance Company **189**: J. Gerard Smith **192**: D. W. Clark **193**: John Manno **194**: J. Gerard Smith **204**: Landon's, Miami **206**: Del Monte Corporation **207**: USDA **210**: J. Gerard Smith **212**: Alfred Fisher/DPI **214**: John Manno **218** *top*: John Manno *bottom*: Hugh Rogers/Monkmeyer **222**: Mimi Forsyth/ Monkmeyer **226**: Pepperidge Farm, Inc. **227, 228, 232**: J. Gerard Smith **233**: John Manno **236**: Marc and Evelyen Bernheim/Woodfin Camp **240**: Jack McConnell **242**: Pepperidge Farm, Inc. **243**: USDA **248**: O. Christian Irgens **249**: E. S. Beckwith **254**: J. Viles/Shostal **262, 264**: Ann Hagen Griffiths/DPI **265**: E. S. Beckwith **267**: Ann Hagen Griffiths/DPI **268**: O. Christian Irgens **270**: John Manno **273**: Ann Hagen Griffiths/DPI **274**: Oscar Mayer & Co. **275, 278**: Ann Hagen Griffiths/DPI **282, 284**: Mimi Forsyth/ Monkmeyer **285**: J. Gerard Smith **287**: W. Hamilton/Shostal **293**: Mimi Forsyth/ Monkmeyer **298**: Jack McConnell **300**: J. Alex Langley/DPI **302**: A. Upitis/Shostal **303**: D'Arazien/Shostal **304**: K. Scholz/ Shostal **306**: Libby Corlett/DPI **307**: S. H. Wood/Shostal **308** *top*: Cynara *bottom*: USDA **Back cover** *first row*: Landon's, Miami; Tom Rowe; Ann Hagen Griffiths/DPI; Jack McConnell; Mimi Forsyth/Monkmeyer *second row*: Mimi Forsyth/Monkmeyer; Jack McConnell; John Hopkins/Nancy Palmer; Jack McConnell; Landon's, Miami *third row*: Mimi Forsyth/Monkmeyer; Jack McConnell; Ann Hagen Griffiths/DPI; Mimi Forsyth/Monkmeyer; Jack McConnell